FILTHY
DIRTY

FILTHY DIRTY JOKES

Edited by Platinum Press, LLC

POCKET BOOKS

New York   London   Toronto   Sydney

Pocket Books
A Division of Simon & Schuster, Inc.
1230 Avenue of the Americas
New York, NY 10020

Copyright © 2005 by Platinum Press, Inc.
Originally published by Platinum Press, Inc.

First Pocket Books paperback edition October 2008

POCKET and colophon are registered trademarks of Simon & Schuster, Inc.

For information about special discounts for bulk purchases, please contact Simon & Schuster Special Sales at 1-800-456-6798 or business@simonandschuster.com.

Cover design by Mary Ann Smith

Manufactured in the United States of America

10

ISBN 978-1-4165-8999-0

Contents

FILTHY
DIRTY
JOKES

Business

The beer company held a contest to select a slogan for the new beer they had just developed. They advertised all over and received thousands of submissions.

The panel of judges finally settled on one particular entry—"Love on a Lake."

The president of the company said, "I like the name but I'm puzzled as to how the contestant selected this name. If he can explain the meaning, I'll be happy to award the prize to him."

When asked for the explanation, the winner responded, "Well, 'love on a lake' is f***ing close to water, and that's what this beer tasted like!"

•

After the annual office Christmas-party blowout, John woke up with a pounding headache, cotton-mouthed, and utterly unable to recall the events of the preceding evening. After a trip to the bathroom, he was able to make his way downstairs, where his wife put some coffee in front of him.

"Louise," he moaned, "tell me, what went on last night? Was it as bad as I think?"

"Even worse," she assured him in her most scornful voice. "You made a complete ass of yourself, succeeded in antagonizing the entire board of directors, and insulted the chairman of the company to his face. You said, 'He's an arrogant, self-important prick, piss on him!' And you did, all over his suit. And he fired you."

"Well, f*** him," said John.

"I did. You're back at work on Monday."

•

A company, feeling it's time for a shake-up, hires Marvin as the new CEO. As the new boss, he's determined to rid the company of all slackers. On a tour of the facilities, he notices a guy leaning on a wall. The room is full of workers and Marvin wants to let them know he means business. He walks up to the guy and asks, "And how much money do you make a week?"

The young fellow looks at him and replies, "I make $300 a week. Why?"

Marvin hands the guy $300 in cash and screams, "Here's a week's pay, now *get out* and never come back!"

Feeling pretty good about his first firing, Marvin looks around the room and asks, "Does anyone want to tell me what that goof-off did here?"

One of the workers answers, "He's the pizza delivery guy."

•

A woman entered a pawnshop and asked to see a pistol. She then asked for some bullets. Loading the gun, she ordered the pawnbroker to empty out the cash register. But then she said, "I have an even greater urge. Get into the back room!"

There she ordered him to disrobe and began having sex with him. She got so involved that she dropped the gun.

"For God's sake, lady," he said, "pick it back up. My wife is due anytime now!"

•

Two business partners, both married, were taking turns having intercourse with their attractive secretary, Ruthie. As a result of such frequent screwing, the young lady became pregnant.

One partner, congratulating the other, said, "Ruthie had twins. Unfortunately, mine died!"

•

A city boy, Kenny, moved to the country and bought a donkey from an old farmer for $100. The farmer agreed to deliver the donkey the following day.

The next day the farmer drove up and said, "Sorry, son, but I have some bad news—the donkey died."

Kenny replied, "Well then, just give me my money back."

The farmer said, "Can't do that. I went and spent it already."

Kenny said, "Okay then, just unload the donkey."

The farmer asked, "What you gonna do with him?"

Kenny: "I'm going to raffle him off."

Farmer: "You can't raffle off a dead donkey!"

Kenny: "Sure I can. Watch me. I just won't tell anybody he's dead."

A month later, the farmer met up with Kenny and asked, "What happened with that dead donkey?"

Kenny: "I raffled him off. I sold five hundred tickets at two dollars each and made a profit of $898."

Farmer: "Didn't anyone complain?"

Kenny: "Just the guy who won. So I gave him his two dollars back."

Kenny grew up and eventually became the chairman of Enron.

•

A businessman flew to Vegas for the weekend to gamble. He lost the shirt off his back and had nothing left but a quarter and the second half of his round-trip ticket. If he could just get to the airport, he could get himself home. So he went out to the front of the casino where a cab was waiting.

He got in and explained his situation to the cabbie. He promised to send the driver money from home. He offered him his credit card numbers, his driver's license number, his address, all to no avail.

The cabbie said, "If you don't have fifteen dollars, get the hell out of my cab!" So the businessman was forced to hitchhike to the airport and was barely in time to catch his flight.

One year later the businessman, having worked long and hard to regain his wealth, returned to Vegas, and this time he won big. Feeling pretty good about himself, he went out to the front of the casino to get a cab ride back to the airport.

Well, whom should he see out there, at the end of a long line of cabs, but his old buddy who had refused to give him a ride when he was down on his luck. The businessman thought for a moment about how he could make the guy pay for his lack of charity, and he hit on a plan.

The businessman got in the first cab in the line and asked, "How much for a ride to the airport?"

"Fifteen bucks," came the reply.

"And how much for you to give me oral sex on the way?"

"What? Get the hell out of my cab!"

The businessman got into the back of each cab in the long line and asked the same questions, with the same result. When he got to his old friend at the back of the line, he got in and asked, "How much for a ride to the airport?"

The cabbie replied, "Fifteen bucks."

The businessman said, "Okay," and away they went.

Then, as they drove slowly past the long line of cabs, the businessman gave a big smile and a thumbs-up to each driver.

•

A guy phones his boss but gets the boss's wife instead.

"I'm afraid he died last week," she explains.

The next day the man calls again and asks for the boss.

"I told you," the wife replies, "he died last week."

The next day he calls again and once more asks to speak to his boss.

By this time the wife is getting upset and shouts, *"I've already told you twice, my husband, your boss, died last week! Why do you keep calling?"*

"Because," he replied, laughing, "I just love hearing it."

•

Mr. Smith owned a small business. He had two employees, Sarah and Jack. They were both extremely good employees— always willing to work overtime and chip in where needed.

Mr. Smith was looking over his books one day and decided that he wasn't making enough money to warrant two employees, and he would have to lay one off. But both Sarah and Jack were such good workers he was having trouble finding a fair way to do it. He decided that he would watch them work, and the first one to take a break would be the one he would lay off.

So he sits in his office and watches them work.

Suddenly, Sarah gets a terrible headache and needs to take an aspirin. She gets the aspirin out of her purse and goes to the watercooler to get something to wash it down with.

Mr. Smith follows her to the watercooler, taps her on the shoulder, and says, "Sarah, I'm going to have to lay you or Jack off."

Sarah says, "Can you jack off? I have a headache."

•

At one ad agency, a guy in production was fired when they discovered he was the Xerox Flasher. Every morning he photocopied his privates, made copies, and left them in the secretaries' desks.

The boss said, "Hell, he's the only person in the building who isn't guilty of false advertising!"

His secretary said, "Well, not exactly."

The boss said, "Oh, God! Don't tell me!"

She said, "Yes, sir. He was using the enlarger."

•

A man with no ears is trying to find a new reporter for his news show. The first guy walks in and the boss says, "This job requires you noticing a lot of details. What is one thing you notice about me?"

And the guy says, "Well, shit! You got no ears, man!"

So the boss yells, "Get the f*** out!"

So the next guy comes in and the boss says to him, "This job requires you noticing a lot of details. What is something you notice about me?"

And the guy says, "That's easy. You got no ears!"

So the boss says to him, "Get the f*** out!"

As the second guy leaves, he sees the third guy about to go in and says to him, "The boss has no ears but don't say anything about them, he is really sensitive about it."

So the guy goes in and the boss says, "This job requires you to notice a lot of details. What is one that you notice about me?"

So the guy says, "You're wearing contacts!"

And the boss says, "Yeah, how did you know?"

So the guy replies, "Well, shit, you can't wear glasses 'cause you ain't got no ears."

•

Joan goes into Wal-Mart and tells the clerk she wants a refund for the toaster she bought because it doesn't work. The clerk tells her that he can't give her a refund because she bought it on special. All of a sudden, Joan throws her arms up in the air and starts screaming, *"Grab my breasts! Grab my breasts!"*

The clerk, not knowing what to do, runs to get the store manager. The manager comes up to Joan and asks, "What's wrong?"

She explains the situation with the toaster.

He tells her that he can't give her a refund because she bought it on special.

Once again, Joan throws her arms up in the air and starts screaming, *"Grab my breasts!"*

In shock, the store manager pleads, "Ma'am, why are you saying that?"

In a huff, Joan says, *"Because I like to have my breasts grabbed when I'm getting screwed."*

•

A businessman was confused about a bill he had received, so he asked his secretary for some mathematical help.

"If I were to give you $25,000, minus eighteen percent, how much would you take off?" he asked.

The secretary replied, "Everything but my earrings."

•

A man advertises for a secretary at $1,000 a week. He hires one.

He: "Now the first thing, take off your clothes and we'll make love."

She does not want to jeopardize her job, so she obliges the boss. When finished, he says, "You're fired. Here's a half hour's pay."

•

The prostitute wants to leave her employer.

The madam: "But why? You're the most popular girl in

the house. Why, you go upstairs at least twenty-five times a day."

Prostitute: "That's just it . . . my feet are killing me."

•

Memo from the secretary to the boss:

I've got good news and bad news. The good news is that you're not sterile.

•

The madam had assembled some of her girls for the men in town for the accountants' convention. "This is Dolores," she said, smiling. "For $250, I can promise you an exciting evening starting with a hot tub.

"And this is Connie, available for $375. She's rigged an Oriental Swing in her room.

"Now lovely Maria," she continued, "can be yours for both straight and kinky sex, including bondage. She's yours for the night for only $300.

"And if you take a fancy to tantalizing Jenny here, why she can—"

"Just a minute," interrupted one of the accountants. "Don't you have any generic sluts?"

•

A prosperous and somewhat amorous businessman propositioned a beautiful chorus girl of well-proportioned figure to spend the night with him for $500.

When he was ready to leave the next morning, certain things having transpired, he told her he didn't have that much money with him, but would have his secretary mail her a check for it made out with a memo of *Rent for apartment*, to avoid any embarrassment.

On the way to the office, however, after thinking the matter over carefully, he decided the night hadn't been worth what he'd agreed to pay. As a result, he had his secretary send a check for $250 instead and enclosed the following explanatory note:

> *Dear Madam:*
>
> *Enclosed is a check for the amount of $250 for rent on your apartment. I am sending this amount instead of the amount originally agreed upon, because when I rented this apartment, I was under the impression that . . .*
>
> *1. It had never been occupied.*
> *2. There was plenty of heat.*
> *3. It was small.*
>
> *Last night I found that it had been occupied many times, that there wasn't any heat, and that it was entirely too large!*

Upon receipt of the note, the chorus girl immediately returned the check, with this note:

> *I am returning the check for $250. I cannot understand how you could expect such a beautiful apartment to remain unoccupied. As for the heat . . . there is plenty of it there if you know how to turn it on. As for the size, it's not my fault if you didn't have enough furniture to furnish it.*

Medical

Just after Dave was admitted to the hospital, he heard a knock at the door of his room. "Come in," Dave said, and in came a woman.

"I'm your doctor," she said. "Please take off your clothes."

Dave asked her if she meant for him to remove all of his clothing, and she told him that was just what she did mean. So he took off all his clothes and she examined him: nose, throat, chest, stomach, thighs, feet. When she finished examining him, she announced, "You may get into bed. Do you have any questions?"

"Just one," said Dave. "Why did you knock?"

•

A cardiac specialist died, and at his funeral the coffin was placed in front of a huge mock-up of a heart made of flowers. After the pastor finished with the sermon and eulogy and everyone said their good-byes, the heart opened, the coffin rolled inside, and the heart closed. Just then one of the mourners burst into laughter.

The guy next to him asked, "Why are you laughing?"

"I was thinking about my own funeral," the man replied.

"What's so funny about that?"

"I'm a gynecologist."

•

A physician claims these are actual comments his patients made while he was performing colonoscopies:

1. "Take it easy, Doc, you're boldly going where no man has gone before."
2. "Find Amelia Earhart yet?"
3. "Can you hear me *now*?"
4. "Are we there yet? Are we there yet?"
5. "You know, in Arkansas, we're now legally married."
6. "Any sign of the trapped miners, chief?"
7. "You put your left hand in; you take your left hand out. You do the hokeypokey . . ."
8. "Hey! Now I know how a Muppet feels!"
9. "If your hand doesn't fit, you must acquit!"
10. "Hey, Doc, let me know if you find my dignity."

And the *best* one . . .

11. "Could you write me a note for my wife, saying that my head is not, in fact, up there?"

•

A patient asked through his oxygen mask, "Nurse, are my testicles black?"

The nurse replied, "I can't tell. I'm only here to wash your face and hands."

The head nurse was passing and saw the man getting a little distraught so she marched over to inquire what was wrong.

"Nurse," he mumbled, "are my testicles black?"

Being a nurse of long standing, she was undaunted. She whipped back the bedclothes, pulled down his pajama trousers, moved his penis out of the way, had a good look, pulled up the pajamas, replaced the bedclothes, and announced, "There's nothing wrong with them!"

Startled, the man pulled off his oxygen mask and exclaimed, *"I said, are my test results back?"*

•

As the manager of our hospital's softball team, I was responsible for returning equipment to the proper owners at the end of the season. When I walked into the surgery department carrying a bat that belonged to one of the surgeons, I passed several patients and their families in a waiting area.

"Look, honey," one man said to his wife. "Here comes your anesthesiologist."

•

A young lady who thought she was overweight went to see a dietitian. She walked into his office and asked several questions about dieting, exercise, and other things. Her final question to the dietitian sparked interest in him. She asked, "How many calories are in sperm?"

"Why?" he replied.

She explained some of the things she liked to do.

After thinking a minute he said, "I really have no clue, but if you are consuming that much of it, then no guy is going to care if you're a little chunky!"

•

One day a young man and woman were in their bedroom making love. All of a sudden, a bumblebee entered the bedroom window. As the young lady parted her legs, the bee entered her vagina. The woman started screaming, "Oh my God, help me, there's a bee in my vagina!"

The husband immediately took her to the local doctor and explained the situation.

The doctor thought for a moment and said, "Hmm, tricky situation. But I have a solution to the problem if young sir would permit."

The husband, concerned, agreed that the doctor could use any method to get the bee out of his wife's vagina.

The doctor said, "Okay, what I'm going to do is rub some honey over the top of my penis and insert it into your wife's vagina. When I feel the bee getting closer to the tip of my dick, I shall withdraw it and the bee should hopefully follow my penis out of your wife's vagina."

The husband nodded and gave his approval. The young lady said, "Yes, yes, whatever, just get on with it."

So the doctor, after covering the tip of his penis with honey, inserted it into the young lady's vagina. After a few gentle strokes, the doctor said, "I don't think the bee has noticed the honey yet. Perhaps I should go a bit deeper."

So the doctor went deeper and deeper. After a while the doctor began shafting the young lady very hard indeed. The young lady began to quiver with excitement; she began to moan and groan aloud. "Oh, Doctor, Doctor!" she shouted.

The doctor, concentrating hard, looked to be enjoying himself. He then put his hands on the young lady's breasts and started making loud noises.

The husband, at this point, suddenly became annoyed and shouted, *"Now wait a minute, what the hell do you think you're doing?"*

The doctor, still concentrating, replied, "Change of plan. I'm gonna drown the bastard!"

•

A woman went to a doctor and said, "Doctor, I have a problem. Every time I sneeze, I have an orgasm."

The doctor said, "Oh, really, what have you been doing for it?"

The woman replied, "Snorting pepper."

•

Three women were in the waiting room of a gynecologist's office, and each of them was knitting a sweater for her baby-to-be. The first one stopped and took a pill. "What was that?" the others asked her.

"Oh, it was vitamin C—I want my baby to be healthy."

A few minutes later, the second woman took a pill.

"What was that?" the others asked.

"Oh, it was iron—I want my baby to be big and strong."

They continued knitting. Finally the third woman took a pill.

"What was that?" the others asked her.

"It's thalidomide," she said. "I just can't get the arms right on this f***ing sweater!"

•

The dentist was striving to extract a tooth, but every time he got ready to proceed, the patient clamped his jaws. At last, the dentist took his assistant aside and told her that at the very moment he poised the forceps, she should give the patient's balls a vicious pinch.

The pinch was administered, the nervous patient's mouth flew open, and the tooth was easily removed.

"Didn't hurt, did it?" asked the dentist.

"Not too much," replied the patient, "but who would have thought the root went that deep?"

•

This beautiful woman walks into a doctor's office and the doctor is bowled over by how stunningly awesome she is. All his professionalism goes right out the window.

He tells her to take off her pants. She does, and he starts rubbing her thighs.

"Do you know what I am doing?" asks the doctor.

"Yes, checking for abnormalities," she replies.

He tells her to take off her shirt and bra. She takes them off. The doctor begins rubbing her breasts and asks, "Do you know what I am doing now?"

She replies, "Yes, checking for cancer."

Finally, he tells her to take off her panties, lays her on the table, gets on top of her, and starts having sex with her. He says to her, "Do you know what I am doing now?"

She replies, "Yes, getting the clap—that's why I'm here."

•

Dr. Jones completed his examination of a teenage girl and took her mother aside. "I'm afraid," he said, "that your daughter has syphilis."

"Oh, my!" exclaimed the embarrassed woman. "Tell me, could she possibly have caught it in a public lavatory?"

After giving it a little thought, Dr. Jones responded, "It's possible." Then he added, "But it would certainly have been uncomfortable."

•

A lady goes to the doctor to see about getting a face-lift.

"Well," says the doctor, "I can do the face-lift, and then you'll have to come back in six months for a follow-up."

"Oh, no," the woman replies. "I want it all done in one shot. I don't want to have to come back."

The doctor thinks for a second, then offers, "There is a new procedure where we put a screw in the top of your head. Then anytime you see wrinkles appearing, you just give it a little turn, which pulls the skin up, and they disappear."

"That's what I want!" exclaims the lady. "Let's do that."

Six months later, the lady charges into the doctor's office. "Well, how's the procedure holding up?" the doctor asks.

"Terrible!" the lady bellows. "It's the worst mistake I've ever made."

"What's wrong?"

"Just look at these bags under my eyes!" she hollers.

"Lady," the doctor retorts, "those aren't bags, those are your breasts. And if you don't leave that screw alone, you're going to have a beard!"

•

Last time I was in the hospital, I really enjoyed myself: patting the bottoms of the pretty nurses, offering to show them my circumcision scar, and the like. One nurse finally had all she could stand of my crude behavior and said, "A pervert like you should be living in a house of prostitution!"

I grinned and said, "Well, it *would* be cheaper than here, but I can't get my insurance to pay for it!"

•

Bill was a clerk in a small drugstore, but he was not much of a salesman. He could never find the item the customer wanted. Dave, the owner, had had about enough and warned Bill that the next sale he missed would be his last.

Just then a man came in coughing and asked Bill for their best cough syrup. Try as he might, Bill could not find the cough syrup. Remembering Dave's warning, he sold the man a box of laxatives and told him to take it all at once. The customer did as Bill said, then walked outside and leaned against a lamppost.

Dave had seen the whole thing and came over to ask Bill what had transpired.

"He wanted something for his cough, but I couldn't find the cough syrup. I substituted a laxative and told him to take it all at once," Bill explained.

"Laxatives won't cure a cough!" Dave shouted angrily.

"Sure it will," Bill said, pointing at the man leaning on the lamppost. "Look at him. He's afraid to cough."

•

"I've got some good news and some bad news," the doctor says.

"What's the bad news?" asks the patient.

"The bad news is that unfortunately you've only got three months to live."

The patient is taken aback. "What's the good news then, Doctor?"

The doctor points over to the secretary at the front desk. "You see that blonde with the big breasts?"

The patient nods his head.

The doctor replies, "I'm f***ing her."

•

A guy walks into a clinic to have his blood type taken. The nurse goes about taking the blood sample from his finger. After finishing, she looks around for a piece of cotton to wipe away the excess blood. She can't find it, so she looks innocently at the guy and takes his finger and sucks it.

The guy is so pleased, he asks, "Do you think I could have a urine test done?"

•

A young woman was having a physical examination and was embarrassed because of her weight. As she removed her last bit of clothing, she blushed. "I'm so ashamed, Doctor," she said. "I guess I let myself go."

The physician was checking her eyes and ears. "Don't feel ashamed, miss. You don't look that bad."

"Do you really think so, Doctor?" she asked.

The doctor held a tongue depressor in front of her face and said, "Of course. Now just open your mouth and say moo."

•

A handsome young lad went into the hospital for some minor surgery, and the day after the procedure a friend stopped by to see how the guy was doing. His friend was amazed at the number of nurses who entered the room in short intervals with refreshments, offers to fluff his pillow, make the bed, give back rubs, etc. "Why all the attention?" the friend asked. "You look fine to me."

"I know!" The patient grinned. "But the nurses kind of formed a little fan club when they all heard that my circumcision required twenty-seven stitches."

•

There's a student in medical school who wants to specialize in sexual disorders, so he makes arrangements to visit the sexual disorder clinic. The chief doctor is showing him around, discussing cases and the facility, when the student sees a patient masturbating right there in the hallway.

"What condition does he have?" the student asks.

"He suffers from Seminal Buildup Disorder," the doctor replies. "If he doesn't obtain sexual release ten to twenty times a day, he'll pass into a coma."

The student takes some notes on that, and they continue down the hall. As they turn the corner, he sees another patient with his pants around his ankles, receiving oral sex from a beautiful nurse.

"What about him?" the student asks. "What's his story?"

"Oh, it's the same condition," the doctor replies. "He just has a better health plan."

•

In a mental institution, a nurse walks into a room and sees a patient acting as if he's driving a car. The nurse asks him, "Charlie! What are you doing?"

He says, "Can't talk right now . . . I'm driving to Chicago!"

The nurse wishes him a good trip and leaves the room. The next day, the nurse enters Charlie's room just as he stops driving his imaginary car, and she asks, "Well, Charlie, how are you doing?"

Charlie says, "I'm exhausted, I just got into Chicago and I need some rest."

"That's great," replies the nurse. "I'm glad you had a safe trip." The nurse leaves Charlie's room and goes across the hall into Fred's room and finds Fred sitting on his bed masturbating vigorously. With surprise she asks, "Fred, what the hell are you doing?"

Fred smiles and replies, "I'm f***ing Charlie's wife. He's in Chicago!"

•

Dr. Dave had sex with one of his patients and felt guilty all day long. No matter how much he tried to forget about it, he couldn't. The guilt and sense of betrayal were overwhelming. But every once in a while he'd hear an internal, reassuring voice that said:

"Dave, don't worry about it. You aren't the first doctor to have sex with one of their patients and you won't be the last. And you're single. Let it go."

But invariably the other voice would bring him back to reality.

"Dave, you're a vet."

•

Matt went into the doctor's office for his annual checkup, and the doc asked if there was anything unusual he should know about.

That left it pretty wide-open, so he told the doctor that he found it real strange how his suit must have shrunk just sitting in his closet because it didn't fit when he went to get ready for a wedding recently.

The doc said, "Suits don't shrink just sitting there. You probably just put on a few pounds, Matt."

"That's just it, Doc, I know I haven't gained a single pound since the last time I wore it."

"Well, then," said the doc, "you must have a case of Furniture Disease."

"What in the world is Furniture Disease?"

"Furniture Disease is when you reach that stage in life when your chest starts sliding down into your drawers."

•

The doctor said, "Joe, the good news is I can cure your headaches. The bad news is that it will require castration. You have a very rare condition that causes your testicles to press on your spine, and the pressure creates one hell of a headache. The only way to relieve the pressure is to remove the testicles."

Joe was shocked and depressed. He wondered if he had anything to live for. He couldn't concentrate long enough to answer, but decided he had no choice but to go under the knife.

When he left the hospital, he was without a headache for the first time in twenty years, but he felt as if he was missing an important part of himself. As he walked down the street, he realized that he felt like a different person. He could make a new beginning and live a new life. He saw a men's clothing store and thought, "That's what I need—a new suit."

He entered the shop and told the salesman, "I'd like a new suit."

The elderly tailor eyed him briefly and said, "Let's see . . . size 44 long."

Joe laughed. "That's right, how did you know?"

"Been in the business sixty years!"

Joe tried on the suit. It fit perfectly. As Joe admired himself in the mirror, the salesman asked, "How about a new shirt?"

Joe thought for a moment, then said, "Sure."

The salesman eyed Joe and said, "Let's see, 34 sleeve and 16½ neck."

Again Joe was surprised. "That's right, how did you know?"

"Been in the business sixty years!"

Joe tried on the shirt, and it fit perfectly. As Joe adjusted the collar in the mirror, the salesman asked, "How about new shoes?"

Joe was on a roll and said, "Sure."

The salesman eyed Joe's feet and said, "Let's see . . . size 9½ E."

Joe was astonished. "That's right, how did you know?"

"Been in the business sixty years!"

Joe tried on the shoes and they fit perfectly. He walked comfortably around the shop and the salesman asked, "How about some new underwear?"

Joe thought for a second and said, "Sure."

The salesman stepped back, eyed Joe's waist, and said, "Let's see . . . size 36."

Joe laughed. "Aha! I got you! I've worn size 34 since I was eighteen years old."

The salesman shook his head. "You can't wear a size 34. A size 34 underwear would press your testicles up against the base of your spine and give you one hell of a headache."

•

A little old lady goes to the doctor and says, "Doctor, I have this problem with gas, but it really doesn't bother me too much. It never smells and it's always silent. As a matter of fact, I've farted at least ten times since I've been here in your office. You didn't know I was farting because it doesn't smell and you didn't hear anything."

The doctor says, "I see. Take these pills and come back to see me next week."

The lady returns the following week. "Doctor," she says, "I don't know what the heck you gave me, but now my farts, although still silent, stink terribly."

"Good," the doctor says. "Now that we've cleared up your sinuses, let's work on your hearing."

•

Two men are in a doctor's office. Each of them is to get a vasectomy. The nurse comes into the room and tells them, "Strip and put on these gowns before going in to see the doctor to have your procedures done." A few minutes later she returns and reaches into one man's gown and fondles and ultimately begins to masturbate him.

Shocked, he asks, "Why are you doing that?"

She replies, "We have to vacate the sperm from your system to have a clean procedure." The man, not wanting to be a problem and enjoying it, allows her to complete her task. After she is through, she proceeds to the next man. She starts to fondle the man as she had the previous man, but then drops to her knees to give him oral sex.

Upon seeing this, the first man quickly says, "Hey! Why is it that I get masturbated and he gets a blow job?"

The nurse simply replies, "Sir, there *is* a difference between HMO and Complete Coverage."

•

A young woman took her troubles to a psychiatrist. "Doctor, you must help me," she pleaded. "It's gotten so that every time I date a nice guy, I end up in bed with him. And then afterward, I feel guilty and depressed for a week."

"I see." The psychiatrist nodded. "And you, no doubt, want me to strengthen your willpower and resolve in this matter."

"For God's sake, *no!*" exclaimed the woman. "I want you to fix it so I won't feel guilty and depressed afterward."

•

A man visits his doctor and is told that his penis must be amputated. He goes to another doctor, same diagnosis. He finally sees a sign for an Asian physician. The doctor assures him amputation is not necessary. The man sighs in relief and starts to leave, and the doctor finishes his diagnosis: "No need to amputate, wait two weeks and it fall off by itself."

•

A man goes into the doctor's office feeling really bad. After a thorough examination, the doctor says, "I have some bad news. You have HAGS."

"What is HAGS?" the man asks.

"It's herpes, AIDS, gonorrhea, and syphilis," says the doctor.

"Oh my God," says the man. "What are you going to do?"

"We are going to put you in an isolated room and feed you pancakes and pizza."

"Is that going to help me?"

"No," says the doctor. "But it's the only food we can think of that we can slide under the door."

•

One day a guy goes to his doctor and says, "Doc, I have these real bad headaches. What should I do?"

The doctor replies, "Well, to get rid of *my* headaches, I just have sex with my wife." They both laugh.

A week later the patient returns. The doctor asks, "How are you feeling?"

The patient smiles and replies, "You were right! I feel so much better. And by the way, Doc, you have a lovely home."

•

A man goes into the hospital for a vasectomy. Shortly after he recovers from his anesthesia, his surgeon comes in and tells him, "Well, I've got good news and I've got bad news for you."

"Give me the bad news first, Doc," says the patient.

"I'm afraid that we accidentally cut your balls off during surgery, son."

"Oh my God!" the patient cries, breaking into tears.

"But the good news," the doctor adds, "is that we had them biopsied and you'll be relieved to know that they weren't malignant."

•

A guy says, "Doc, I think I've got a sex problem. I can't get it up for my wife anymore."

The doctor says, "Come back tomorrow and bring her with you."

The next day, the guy shows up with his wife.

The doctor says to the wife, "Take off your clothes and lie on the table."

She does, and the doctor walks around the table a few times looking her up and down.

He pulls the guy to the side and says, "You're fine. She doesn't give me a hard-on either."

•

A female bodybuilder runs into the doctor's office. "Doctor! It's the steroids you've been giving me! I've got hair growing all over my chest!"

"How far down does it go?"

"That's another thing I've got to talk to you about—it goes all the way down to my balls."

•

A man with a bump growing on his forehead goes to the doctor. After many tests, the doctor announces, "You're growing a second penis out of your forehead, and with the way your skull and brain are forming around it, we're not going to be able to operate, or do anything to stop it."

The man says, "You mean I'm going to wake up every morning, look in the mirror, and see a penis hanging from my forehead?"

The doctor replies, "No, no. That won't happen . . . we figured it out, and the balls should be hanging right over your eyes."

•

A fat man says to his doctor, "Doc, it's my penis . . . I haven't been able to see it for years. Please check and make sure everything's okay!"

The doctor says, "My God! You should diet!"

The man asks, "What color?"

Husband/Wife

A young couple were in their honeymoon suite on their wedding night.

As they were undressing for bed, the husband, who was a big, burly man, tossed his pants to his bride and said, "Here, put these on."

She put them on, and the waist was much too big.

"I can't wear your pants," she said.

"That's right," said the husband, "and don't you ever forget it. I'm the man who wears the pants in this family."

She then flipped him her panties and said, "Try these on."

He tried them on and found he could only get them on as far as his kneecaps.

"Heck," he said. "I can't get into your panties!"

She replied, "That's right, and that's the way it's going to be until your attitude changes!"

•

A man says to his wife, "I feel like having kinky sex—how about I blow my load in your ear?"

The wife hastily replies, "No, I might go deaf!"

To which the man responds, "I've been shooting my love wads in your mouth for the last twenty years and you're still f***ing talking, aren't you?"

•

A husband and his wife who have been married twenty years are doing some yard work. The man is working hard cleaning the BBQ grill while his wife is bending over weeding in the flowerbed. So the man says to his wife, "Your rear end is almost as wide as this grill."

She ignores the remark.

A little later, the husband takes his measuring tape and measures the grill, then he goes over to his wife while she is bending over, measures her rear end, and gasps, "Jeez, it really *is* as wide as the grill!" She ignores this remark as well.

Later that night while in bed, the husband starts to feel frisky. The wife calmly responds, "If you think I'm gonna fire up the grill for one little wiener, you are sadly mistaken."

•

An old man goes to a wizard to ask him if he can remove a curse he has been living with for the last forty years. The wizard says, "Maybe, but you will have to tell me the exact words that were used to put the curse on you."

The old man says without hesitation, "'I now pronounce you man and wife.'"

•

If your dog is barking at the back door and your wife is yelling at the front door, whom do you let in first?

The dog, of course. He'll shut up once you let him in.

•

I married Miss Right. I just didn't know her first name was Always.

•

I haven't spoken to my wife for eighteen months; I don't like to interrupt her.

•

Scientists have discovered a food that diminishes a woman's sex drive by 90 percent. It's called a wedding cake.

•

Marriage is a three-ring circus: engagement ring, wedding ring, suffering.

•

A man inserted an advertisement in the classifieds: "Wife Wanted."

The next day he received a hundred letters. They all said the same thing: *You can have mine.*

•

Mrs. Smith hires a maid with beautiful blond hair. The first morning the girl pulls off the hair and says, "I wear a wig because I was born totally hairless. Not a hair on my body, not even down there."

That night Mrs. Smith tells her husband.

He says, "I've never seen anything like that. Please, tomorrow, ask her to go into the bedroom and show you. I want to hide in the closet so I can have a look."

The next day, Mrs. Smith asks the girl. The two of them go into the bedroom and the girl strips and shows her. Then the girl says, "I've never seen one with hair on it. Can I see yours?"

So Mrs. Smith pulls off her clothes and shows her. That night Mrs. Smith says to her husband, "I hope you're satisfied, because I was pretty embarrassed when that girl asked to see mine."

Her husband says, "You think you were embarrassed . . . I had the four guys I play poker with in the closet with me."

•

It's a beautiful, warm spring day, and a man and his wife are at the zoo. She's wearing a low-cut, loose-fitting, pink spring dress, sleeveless with straps. As they walk through the ape exhibit and pass in front of a large gorilla, the gorilla goes wild. He jumps up on the bars, holding on with one hand and two feet, grunting and pounding his chest with his free hand. He is obviously excited at the pretty lady in the wavy dress.

The husband, noticing the excitement, suggests that his wife tease the poor fellow. The husband suggests she pucker her lips, wiggle her bottom, and play along. She does, and Mr. Gorilla gets even more excited, making noises that would wake the dead. Then the husband suggests that she let one of her straps fall, she does, and Mr. Gorilla is just about to tear the bars down. "Now try lifting your dress up your thighs, and showing him your bush," he says, so she does, and this drives the gorilla absolutely crazy.

Then, quickly, the husband grabs his wife by the hair, rips open the door to the cage, slings her in with the gorilla, and says, "Now, tell *him* you have a f***ing headache."

•

Two men were talking one day. "My wife asked me to buy *organic* vegetables from the market garden," said the first man.

"So were you able to find some?" the second man asked.

"Well, when I got to the market, I asked the gardener, 'These vegetables are for my wife. Have they been sprayed with any poisonous chemicals?' The gardener said, 'No, you'll have to do that yourself.'"

•

Three couples want to join a church. They all talk to the pastor to see what must be done to be accepted.

He says, "You must go without sex for three weeks." Each couple agrees.

Three weeks later all the couples return. The pastor says to the first couple, "How did you do?"

"Oh, Father," they reply, "we did fine. We've been married for twenty years! We're used to going without sex."

"Very good," says the father. "Welcome to my church."

He then asks the second couple how they did.

"It was kind of hard, Father. We've gone up to two

weeks without it, but never three. Somehow we managed, though."

"Good, welcome to my church," he says.

"Well?" He turns to the third couple.

"Oh, Father! We did fine up until this morning! We were at breakfast and my wife bent over to retrieve her napkin, and I just had to do her right then and there!"

"I'm sorry," says the pastor. "You are no longer allowed in my church."

"That's okay," says the wife. "We're not allowed at that restaurant anymore either."

•

The other day I was invited out for a night with "the girls." I told my husband that I would be home by midnight: "I promise!"

Well, the hours passed and the champagne was going down way too easy. Around 3 a.m., drunk as a skunk, I headed for home. Just as I got in the door, the cuckoo clock in the hall started up and cuckooed three times. Quickly, realizing he'd probably wake up, I cuckooed another nine times. I was really proud of myself for coming up with such a quick-witted solution (even when smashed) to escape a possible conflict with him.

The next morning, my husband asked me what time I got in, and I told him twelve. He didn't seem disturbed at all. Whew! Got away with that one!

Then he said, "We need a new cuckoo clock."

When I asked him why, he said, "Well, last night our clock cuckooed three times, then said, 'Oh, shit,' cuckooed four more times, cleared its throat, cuckooed another three times, giggled, cuckooed twice more, then tripped over the cat and farted."

•

A man and a woman go to a marriage counselor. The woman says that her husband, Morris, is driving her crazy. The counselor explains, "She says that you've got these habits that are driving her crazy. First, you're always acting strange in public—looking at the floor and never going near anyone else."

Morris looks concerned. "Oh, you don't understand! It's one of the few things my father told me to do on his deathbed, and I swore I'd obey everything he said."

"What did he say?"

"He said that I should never step on anyone's toes!"

The counselor looks amused. "Actually, that means that you should not do anything that would cause anyone else to get angry."

The husband looks sheepish. "Oh, that's what he meant. Okay."

The counselor continues, "And you keep picking your nose in public."

"Well, it's another thing my father specifically commanded me to do! He told me to always keep my nose clean."

The counselor explains, "That means that you should not indulge in any criminal activity."

"Oh," says the husband, looking stupid.

"And finally, she says that you never allow her to be on top during your lovemaking."

"This," says the husband seriously, "is the last thing my father commanded me to do on his deathbed, and it's the most important thing."

"What did he say?"

Morris replies, "In his dying breath, he said, 'Don't f*** up.' "

•

The FBI is considering three men to be hired. They bring them in separately to speak with the interviewer. The first man comes in and sits down. The interviewer asks him, "Do you love your wife?"

He replies, "Yes, I do, sir."

"Do you love your country?" asks the interviewer.

"Yes, I do, sir."

The interviewer continues, "What do you love more, your wife or your country?"

"My country, sir."

The interviewer looks at the man. "Okay. We brought in your wife. Take this gun and go into the next room and kill her."

The man goes into the room, and all is silent for about five minutes. He comes back with his tie loosened and he is all sweaty. He puts down the gun and leaves.

The second guy comes in and sits down. The interviewer asks him the same questions, and the responses are the same. The interviewer gives him a gun and tells him to go kill his wife. The guy puts the gun down and says, "I can't do it."

The third guy comes in, the same thing happens. The interviewer gives him a gun and tells him to go kill his wife. The guy goes into the room, and *Blam! Blam! Blam! Blam! Blam! Blam!* This is followed by a bunch of crashing sounds that end after a few minutes. The guy comes out of the room with his tie loosened and puts the gun on the table.

The interviewer looks at him and says, "What happened?"

The guy replies, "The gun you gave me was filled with blanks, so I had to strangle her."

•

An old man and an old lady are getting ready for bed one night when all of a sudden the woman bursts out of the bathroom, flings open her robe, and yells, "Super Pussy!"

The old man says, "I'll have the soup."

•

A minister gave a talk on sex to the Lions Club. When he got home, he couldn't tell his wife that he had spoken about sex, so he said he had discussed horseback riding with the members.

A few days later, she ran into some men at the shopping center, and they complimented her on her husband's speech.

She said, "Yes, I hear. I was surprised about the subject matter, as he's only tried it twice. The first time he got so sore he could hardly walk, and the second time he fell off."

•

A young couple had just returned from their honeymoon and were settling down in their new apartment. Coming home from work one night, the landlady met the man in the hallway.

She said, "I have a couple of extra tickets to a play tonight, and I wonder if you and your bride would like to have them."

"I'll ask her," the young man responded. He opened his door and called out, "Honey, would you like to see *Oliver Twist* tonight?"

"Hey, pal," she retorted. "If you show me one more trick with that thing, I'm going home to Mother."

•

David returned home one night to find his wife lying naked in bed. His eyes went wide and he began to strip, only to stop suddenly when he saw a cigar in the ashtray beside the bed.

"All right," David demanded, "I'll kill you unless you tell me where the cigar came from!"

A muffled voice came from under the bed: "Havana."

•

A couple has just gotten married, and on the night of their honeymoon before passionate love, the wife tells the husband, "Please be gentle, I'm still a virgin."

The husband, shocked, replies, "How's this possible? You've been married three times before."

The wife responds, "Well, my first husband was a gynecologist, and all he wanted to do was look at it. My second husband was a psychiatrist, and all he wanted to do was talk about it. Finally, my third husband was a stamp collector, and all he wanted to do was . . . oh, do I miss him!"

•

On their first night together, a newlywed couple goes to change. The new bride comes out of the bathroom showered and wearing a beautiful robe.

The proud husband says, "My dear, we are married now—you can open your robe."

The beautiful young woman opens her robe, and he is astonished. "Oh, oh, aaaahh!" he exclaims. "My God, you are so beautiful. Let me take your picture."

Puzzled, she asks, "My picture?"

"Yes, my dear, so I can carry your beauty next to my heart forever."

She smiles and he takes her picture, then he heads into the bathroom to shower. He comes out wearing his robe and the new wife asks, "Why do you wear a robe? We are married now."

At that the man opens his robe and she exclaims, "*Oh, oh, oh my,* let me get a picture."

He beams and asks why, and she answers, "So I can get it enlarged!"

•

A man and his wife went to their honeymoon hotel for their twenty-fifth anniversary.

As the couple reflected on that magical evening twenty-five years ago, the wife asked the husband, "When you first saw my naked body in front of you, what was going through your mind?"

The husband replied, "All I wanted to do was to f*** your brains out and suck your tits dry."

Then, as the wife undressed, she asked, "What are you thinking now?"

He replied, "It looks as if I did a pretty good job."

•

The angry wife met her husband at the door. He had alcohol on his breath and lipstick on his collar.

"I assume," she snarled, "that there is a very good reason for you to come waltzing in here at six o'clock in the morning?"

"There is," he replied. "Breakfast."

•

Mr. Jones, who had been away on an extended trip, had romantic plans for his first night home. He told them to his wife, who promptly said, "Oh, I'm sorry, dear, but I've got to do all of this laundry. Another time, please."

The next night Jones tried again, and his wife said, "Oh my, I would like to, dear, but it wouldn't be any good. I've got this terrible headache. Please give me a rain check."

By the third night, Jones was rather impatient. "How about it?" he said urgently.

Mrs. Jones snapped back, "This is the third night in a row you've asked. What are you? Some kind of a sex maniac?"

•

A man is lying in bed with his wife, reading a book. He reaches down to tease her pussy.

"You want sex, babe?" she asks.

"No," he replies, "I'm just wetting my finger to turn the page."

•

Two deaf people get married. During the first week of marriage, they are unable to communicate in the bedroom when they turn off the lights (because they can't see each other using sign language). After several nights of fumbling around and misunderstandings, the wife proposes a solution.

"Honey," she signs, "why don't we agree on some simple signals? For instance, at night, if you want to have sex with me, reach over and squeeze my left breast one time. If you don't want to have sex, reach over and squeeze my right breast one time."

The husband thinks this is a great idea and signs back to his wife, "Great idea! Now, if you want to have sex with *me*, reach over and pull on my penis one time. And if you don't want to have sex, reach over and pull on my penis fifty times."

•

Husband and wife had a bitter quarrel on the day of their fortieth wedding anniversary.

The husband yells, "When you die, I'm getting you a headstone that reads, 'Here Lies My Wife—Cold as Ever.'"

"Yeah," she replies, "when you die, I'm getting you a headstone that reads, 'Here Lies My Husband—Stiff at Last.'"

•

Not long after their wedding, John and Mary awoke early one morning. The couple had been up for quite a while before they met up in the kitchen. Marriage was agreeing with John, and he greeted his new wife with glee and excitement that morning.

"If you'll make the toast and pour the juice, sweetheart," said Mary, the newlywed bride, "breakfast will be ready."

"Great! What are we having for breakfast?" asked John.

"Toast and juice," replied Mary.

•

After the big Super Bowl party, John figures he'd better spend some quality time with his wife. He climbs upstairs, walks in the bedroom, and crawls into bed.

"All right, honey," he says, "give me a play you want me to run."

"How about foreplay?" his wife replies.

"What's the Four Play?" says John.

"You know," the wife says, "it happens before the two-minute warning."

•

A couple has a male friend who's visiting from out of state when an unexpected blizzard blows in and keeps him from traveling. Since the couple has no guest room, he says he'll find a nearby hotel and be on his way in the morning.

"Nonsense," says the wife. "Our bed is plenty big enough for all three of us, and we're all friends here."

The husband concurs, and before long they're settled in: husband in the middle, wife on his left, friend on his right.

After a while, the husband begins snoring, and the wife sneaks over to the friend's side of the bed and invites him to have sex with her. Naturally, he'd like to, but he's reluctant. "We're in the same bed with your husband! He'll wake up, and he'll kill me."

"Don't worry about it," she says, "he's such a sound sleeper, he'll never notice. If you don't believe me, just yank a hair off his butt. He won't even wake up."

So the friend yanks a hair off the husband's butt, and sure enough, she's right . . . her husband sleeps right through. So, she and the friend have sex, then she goes back to her side of the bed.

After about twenty minutes, though, she's back on his side of the bed, asking him to do it again. The same argument follows, another hair is yanked from the husband's butt, and again they have sex. This keeps up for about half the night, until after about the fourth time, when the wife goes back to her side.

Then the husband rolls over and whispers to his friend, "I don't mind that you're f***ing my wife, but do you really have to use my butt as your scoreboard?"

•

A man and his wife are in the bedroom one night and they have just finished making love.

"Honey, did you enjoy the fun we just had?" he asks.

"Yes, of course, dear. Didn't you hear me laughing?"

•

Tom's wife wasn't very attractive, but he was no oil painting, either. After the wedding ceremony, Tom asked the minister how much the cost was.

"Just give me what you think it is worth to have this lady for your wife," replied the minister.

Tom looked at his wife and handed the minister $50.

The minister looked at Tom's wife and gave him $42 change.

•

Bill: "Anne! Help me! I'm a sex-crazed beast that can never get enough no matter how many times I do it! You work in a doctor's office—is there something you can give me for it?"

Anne (after rifling through her purse for a moment): "Sixty dollars and my wedding ring."

•

This guy called up his lawyer to tell him he was filing for divorce, and the lawyer inquired as to the grounds for the suit.

"I've got grounds, all right," sputtered the irate husband. "Can you believe my wife told me I'm a lousy lover?"

"That's why you're suing?"

"Of course not. I'm suing because she knows the difference."

•

Pa and Ma were taking a load of produce into town to sell. Pa
held the reins as the old horse trotted down the road.

Ma said softly, "Pa, hold my hand."

Pa obliged.

A bit later, Ma said, "Pa, kiss me?" So he kissed her.

A little farther along, she said, "Pa—"

"Damn it, Ma!" snapped Pa. "Get off the cucumbers and sit
on the melons!"

•

A woman had gained a few pounds. It was most noticeable to
her when she squeezed into a pair of her old blue jeans.

Wondering if the added weight was noticeable to everyone
else, she asked her husband, "Honey, do these jeans make me
look like the side of the house?"

"No, dear, not at all," he replied. "Our house isn't blue."

•

An old Jewish couple is sitting around one evening and the
man says to his wife, "We are about to celebrate our fiftieth
wedding anniversary. We've had a wonderful life together,
full of contentment and blessing. But there's something I've
always wondered about: tell me, have you ever been unfaith-
ful to me?"

She hesitates a while, then says, "Yes, three times."

"Three times? How did it happen?"

The wife begins slowly, "Well, do you remember right after
we were married and we were broke and the bank was going
to foreclose on our little house?"

"Yes, that was really a terrible time," replies the man.

"And remember when I went to see the bank manager one
night and the next day the bank extended our loan?"

"It's hard to take," the man says, "but I guess it really was for us and I can forgive you. What was the second time?"

"Well, do you remember years later when you almost died from the heart problem because we couldn't afford the operation?"

"Yes, I do."

"Then you remember that right after I went to see the doctor he did your operation at no cost?"

"Yes," says the husband. "That shocks me, too, but I understand you did it because of your love for me, and I forgive you. But what was the third time?"

The wife lowers her head. "Remember when you ran for president of our synagogue and needed sixty-two more votes?"

•

A man approached a beautiful woman in a large supermarket and said, "I've lost my wife here in the supermarket. Can you talk to me for a couple of minutes?"

The woman looked puzzled. "Why talk to me?"

"Because every time I talk to a woman with tits like yours, my wife appears out of nowhere!"

•

A professor of mathematics sent this fax to his wife:

> *Dear Wife: You must realize that you are fifty-four years old, and I have certain needs that you are no longer able to satisfy. I am otherwise happy with you as my wife, and I sincerely hope you will not be hurt or offended to learn that by the time you receive this letter I will be at the Grand Hotel with my eighteen-year-old teaching assistant. I'll be home before midnight. —Your Husband*

When he arrived at the hotel, a fax was waiting for him that read as follows:

Dear Husband: You, too, are fifty-four years old, and by the time you receive this letter, I will be at the Breakwater Hotel with the eighteen-year-old pool boy. Being the brilliant mathematician that you are, you can easily appreciate the fact that 18 goes into 54 a lot more times than 54 goes into 18. Don't wait up.

•

Jack wakes up in his bedroom with a terrible hangover. He painfully opens his eyes, and the first thing he sees is a couple of aspirins and a glass of water on the night table. He sits up and sees a clean shirt and a freshly pressed suit hanging on the closet door.

He takes the aspirins and notices a note propped on the dresser that says, *Honey, fresh orange juice and cereal are on the kitchen table. I left early to go shopping. Love you.*

So he makes his way down to the kitchen, and sure enough there's his breakfast and the morning newspaper. His teenage son is at the table eating.

Jack asks, "Bobby, what happened here last night?"

His son looks at him and says, "Dad, you came home drunk at three a.m. You knocked over the china cabinet, barfed in the front hall, and passed out on the stairs. Mom and I dragged you upstairs to bed."

Puzzled, Jack asks, "So, why is your mother being so nice to me? She laid out my clothes and had my breakfast on the table."

Bobby replies, "We got you on the bed and Mom tried to undress you. You said, 'Leave me alone, lady, I'm married.' "

•

A man and his wife were having some problems at home and were giving each other the silent treatment. The next day, the man realized that he would need his wife to wake him at 5 a.m. for an early-morning business flight to Chicago. Not wanting to be the first to break the silence (*and lose*), he wrote on a piece of paper, *Please wake me at 5 a.m.*

The next morning the man woke up only to discover it was 9 a.m. and that he had missed his flight. Furious, he was about to go see why his wife hadn't awakened him when he noticed a piece of paper by the bed. It said, *It is 5 a.m. Wake up.*

•

A businessman entered a tavern, sat down at the bar, and ordered a double scotch. After he finished the drink, he peeked inside his shirt pocket, then ordered another double scotch. After he finished that one, he again peeked inside his shirt pocket and ordered another double scotch.

Finally, the bartender said, "Look, buddy, I'll bring you drinks all night long. But you gotta tell me why you look inside your shirt pocket before you order another drink."

The customer replied, "I'm looking at a photo of my wife. When she starts to look good, I know it's time to go home."

•

Wife: "Oh, come on."

Husband: "Leave me alone! I won't be able to sleep afterwards."

Wife: "I can't sleep without it."

Husband: "Why do you think of things like this in the middle of the night?"

Wife: "Because I'm hot."

Husband: "You get hot at the weirdest times."

Wife: "If you loved me, I wouldn't have to beg you."

Husband: "If you loved me, you'd be more considerate."

Wife: "You don't love me anymore."

Husband: "Yes, I do, but let's forget it for tonight."

Wife: (Sob, sob)

Husband: "All right, I'll do it."

Wife: "What's the matter? Need a flashlight?"

Husband: "I can't find it."

Wife: "Oh, for heaven's sake, feel for it!"

Husband: "There! Are you satisfied?"

Wife: "Oh, yes, honey."

Husband: "Is it up far enough?"

Wife: "Oh, that's fine."

Husband: "Now go to bed. And from now on when you want the window open, do it yourself."

•

When the groom removed his socks, his new wife asked, "Ewww, what's wrong with your feet? Your toes look all mangled and weird. Why are your feet so gross?"

"I had tolio as a child," he answered.

"You mean polio?"

"No, tolio. The disease only affected my toes."

The bride was satisfied with this explanation, and they continued undressing. When the groom took off his pants, his bride once again wrinkled up her nose.

"What's wrong with your knees?" she asked. "They're all lumpy and deformed!"

"As a child, I also had kneasles."

"You mean measles?"

"No, kneasles. It was a strange illness that only affected my knees."

The new bride had to be satisfied with this answer. As the undressing continued, her husband at last removed his underwear.

"Don't tell me," she said. "Let me guess . . . Smallcox?"

•

Morris returns from the doctor and tells his wife that the doctor has told him he has only twenty-four hours to live. Given the prognosis, Morris asks his wife for sex. Naturally, she agrees, so they make love.

About six hours later, the husband goes to his wife and says, "Honey, you know I now have only eighteen hours to live. Could we please do it one more time?" Of course, the wife agrees, and they do it again.

Later, as the man gets into bed, he looks at his watch and realizes that he now has only eight hours left. He touches his wife's shoulder and asks, "Honey, please . . . just one more time before I die?"

She says, "Of course, dear," and they make love for the third time.

After this session, the wife rolls over and goes to sleep. Morris, however, worried about his impending death, tosses and turns, until he's down to four more hours. He taps his wife, who rouses. "Honey, I have only four more hours. Do you think we could . . . ?"

At this point, the wife sits up and says, "Listen, Morris, I have to get up in the morning . . . you don't."

•

Fresh from her shower, a woman stands in front of the mirror, complaining to her husband that her breasts are too small. Instead of characteristically telling her it's not so, the husband uncharacteristically comes up with a suggestion.

"If you want your breasts to grow, then every day take a piece of toilet paper and rub it between your breasts for a few seconds."

Willing to try anything, the wife fetches a piece of toilet paper and stands in front of the mirror, rubbing it between her breasts. "How long will this take?" she asks.

"They'll grow larger over a period of years," he replies.

The wife stops. "Why do you think rubbing a piece of toilet paper between my breasts every day will make my breasts grow over the years?"

"Worked for your butt, didn't it?"

•

A woman rushes into her house one morning and yells to her husband, "Sam, pack up your stuff. I just won the lottery!"

"Shall I pack for warm weather or cold?"

"Whatever. Just so you're out of the house by noon!"

•

It is two o'clock in the morning, and a husband and his wife are asleep when suddenly the phone rings. The husband picks up the phone, and before he can say anything, some talking comes from the other end of the line and the husband says, "How the heck do I know? What am I, the weatherman?" and promptly slams the phone down.

His wife rolls over and asks, "Who was that?"

The husband replies, "I don't know. It was some guy who wanted to know if the coast was clear."

•

The distressed-looking man had downed several drinks in rapid succession before the bartender asked him, "You trying to drown your sorrows, buddy?"

"You could say that," the guy replied.

"It usually doesn't work, you know."

"No shit," the man moaned. "I can't even get my wife anywhere near the water!"

•

A woman pregnant with her first child paid a visit to her obstetrician's office. After the exam, she shyly said, "My husband wants me to ask you . . ."

To which the doctor replies, "I know, I know," placing a reassuring hand on her shoulder. "I get asked that all the time. Sex is fine until late in the pregnancy."

"No, that's not it," the woman confessed. "He wants to know if I can still mow the lawn."

•

Charlie marries a virgin. On their wedding night he's on fire, so he gets naked, jumps into bed, and immediately begins groping her.

"Charles, I expect you to be as mannerly in bed as you are at the dinner table."

So, Charlie folds his hands and says, "Is this better?"

"Much better!" she replies with a smile.

"Okay, then, now will you please pass the pussy?"

•

A woman wanted to surprise her husband, so she bought a pair of crotchless panties. When her husband got home from work, he found his wife spread-eagled on the floor with the panties on.

"You want some of this?" she asked.

The husband replied, "Hell no! Look what it did to your underwear!"

•

I went into a drugstore and said, "I need one of them condoms with insecticide."

Trying to hold back a laugh, the druggist replied, "You mean with spermicide?"

I said, "No. I mean insecticide. My wife has a bug up her ass and I aim to kill the son of a bitch."

•

Having gone to his secretary's apartment for some hot overtime, Mersky was astonished to wake up and find that it was three in the morning. "My wife is going to kill me!"

Unsure of how he would explain it, he ran out to the nearest pay phone and called his wife excitedly.

"Honey, thank God!" he began. "Don't pay the ransom. I escaped!"

•

John came home from work one afternoon and, being horny as hell, took his beautiful girlfriend, Suzy, upstairs to the bedroom. He undressed her, but before he took his pants off, he removed a packet of condoms from his pocket. "What are those?" Suzy asked.

"Olympic condoms," replied John.

"What makes them Olympic?"

"There are three colors: gold, silver, and bronze."

"Which color are you planning to wear tonight?" asked Suzy.

"Gold, of course!"

"Well," said Suzy, "why don't you wear silver and come second for a change!"

•

On their wedding night, the young bride went up to her new husband.

"Since we're married now, we can arrange our sex life like this: In the evening, if my hair is done, that means I don't want sex at all. If my hair is somewhat undone, that means I may or may not have sex, and if my hair is completely undone, that means I want sex."

"Okay, sweetheart," the groom replied. "When I come home, I usually have a drink. If I have only one drink, that means I don't want sex. If I have two drinks, I may or may not want sex. But if I have three drinks, your hair doesn't matter!"

•

One night, an eighty-seven-year-old woman came home from playing bingo to find her husband in bed with another woman. Angry, she became violent and ended up pushing him off the balcony of their twentieth-floor apartment, killing him instantly.

When brought before the court on charges of murder, she was asked if she had anything to say in defense of herself.

"Well, Your Honor," she began coolly, "I figured that at ninety-two, if he could f***, he could fly."

•

It's after dinner when a man realizes he's out of cigarettes. He decides to pop down to the local bar for a pack, telling his wife he'll be right back.

He's persuaded by the bartender to share a cold one. As he's nursing it, a gorgeous blonde comes in the door, but he looks the other way. She comes over and sits down. One thing leads to another and she invites him home.

Back at her place, they screw like rabbits, until the next thing he knows, it's four o'clock in the morning. Jumping out of bed, he shakes the woman awake, asking if she has any baby powder.

"In the bathroom cabinet," she says.

He dusts his hands, drives home doing ninety, and pulls into the driveway to find his wife waiting up for him, rolling pin in hand.

"Where the hell have you been?" she screams.

"Well, you see, honey," he stammers, "I only went out for cigarettes, but Jake offered me a beer, and then this beautiful blonde walked in and we got to talking and drinking, and I ended up back at her place making love—"

"Wait a minute," snapped his wife. "Let me see your hands." Turning on him furiously, she says, "Don't lie, you rotten little shit . . . you've been bowling again!"

•

One night, as a couple lies down for bed, the husband gently taps his wife on the shoulder and starts rubbing her arm. The wife turns over and says, "I'm sorry, honey, I've got a gynecologist appointment tomorrow and I want to stay fresh."

The husband, rejected, turns over and tries to sleep. A few minutes later, he rolls back over and taps his wife again. This time he whispers in her ear, "Do you have a dentist appointment tomorrow, too?"

•

A man was visiting his wife in the hospital, where she had been in a coma for several years. On this visit, he decides to rub her left breast instead of just talking to her. As he does this, she lets out a sigh.

The man runs out and tells the doctor, who says this is a good sign and suggests he try rubbing her right breast to see if there is any reaction.

The man goes in and rubs her right breast, and this brings a moan. From this, the doctor suggests that the man should go in and try oral sex, saying he will wait outside, as it is a personal act and he doesn't want the man to be embarrassed.

The man goes in, then comes out about five minutes later, white as a sheet, and tells the doctor his wife is dead. The doctor asks what happened, to which the man replies, "She choked."

•

A guy walks into a bar with a pet alligator by his side. He puts the alligator up on the bar. He turns to the astonished patrons. "I'll make you a deal. I'll open this alligator's mouth and place my genitals inside. Then the gator will close his mouth for one minute. He'll then open his mouth and I'll remove my unit unscathed. In return for witnessing this spectacle, each of you will buy me a drink."

The crowd murmured their approval. The man stood up on the bar, dropped his trousers, and placed his privates in the alligator's open mouth. The gator closed his mouth as the crowd gasped. After a minute, the man grabbed a beer bottle and rapped the alligator hard on the top of his head. The gator opened his mouth and the man removed his genitals unscathed as promised. The crowd cheered and the first of his free drinks were delivered.

The man stood up again and made another offer. "I'll pay

anyone $100 who's willing to give it a try." A hush fell over the crowd.

After a while, a hand went up in the back of the bar. A woman timidly spoke up. "I'll try, but you have to promise not to hit me on the head with the beer bottle."

•

A man takes his wife to the livestock show. They start heading down the alley that houses the bulls. They come up to the first bull, whose sign states, "This bull mated fifty times last year."

The wife turns to her husband and says, "He mated fifty times in a year, you could learn from him."

They proceed to the next bull, whose sign states, "This bull mated sixty-five times last year."

The wife turns to her husband and says, "This one mated sixty-five times last year. That is over five times a month. You could learn from this one also."

They proceed to the last bull and his sign says, "This bull mated 365 times last year."

The wife's mouth drops open and she says, "*Wow!* He mated 365 times last year. That is *once a day*! You could really learn from this one!"

The man turns to his wife and says, "Go up and inquire if it was 365 times with the same cow."

•

A woman is married to a nature lover and nudist. One day she sees him sunbathing in the nude near the swimming pool.

She: "Go in the house before the neighbors see you— they'll think I married you for your money."

•

Jake is calling his wife, Becky, on the phone. They have been married a long, long time.

"Becky, I'm feeling the urge. I'm coming home, get ready.

I feel it coming; it's my semiannual hard-on. Put on the silk sheets."

Becky: "No, Jake, it's your annual semi-hard-on."

•

Abe and Becky are honeymooning.

At 1 a.m. Becky says, "When are you gonna?"

At 2 a.m. Becky says, "When are you gonna?"

Abe at 4 a.m. finally responds, "When am I gonna what?"

Becky: "When are you gonna get off?"

•

A lady had just married a man who was not giving her any sex. She was getting pretty pissed because every night her husband went to the bar and got so drunk that he was unfit for any sexual activities.

One night the young lady decided to take action. She got dressed in her sexiest outfit and sat on the couch in her lacies until at last her husband came home.

"Come upstairs with me to the bathroom," he said awkwardly.

Oh, yes, I'm getting some action now, the young lady thought.

They walked upstairs and she began undressing herself for him.

"Do a handstand in front of the mirror for me," he said.

I'm almost there, she thought.

The guy put his chin on her pussy and said, "The guys at the bar were right—a beard does look good on me."

•

A distinguished-looking lady walks into a tattoo shop and sits down.

The owner, amazed at seeing such a sophisticated lady in his shop, runs over immediately and asks if he can help her. To his shock and utter delight, she lifts up her silk dress and points to her right inner thigh . . . high up.

"Right here," she says, "I want you to tattoo a turkey, and underneath it, I want the word *Thanksgiving*."

Then she points to her left thigh . . . just as high up, and says, "On this side, I want you to tattoo an evergreen tree with lights and tinsel and an angel on top, and I want the word *Christmas* underneath it."

The owner looks at her. "Okay, lady, it's none of my business, but that is probably the most unusual request I've ever heard. Why in the world do you want to do that?"

"Well," the lady said, "I'm sick and tired of my husband always complaining that there's never anything good to eat between Thanksgiving and Christmas."

•

A newly married couple came home from their honeymoon and moved into the upstairs apartment they'd rented from the groom's parents.

That night, the mother of the groom awakened her husband from his sleep. "Tony, listen!" she whispered. Upstairs, the bed was creaking in rhythm.

The wife said, "Come on, Tony! Let's make love!"

So Tony climbed on top of his wife and pounded the old bone home.

As he was trying to fall back asleep fifteen minutes later, the bed upstairs started creaking in rhythm again.

"Come on, Tony!" said the wife. "Let's make love again!"

Once again, Tony climbed on top of his wife and screwed her as hard as he could.

As he was trying to fall back asleep fifteen minutes later, the bed upstairs started creaking in rhythm again.

"Come on, Tony!" said the wife. "Let's do it again!"

So, Tony grabbed a broom and pounded on the ceiling as he shouted, "Hey, kids, cut it out! You're killing your old man down here!"

•

A woman recently lost her husband. Their marriage had been lousy, and she was relieved that he was finally gone.

She had him cremated and brought his ashes home.

Picking up the urn that he was in, she poured him out on the counter.

Then she started talking to him, and tracing her fingers in the ashes, she said, "You know that fur coat you promised me?"

She answered, "I bought it with the insurance money!"

She then said, "Remember that new car you promised me?"

She answered, "Well, I bought it with the insurance money!"

Still tracing her finger in the ashes, she said, "Remember that blow job I promised you? Well . . . here it comes."

•

"I'm worried that I'm losing my wife's love," the husband told the counselor.

"Has she started to neglect you?"

"Not at all," the dejected man replied. "She meets me at the door with a cold drink and a warm kiss. My shirts are always ironed; she's a great cook. The house is always neat, and she keeps the kids out of my hair. She even lets me choose the television shows we watch, and she never objects to kinky sex or says she has a headache."

"So what's the problem?"

"Maybe I'm just being too sensitive," the husband ventured, "but at night, when she thinks I'm sleeping, she puts her lips close to my ear and whispers, 'Die! Die, you son of a bitch!'"

•

Two buddies were sharing drinks while discussing their wives. "Does your wife ever . . . well, you know . . . does she . . .well, let you do it doggie style?" asked one of the two.

"Well, not exactly," his friend replied. "She's more into the dog-trick aspect of it."

"Oh, I see. Kinky stuff, huh?"

"Well, not exactly. Whenever I make a move, she's most likely to roll over and play dead."

•

Will came home dejected because a boyhood friend was about to be executed by hanging for murder. His mood wasn't improved when his bitchy wife started berating him after dinner for one thing after another.

"That's enough!" he finally announced. "Poor Sam Wright is going to die tonight, and all you can do is yell at me. I'm going upstairs."

Alone, watching TV, the woman had begun to regret her conduct when a newscaster reported that the condemned man had been given a last-hour reprieve. She hurried upstairs, heard water running, burst into the bathroom, yanked open the shower-stall door, and shouted, "They're not hanging Wright tonight!"

"Good God, woman!" shouted back her husband. "Isn't there anything about me that satisfies you?"

•

Three women always hang their laundry out in the backyard. When it rains, the laundry always gets wet. All the laundry, that is, except for Sophie's. The other two women wonder why Sophie never has her laundry out on the days it rains. So one day, they are all out in the backyard putting their clothes on the line when one of the women says to Sophie, "Say, how come when it rains, your laundry is never out?"

"Well," says Sophie, "when I wake up in the morning, I look over at Saul. If his penis is hanging over his right leg, I know it's going to be a great day and I can hang out the wash. If his penis is hanging over his left leg, I know it's going to rain, so I don't hang out the wash."

"What if he has an erection?" asks one of the women.

"Honey," says Sophie, "on a day like that, you don't do the laundry!"

•

A couple had been married for twenty years. Every time they made love the husband always insisted on shutting off the lights.

Well, after twenty years the wife felt this was ridiculous. She figured she would break him of this crazy habit. So one night, while they were in the middle of a wild, screaming, passionate session, she turned on the lights.

She looked down and saw her husband was holding a battery-operated pleasure device . . . a vibrator . . . soft, wonderful, and larger than a real "one."

She went completely ballistic. "You impotent fake," she screamed at him, "how could you be lying to me all of these years. You better explain yourself!"

The husband looked her straight in the eyes and said calmly, "I'll explain the toy . . . if you explain the kid."

•

A newlywed couple were spending their honeymoon in a remote log-cabin resort way up the mountains. They had registered on Saturday and had not been seen for five days. An elderly couple ran the resort, and they were getting concerned about the welfare of these newlyweds. The old man decided to go see if they were all right. He knocked on the door of the cabin, and a weak voice from inside answered. The old man asked if they were okay.

"Yes, we're fine. We're living on the fruits of love."

The old man replied, "I thought so. Would you mind not throwing the peelings out the window—they're choking my ducks!"

Viagra

The boss of a company called a staff meeting in the middle of a particularly stressful week. When everyone gathered, the employer, who understood the benefits of having fun, told the burnt-out staff that the purpose of the meeting was to have a quick contest, whose theme was Viagra advertising slogans.

As they divided into groups, the only rule was that they had to use past ad slogans to capture the essence of Viagra.

About seven minutes later, they turned in their suggestions and created a Top Ten list.

10. Viagra, it's "Whaazzzz up!"
9. Viagra, the quicker pecker upper.
8. Viagra, like a rock.
7. Viagra, when it absolutely, positively has to be there tonight.
6. Viagra, be all that you can be.
5. Viagra, reach out and touch someone.
4. Viagra, strong enough for a woman, but made for a man.
3. Viagra, tastes great! . . . More filling!
2. Viagra, we bring good things to life!

And the unanimous #1 slogan:

1. This is your penis. This is your penis on drugs.
   Any questions?

•

A wife says to her husband, "Are you hungry for breakfast?"

He replies, "No, it must be the Viagra."

A few hours later she says, "Do you want to eat lunch?"

He answers, "No, it must be the Viagra."

Later still, she asks him, "How about supper?"

He says, "No, it must be the Viagra."

She says, "Well, get the f*** off me, I'm starving."

•

A doctor is making his rounds in the hospital when he comes upon a guy with the worst case of sunburn he has ever seen. The poor guy is burnt raw from head to toe and is in agony. He says to the doctor, "Is there anything you can give me to ease this terrible pain?"

So the doctor says, "Yes, I'll prescribe some Viagra for you."

"Viagra?" asks the guy. "How will that help my sunburn?"

"It won't help your sunburn much," the doc says, "but at least it'll keep the sheets off it!"

•

Pfizer corporation is making the announcement today that Viagra will soon be available in liquid form and will be marketed by Pepsi as a power beverage suitable for use "as is" or as a mixer.

Pepsi's proposed ad campaign claims, "It will now be possible for a man to literally pour himself a stiff one." Obviously, we can no longer call this a "soft drink." This additive gives new meaning to the names *cocktails, highballs,* and just a good old-fashioned *stiff drink.*

Pepsi will market the new concoction by the name *Mount and Do.*

Gay

A golfer is looking for his ball in the woods when he comes up to another man hugging a tree with his ear firmly against it.

Seeing this, the golfer inquires, "Just out of curiosity, what the heck are you doing?"

"I'm listening to the music of the tree."

"You gotta be kiddin' me."

"No, would you like to give it a try?"

"Well, okay . . ." So the golfer wraps his arms around the tree and presses his ear up against it. With this the other guy slaps a set of handcuffs on him on the other side of the tree, takes his wallet, jewelry, and car keys, then strips him naked and leaves.

Two hours later another nature lover strolls by, sees this guy handcuffed to the tree, stark naked, and asks, "What the heck happened to you?"

So the golfer tells the guy the whole story about how he got there. While he's telling his story, the other guy shakes his head in sympathy, walks around behind him, kisses him behind the ear, and says, "This just ain't gonna be your day."

•

These two gay guys give each other anal each night. One night, beforehand, one of the guys has to go to the toilet. So the other guy says, "Okay, but don't wank in there, save it for later." And the first guy agrees.

This guy was in the toilet for a while so the other guy decides to check on him. When he opens the door, he sees lots of semen everywhere. He gets angry and yells, "I thought I told you not to wank and to save it for later!"

The first guy replies, "I didn't wank, I just farted."

•

Two lesbians were walking down the street and passed a beautiful woman.

"Unh-unh," mumbled one of the lesbians.

It continued like that; anytime they passed a gorgeous woman and the first one waxed lyrical about her, the other would just mumble, "Unh-unh."

When they got to the bar, the first lesbian turned to the other. "Hey, what's with all the mumbling back there when we came across all those beautiful women?"

"I'm sorry," said the second lesbian, "my tongue got hard!"

•

While enjoying a drink with a buddy one night, this guy decides to try his luck with an attractive young girl sitting alone by the bar. To his surprise, she asks him to join her for a drink and eventually asks him if he'd like to come back to her place. The pair jump into a taxi and go to her place, where they make passionate love.

Later, the young man pulls out a cigarette from his jeans and searches for his lighter. Unable to find it, he asks the girl if she has one.

"There might be some matches in the top drawer," she replies.

Opening the drawer of the bedside table, he finds a box of matches sitting neatly on top of a framed picture of another man. Naturally, the guy begins to worry.

"Is this your husband?" he inquires nervously.

"No, silly," she replies, snuggling up to him.

"Your boyfriend then?"

"No, don't be silly." She nibbles at his ear.

"Well, who is he then?" demands the bewildered fellow.

Calmly, the girl takes a match, strikes it, and replies, "That's me before the operation."

•

A guy met this girl in a bar and asked, "May I buy you a drink?"

"Okay," she said, "but it won't do you any good."

A little later, he asks, "May I buy you another drink?"

"Okay," she says again, "but it won't do you any good."

He invites her up to his apartment and she replies, "Okay, but you know it won't do you any good."

They get to his apartment and he says, "You are the most beautiful thing I have ever seen. I want you for my wife."

"Oh, well that's different," she says. "Where is she? Send her in!"

•

A girl goes into the doctor's office for a checkup. As she takes off her blouse, he notices a red *H* on her chest.

"How did you get that mark on your chest?" asks the doctor.

"Oh, my boyfriend went to Harvard, and he's so proud of it that he never takes off his Harvard sweatshirt, even when we make love," she replies.

A couple of days later, another girl comes in for a checkup. As she takes off her blouse, the doctor notices a blue *Y* on her chest.

"How did you get that mark on your chest?" asks the doctor.

"Oh, my boyfriend went to Yale and he's so proud of it that he never takes off his Yale sweatshirt, even when we make love," she replies.

A couple of days later, another girl comes in for a checkup. As she takes off her blouse, the doctor notices a red *M* on her chest. "Do you have a boyfriend at Michigan?" asks the doctor.

"No, but I have a girlfriend at Wisconsin. Why do you ask?"

•

A gay guy walks into a bar and has a drink. All he ever wanted was a hairy chest. This guy next to him has hair sticking out of his shirt.

"Hey, man, how did you get such a hairy chest?"

"Well, I take Vaseline and rub it all over my chest every day to make the hair grow."

So the guy goes home, gets the Vaseline out, and starts rubbing it all over his chest. His boyfriend comes home and says, "What the f*** are you doing?"

He tells him the story from the bar, and his boyfriend says, "If that were true, you'd have a ponytail growing out of your ass by now."

•

A guy comes to the Wild West and, tired from his trip, goes to a saloon to have a beer. As soon as he gets in, he sees everybody else leaving in a hurry. He leans on the counter and asks the bartender, "What's happening?"

"Don't you know? The Black Rider will be here in a few minutes."

The guy asks, "Who the f*** is the Black Rider?"

The bartender replies, "I can't believe you don't know. He's the most dangerous guy I've ever seen. You better get lost before he gets here, or God knows what he will do if he finds you here. I'm just about to leave myself."

The guy thinks, "F*** the Black Rider. I'll stay here and have my beer in peace, and when he comes, I'll show him."

So there he is, all alone in the bar drinking his beer; everybody's gone already, so the whole place is a bit creepy. All of a sudden he hears some steps outside the saloon, the door opens, and a six-foot-five-inch man comes in, all dressed in black—black hat, black shirt, black cowboy boots. The guy can feel his knees tremble—the Black Rider is here!

The man leans on the counter and says, "Hey, you!"

The guy stammers, "Wwwhhho, mmme?"

"Yes, you, come over here," the man demands.

He goes. "Yes, sir, how can I help you, sir?" His voice is shaking, and he can barely stand.

The man says, "Blow me."

The guy thinks, what else can he do—that's the Black Rider he's talking to and he can kill him any second, so he starts doing the job. The man starts moaning.

He asks, "Is everything okay, sir?"

The man replies, "Yes, it's okay, but just hurry up a bit. The Black Rider will be here any minute, and then we're both dead."

•

A man with a bad stomach goes to his doctor and asks him what he can do.

The doctor replies that the illness is quite serious but can be cured by inserting a suppository up his anus.

The man agrees, and so the doctor warns him of the pain, tells him to bend over, and shoves the thing way up his behind.

The doctor then hands him a second dose and tells him to do the same thing in six hours.

So the man goes home and later that evening tries to get the second suppository inserted, but he finds that he cannot reach himself properly to obtain the required depth.

He calls his wife over and tells her what to do.

The wife nods, puts one hand on his shoulder to steady him, and with the other shoves the medicine home.

Suddenly the man screams, *"Damn!"*

"What's the matter?" asks the wife. "Did I hurt you?"

"No," replies the man, "but I just realized that when the doctor did that, he had *both* hands on my shoulders!"

•

Two priests are in a Vatican bathroom using the urinals. One of them looks at the other's penis and notices a Nicoderm patch on it. He turns to the other priest and says, "I believe you're supposed to put that patch on your arm or shoulder, not your penis."

The first priest replies, "It's working just fine. I'm down to two butts a day."

•

Three desperately ill men met with their doctor one day to discuss their options. One was an alcoholic, one was a chain smoker, and one was a gay sex addict. The doctor, addressing all three of them, said, "If any of you indulge in your vices one more time, you will surely die."

The men left the doctor's office, each convinced that he would never again indulge himself in his vice.

While walking toward the subway for their return trip to the suburbs, they passed a bar. The alcoholic, hearing the loud music and smelling the booze, could not stop himself. His buddies accompanied him into the bar, where he had a shot of whiskey. No sooner had he replaced the shot glass on the bar than he fell off his stool, stone-cold dead. His companions, somewhat shaken, left the bar, realizing how seriously they must take the doctor's words. As they walked along, they came upon a cigarette butt lying on the ground, still burning.

The homosexual looked at the chain smoker and said, "You know if you bend over to pick that up, we're both dead."

•

An old cowboy sat down at a bar and ordered a drink. As he sat sipping his drink, a young woman sat down next to him.

She turned to the cowboy and asked, "Are you a real cowboy?"

He replied, "Well, I've spent my whole life breaking colts, working cows, going to rodeos, fixing fences, pulling calves, baling hay, doctoring calves, cleaning my barn, fixing flats, working on tractors, and feeding my dogs, so I guess I am a cowboy."

She said, "I'm a lesbian. I spend my whole day thinking about women. As soon as I get up in the morning, I think about women. When I shower, I think about women. When I watch TV, I think about women. I even think about women when I eat. It seems that everything makes me think of women."

The two sat sipping in silence.

A little while later, a man sat down on the other side of the old cowboy and asked, "Are you a real cowboy?"

He replied, "I always thought I was, but I just found out I'm a lesbian."

•

A married couple was on holiday in Jamaica. They were touring around the marketplace looking at the goods and such when they passed a small sandal shop.

From inside they heard the shopkeeper with a Jamaican accent say, "You foreigners! Come in! Come into my humble shop." So the married couple walked in.

The Jamaican said to them, "I have some special sandals I tink you would be interested in. Dey make you wild at sex."

Well, the wife was really interested in buying the sandals after what the man claimed, but her husband felt he really didn't need them, being the sex god he was. The husband asked the man, "How could sandals make you into a sex freak?"

The Jamaican replied, "Just try dem on, mon."

Well, the husband, after some badgering from his wife,

finally gave in and tried them on. As soon as he slipped them onto his feet, he got this wild look in his eyes, something his wife hadn't seen before! In the blink of an eye, the husband grabbed the Jamaican, bent him violently over a table, yanked down his pants, ripped down his own pants, and grabbed a firm hold of the Jamaican's thighs.

The Jamaican screamed, *"You got dem on de wrong feet, mon!"*

•

A cowboy enters a saloon and two steps in realizes it's a gay bar. "But what the heck," he says to himself, "I really want a drink."

When the bartender approaches, he says to the cowboy, "What's the name of your penis?"

The cowboy says, "Look, I'm not into any of that. All I want is a drink."

The bartender says, "I'm sorry, but I can't serve you until you tell me the name of your penis. Mine, for instance, is called Nike, for the slogan Just Do It. That guy down at the end of the bar calls his Snickers, because It Really Satisfies."

The cowboy looks dumbfounded so the bartender tells him he will give him a second to think it over. So the cowboy asks the man sitting to his left, who is sipping on a beer, "Hey, bud, what's the name of yours?"

The man looks back and says with a smile, "Timex."

The thirsty cowboy asks, "Why Timex?"

The fella proudly replies, "Because It Takes a Lickin' and Keeps on Tickin'!"

A little shaken, the cowboy turns to the fella on his right, who is sipping a fruity margarita, and says, "So, what do you call yours?"

The man turns to him and proudly exclaims, "Ford, because Quality Is Job One." Then he adds, "Have You Driven a Ford, Lately?"

Even more shaken, the cowboy has to think for a moment before he comes up with a name for his manhood. Finally, he turns to the bartender and exclaims, "The name of my penis is Secret. Now give me a beer."

The bartender begins to pour the cowboy a beer, but with a puzzled look asks, "Why Secret?"

The cowboy says, "Because it's *Strong Enough for a Man, but Made for a Woman!*"

•

A young man goes into a bar and picks up a tall woman. After a night of drinking and dancing they go back to his place. She unzips his fly and starts playing with his dick.

"Wow," he says, "you handle my penis so well."

"I should," she replies, "I used to have one just like it . . . only longer!"

•

Bunny and Bob, two frequent users of a chat room, discovered that they had a lot in common. Eventually, they abandoned the chat room for a more intimate correspondence. After months of virtual kinkiness, the two decided to meet each other face-to-face at a small café. Bunny arrived a little late.

One customer, a short, frail man with an eye patch, sat at the back of the café. "Are you Bob?" asked Bunny.

"Yes, I am," said Bob.

"Unbelievable!" Bunny exclaimed. "You told me that you were tall, dark, and handsome."

"How do you think I feel?" Bob asked, his face turning red. "You told me that you were skinny, blond, and female."

•

A drunk in a bar keeps hitting on a lesbian who is waiting for her date.

The drunk just won't take no for an answer.

"Tell you what. I'll sleep with you if you can name one thing a man can do for me that my vibrator can't!" the lesbian smirks.

The drunk thinks for a moment. "Okay, let's see your vibrator buy the next round of drinks!"

•

Two couples had arranged to spend a long weekend at a country hotel. During the two-hour drive to the hotel, they decided that, to spice up the weekend, they would try a little partner swapping. Having checked into the hotel, each went on to the bedroom with his or her new partner. The sex started immediately. It was hot and heavy.

After half an hour one of the men turned to his new partner and said, "That was terrific. We should have done this years ago. I wonder how the girls are getting on."

•

A gay man goes to the doctor for an HIV test. A week later he goes back and the doctor confirms his worst fears—the test showed positive. The man is destroyed. He breaks down and begs the doctor to prescribe something for him, anything, that'll help.

"Well," the doctor says, "go down to the health-food store and buy a pound of prunes, then go to the drugstore and get some strong laxatives, then wander down to the supermarket and buy a bottle of Tabasco sauce and some chili powder. Go home and blend it all together and heat it on the stove for twenty minutes . . . then drink it."

The man's a bit dubious. "And that'll cure the HIV?"

"No," says the doctor, smiling, "but it'll teach you what your asshole is for!"

•

A gay man finally decided he could no longer hide his sexuality from his parents. He went over to their house and found his mother in the kitchen cooking dinner. He sat down at the kitchen table, let out a big sigh, and said, "Mom, I have something to tell you. I'm gay."

His mother made no reply and gave no response, and the guy was about to repeat it to make sure she'd heard him, when she turned away from the pot she was stirring and said calmly, "You're gay—doesn't that mean you put other men's penises in your mouth?"

The guy said nervously, "Uh, yeah, Mom, that's right."

His mother went back to stirring the pot, then suddenly whacked him over the head with a spoon and said, "Don't you *ever* complain about my cooking again!"

•

A country boy ends up in the big city. He is walking around in awe of everything. He decides to quench his thirst and enters a bar. After a couple of beers he goes to the can. Walking in, he's shocked at what he sees. He quickly leaves.

The barkeep asks, "What's wrong?"

The country boy replies, "You wouldn't believe what is going on in there."

"What?"

The country boy is shaking his head, "Well, there is a guy standing at the urinal being corn-holed by a guy behind him. And that guy is getting his fudge packed by a guy behind *him*."

The bartender leans in closer, gets all serious, and lisps out his next question. "The guy in the middle wouldn't have been wearing a yellow T-shirt, would he?"

"I think he was. Why?"

"Damn fool's lucky at cards, too."

•

Cyril and Cecil are happily driving along in their car. As they come to an intersection, they stop for the red light. All of a sudden a big tractor-trailer comes crunching through the back of their car!

Cyril and Cecil are really pissed. Cyril asks Cecil to get out of the car to tell off the truck driver.

So Cecil gets out of the car and approaches the truck driver, who apparently is one huge mother trucker.

"You bloody idiot! Look at what you've done to our beloved car!" exclaims Cecil. "You're going to pay for this damage!"

"Suck my dick!" shouts the truck driver.

This prompted Cecil to go back to his car, to discuss the situation with Cyril. "I think he wants to settle out of court."

•

Philip fancied himself quite a ladies' man, so when his cruise ship went down in a storm and he found himself stranded on a desert island with six women, he couldn't believe his good fortune. They quickly agreed that each woman would have one night a week with the only man.

Philip threw himself into the arrangement with gusto, working even on his day off, but as the weeks stretched into months, he found himself looking forward to that day of rest more and more eagerly.

One afternoon he was sitting on the beach and wishing for some more men to share his duties when he caught sight of a man waving from a life raft that was bobbing on the waves. Philip swam out, pulled the raft to shore, and did a little jig of happiness.

"You can't believe how happy I am to see you," he cried.

The new fellow eyed him up and down and cooed, "You're a sight for sore eyes, too, you gorgeous thing."

"Shit," sighed Philip, "there go my Sundays."

•

Two gay guys are in a bar and a beautiful blonde walks in wearing a tight T-shirt with no bra. "God, look at that," says one. "It's enough to make you want to be a lesbian."

•

A guy is riding the bus when the most beautiful woman he has ever seen gets on. The only problem is that she is a nun. He decides to approach her anyway.

"Sister, you are the most beautiful woman I've ever seen and I must make love to you," he says.

"I'm sorry but I've given my body to God," she replies, then leaves.

Suddenly the bus driver turns around to the guy and says, "I know a way you can get her in the sack." The bus driver tells the guy about how the nun goes to confession every day at three in the afternoon. The bus driver tells the guy a foolproof plan, and the guy leaves happy knowing he's going to get some.

The next day at three the guy is in the confessional booth dressed as a priest. When the nun approaches in the darkness, he says, "Sister, God has told me I must have sex with you."

She replies, "Well, if God has said it, we must do it. However, because of my strong commitment to God, I will only take it up the ass."

The guy figures this isn't a problem and proceeds to have the best sex ever. After it is over, he whips off his outfit and says, "Surprise, I'm the guy on the bus."

With that, the nun turns around and says, "Surprise, I'm the bus driver."

•

A guy sits down at the bar, orders a drink, and holds his head in his hands. When the bartender comes back, the guy is swearing softly under his breath and shaking his head.

"Hey, Bob, what's happening?" asks the bartender.

"I'm in *deep shit*," replies the customer. "I just got caught screwing my neighbor."

"Oh, wow! Who caught you? Your wife?"

"No, *his* wife!"

•

A guy walks into a bar and orders six tequilas. The bartender asks, "What's wrong?"

The guy says that he just found out that his younger son is gay. The bartender says he's sorry about it.

After a couple of days the guy comes back and orders ten tequilas. The bartender asks, "What's wrong now?"

The guy responds that he found out that his older son was gay, too. The bartender says that he's sorry.

The guy returns a few days later and orders fifteen tequilas. The bartender bursts out, "Isn't anyone in your family gettin' any pussy?"

The guy gets really pissed and says, "Yeah, my wife!"

•

"My wife and I split up because we had too much in common," said the solitary drinker to the bartender.

"Is that so?"

"Yeah—we both like to eat pussy!"

•

Two lesbians were having a drink at the bar when a good-looking woman waved at them from across the room.

"I'd like to get between her legs," said the first lesbian.

"Oh, no, you wouldn't," responded her friend. "She's hung like a doughnut."

•

We had gay burglars the other night. They broke in and re-arranged the furniture.

•

Because of a bad case of hemorrhoids, a gay man went to his doctor. The physician prescribed suppositories, but when it came time to use them, the young man was afraid he would do it wrong. So he went into the bathroom and, bending over, looked through his legs into the mirror to line up the target. All of a sudden, his penis became stiff and blocked his view.

"Oh, stop it," the young man scolded his organ, "it's only me!"

•

"Dad, I think the priest is a homosexual."

"What makes you think that, Son?"

"Because he closes his eyes when I kiss him."

•

What happened when three gays attacked a woman?

Two of them held her down, and the other started doing her hair.

•

Did you hear about the gay man who couldn't tell K-Y jelly from putty?

All his windows fell out.

•

Sam has been in the computer business for twenty-five years and is finally sick of the stress. He quits his job and buys fifty acres of land in Vermont as far away from humanity as possible. Sam sees the postman once a week and gets groceries once a month. Otherwise, it's total peace and quiet. After six months or so of almost total isolation, he's finishing dinner when someone knocks on his door. He opens it and there is a big, bearded Vermonter standing there.

"Name's Enoch . . . your neighbor from miles over the ridge. . . . Having a party Saturday, thought you'd like to come."

"Great," says Sam, "after six months of this, I'm ready to meet some local folks. Thank you."

As Enoch is leaving, he stops. "Gotta warn you, there's gonna be some drinkin'!"

"Not a problem . . . after twenty-five years in the computer business, I can do that with the best of them."

Again, as he starts to leave, Enoch stops. "More 'n likely there's gonna be some fightin', too."

Damn, Sam thinks . . . *tough crowd.* "Well, I get along with people. I'll be there. Thanks again."

Once again, Enoch turns from the door. "I've seen some wild sex at these parties, too."

"Now, that's not a problem," says Sam. "Remember, I've been alone for six months! I'll definitely be there. . . . By the way, what should I wear to the party?"

Enoch stops in the door again and says, "Whatever you want, it's just gonna be the two of us!"

•

The scene is in prison. They've just admitted a new prisoner to share a cell. The veteran prisoner says to the new prisoner, "Let's play house—you wanna be the husband or the wife?"

New man: "Thanks, I'll be the husband."

Veteran: "Okay, now come over and suck Mama's big cock."

•

A belligerent drunk walks into a bar and hollers, "I can lick any man in the place!"

The nearest customer looks him up and down, then says, "Crude, but direct. Tell me, is this your first time in a gay bar?"

•

The monsignor tells three young Irish candidates for the priesthood they have to pass one more test: the celibacy test. The monsignor leads them into a room and tells them to undress, and a small bell is tied to each man's willy.

In comes a beautiful woman, wearing a sexy belly-dancer costume. She begins to dance sensually around the first candidate.

Ting-a-ling.

"Oh, Patrick," says the monsignor, "I am so disappointed in your lack of control. Run along now and take a long, cold shower and pray about your carnal weakness." The candidate leaves.

The dancer continues, dancing around the second candidate, slowly peeling off her layers of veils. As the last veil drops:

Ting-a-ling.

"Joseph, Joseph," sighs the monsignor. "You, too, are unable to withstand your carnal desires. Off you go . . . take a long, cold shower and pray for forgiveness."

The dancer continues, dancing naked in front of the final candidate. Nothing. She writhes up and down against his body. No response. Finally, exhausted, she quits.

"Michael, my son, I am truly proud of you," says the monsignor. "Only you have the true strength of character needed to become a priest. Now, go and join your weaker brethren in the showers."

Ting-a-ling.

•

Visiting a lawyer for advice, the wife said, "I want you to help me get a divorce."

The lawyer says, "Okay, what are your grounds?"

"My husband is getting a little queer to sleep with."

"What do you mean?" asked the attorney. "Does he force you to indulge in unusual sex practices?"

"No," replied the woman, "and neither does the little queer."

Kids

A little kid walks onto a bus and sits right behind the driver. He then starts yelling, "If my father was a bull, and my mother was a cow, I'd be a little bull."

The driver gets annoyed at the noisy kid, who continues, "If my father was an elephant and my mother was a girl elephant, I would be a little elephant."

The kid goes on with several animals until the bus driver gets angry and yells at the kid, "What if your father was a drunk, and your mother was a prostitute?"

The kid smiles and says, "Then I would be a bus driver!"

•

A little farm boy was walking to the school bus one morning when he began kicking farm animals. First he kicked a pig. Then he kicked a chicken. Finally he kicked a cow. His mother, watching from the kitchen window, decided she would handle the situation after he returned from school.

When he comes home, his mother confronts him and says, "I saw you this morning kicking those animals. Since you kicked a pig, you get no ham or bacon for a week. Since you kicked a chicken, you get no eggs for a week. Since you kicked a cow, you get no beef products for a week. Now go wait for your father and tell him what you have done."

The boy waits for his father to arrive. When his father comes home after a particularly hard day at work, he is so mad that he kicks the cat across the front yard.

The boy looks at his mother and says, "You want to tell him no pussy, or shall I?"

•

Two babies were sitting in their cribs and one baby shouted to the other, "Are you a little girl or a little boy?"

"I don't know," replied the other baby, giggling.

"What do you mean, you don't know?" said the first baby.

"I mean I don't know how to tell the difference."

"Well, I do," said the first baby, chuckling. "I'll climb into your crib and find out."

He carefully maneuvered himself into the other baby's crib, then quickly disappeared beneath the blankets. After a couple of minutes, he resurfaced with a big grin on his face.

"You're a little girl, and I'm a little boy," he said proudly.

"You're ever so clever," cooed the baby girl, "but how can you tell?"

"It's quite easy really," replied the baby boy. "You've got pink socks and I've got blue."

•

A college professor was doing a study testing the senses of first-graders using a bowl of Life Savers.

He gave all of the children the same kind of Life Savers one at a time and asked them to identify them by color and flavor.

The children began to say:

"Red . . . cherry."

"Yellow . . . lemon."

"Green . . . lime."

"Orange . . . orange."

Finally, the professor gave them all honey Life Savers.

After eating them for a few moments, none of the children could identify the taste.

"Well," the professor said, "I'll give you all a clue. It's what your mother may sometimes call your father."

One little girl looked up in horror, spit hers out, and yelled, "Everybody, spit them out—they're assholes!"

•

A father who worked away from home all week always made a special effort with his family on the weekends. Every Sunday morning he would take his daughter out for a drive in the car.

One Sunday, however, he had a bad cold, so he didn't really feel like driving at all. Luckily, his wife came to the rescue and decided that for this week she would take their daughter out.

They returned just before lunch and the little girl ran upstairs to see her father.

"Well," the father asked, "did you enjoy your ride?"

"Oh, yes, Daddy," the girl replied, "and do you know what? We didn't see a single bastard!"

•

For his birthday, little Patrick asked for a ten-speed bicycle. His father said, "Son, we'd give you one, but the mortgage on this house is $80,000 and your mother just lost her job. There's no way we can afford it."

The next day the father saw little Patrick heading out the front door with a suitcase. So he asked, "Son, where are you going?"

Little Patrick told him, "I was walking past your room last night and I heard you telling Mom you were pulling out. Then I heard her tell you to wait because she was coming, too. And I'll be damned if I'm staying here by myself with an $80,000 mortgage and no bike!"

•

A well-dressed businessman was walking down the street when a little kid covered in dirt said to him respectfully, "Sir, can you tell me the time?"

The portly man stopped, carefully unbuttoned his coat and jacket, removed a large watch from a vest pocket, looked at it, and said, "It is a quarter to three, young man."

"Thanks," said the boy. "At exactly three o'clock you can kiss my ass."

With that the kid took off running, and with an angry cry, the outraged businessman started chasing him. He had not been running long when an old friend stopped him.

"Why are you running like this at your age?" asked the friend.

Gasping and almost incoherent with fury, the businessman said, "That little brat asked me the time, and when I told him it was a quarter to three, he told me that at exactly three, I should kiss his ass!"

"So what's your hurry?" said the friend. "You still have ten minutes."

•

A little boy walks into his parents' room to see his mom on top of his dad bouncing up and down. The mom sees her son and quickly dismounts, worried about what her son has seen. She dresses quickly and goes to find him. The son sees his mom and asks, "What were you and Dad doing?"

The mother replies, "Well, you know your dad has a big tummy, and I have to get on top of it to help flatten it."

"You're wasting your time," says the boy.

"Why is that?" asks his mom, puzzled.

"Well, when you go shopping, the lady next door comes over and gets on her knees and blows it right back up."

•

On the last day of kindergarten, all the children brought presents for their teacher.

The florist's son handed the teacher a gift. She shook it, held it up, and said, "I bet I know what it is—it's some flowers!"

"That's right!" shouted the little boy.

Then the candy-store owner's daughter handed the teacher a gift. She held it up, shook it, and said, "I bet I know what it is—it's a box of candy!"

"That's right!" shouted the little girl.

The next gift was from the liquor-store owner's son. The teacher held it up and saw that it was leaking. She touched a drop with her finger and tasted it.

"Is it wine?" she asked.

"No," the boy answered.

The teacher touched another drop to her tongue. "Is it champagne?"

"No."

"What is it?"

"A puppy!"

•

A teenager is walking downtown and a girl whispers to him, "Blow job, twenty dollars."

He gives her a strange look and keeps walking. Soon another girl does the same thing. Confused, he keeps walking. The first thing out of his mouth when he returns home is, "Mom, what's a blow job?"

His mom replies, "Twenty dollars, just like downtown!"

•

A young man asks his father, "Dad, how many kinds of breasts are there?"

The father, surprised, answers, "Well, Son, there are three kinds of breasts. In her twenties, a woman's breasts are like melons, round and firm. In her thirties to forties, they are like pears, still nice but hanging a bit. After sixty, they are like onions."

"Onions?"

"Yes, you see them and they make you cry."

•

A young woman asks her mother, "Mom, how many kinds of penises are there?"

The mother, surprised, answers, "Well, Daughter, a man goes through three phases. In a man's twenties, his penis is like an oak, mighty and hard. In his thirties and forties, it is like a birch, flexible but reliable. After his sixties, it is like a Christmas tree."

"A Christmas tree?"

"Yes, dried up and the balls are there for decoration only."

•

A Frenchwoman took her little daughter to the Louvre, where they saw a statue of a nude male.

"What is that?" asked the child, pointing to the penis.

"Nothing, nothing at all, *chérie*," replied the mother.

"I want one," said the child.

The mother tried to focus her daughter's attention on a more suitable subject, but the little girl persisted.

"I want one just like that," she kept repeating.

At last the mother said, "If you are a good girl and stop thinking about it now, when you grow up, you will have one."

"And if I'm bad?" asked the little girl.

"Then," sighed the mother, "you will have many."

•

Having just finished reading a story to my sixth-grade class, I decided to check the students' knowledge of some of the vocabulary that had been used.

"Who knows what the word *adolescent* means?" I asked.

Out of the entire class of thirty-five, not one child raised a hand.

After a few more silent moments, I decided to give them a hint: "Adolescent—it's something all of you are, and I am not."

Finally one boy tentatively raised his hand and in a soft voice said, "Virgins?"

•

A man and his grandson are fishing by a peaceful lake beneath some weeping willows. The man takes out a cigarette and lights it. His grandson says, "Grandpa, can I try some of your cigarette?"

"Can you touch your asshole with your penis?" he says.

"No," says the little boy.

"Then you're not big enough."

A few more minutes pass and the man takes a beer out of his cooler and opens it. The little boy says, "Grandpa, can I have some of your beer?"

"Can you touch your asshole with your penis?" he says.

"No," says the little boy.

"Then you're not old enough."

Time passes and they continue to fish. The little boy gets hungry and reaches into his lunch box, takes out a bag of cookies, and eats one. The grandfather looks at him and says, "Hey, they look good. Can I have one of your cookies?"

"Can you touch your asshole with your penis?" asks the little boy.

"I most certainly can!" says the grandfather.

"Then go f*** yourself," says the boy. "These are my cookies!"

•

A five-year-old boy went to visit his grandmother one day.

While playing with his toys in her bedroom as Grandma

was dusting furniture, he looked up and said, "Grandma, how come you don't have a boyfriend?"

Grandma replied, "Honey, my TV is my boyfriend. I can sit in my bedroom and watch it all day long. The TV evangelists keep me company and make me feel so good. The comedies make me laugh. I'm so happy with my TV as my boyfriend."

Grandma turned on the old TV with rabbit-ears antennae and the picture was horrible. She started adjusting the antennae and knobs trying to get the picture in focus. Frustrated, she started hitting the back of the TV, hoping to fix the problem.

The little boy heard the doorbell ring so he hurried to the door. When he opened the door, there stood Grandma's minister. The minister said, "Hello, son, is your grandma home?"

The little boy replied, "Yeah, she's in the bedroom bangin' her boyfriend."

•

A little boy got on the bus, sat next to a man reading a book, and noticed he had his collar on backward. The little boy asked why he wore his collar that way.

The man, who was a priest, said, "I am a father."

The little boy replied, "My daddy doesn't wear his collar like that."

The priest looked up from his book and answered, "I am the father of many."

The boy said, "My dad has four boys, four girls, and two grandchildren and he doesn't wear his collar that way."

The priest, getting impatient, said, "I am the father of hundreds." And went back to reading his book.

The little boy sat quietly thinking for a while, then leaned over and said, "Maybe you should wear your pants backwards instead of your collar."

•

A seven-year-old is talking to his six-year-old friend.

Seven-year-old: "I just found a condom on the patio."

Six-year-old: "What's a patio?"

•

Youngster: "Mommy, who has more fun, the man or the woman?"

Mommy: "When you scratch your ear, which feels better, the finger or the ear?"

•

Daughter to Mama: "Tell me about sex. When a man puts what he has between his legs between your legs, what do you get?"

Mama: "A baby."

Daughter: "What do you get when he puts what he's got between his legs in your mouth?"

Mama: "Jewelry."

•

The mother has been teaching the young son about the dangers of social diseases. "Never kiss a girl or you will die."

On his next date a girl kisses him, and he starts to yell that he's dying. He says, "I can feel rigor mortis setting in."

•

Two young boys go to a cathouse; it's their first trip ever.

Boy #1: "How much?"

Madam: "Thirty dollars."

Boy #2: "Oh, we only have a dollar."

Madam: "Well, I'll give you a dollar's worth." She raises her skirt and says, "You can take a look and a smell."

The boys do, and one says to the other, "I don't think I could take thirty dollars' worth."

•

Daughter: "What's a penis?"

Mother: "That's the best part of your father."

Daughter: "What's a schmuck?"

Mother: "The rest of him."

•

A daughter is sent to a finishing school. At the end of the first year she requests a copy of *The Book of Etiquette*, and at the end of the second year she asks for *The Book of Etiquette, Volume 2*. And then the daughter arrives home on vacation, pregnant.

Father asks, "Who's the father?"

Daughter: "I don't know."

Father: "We sent you to finishing school and sent you two books on etiquette. Couldn't you at least ask, 'With whom am I having this pleasure?'"

•

A grandfather and his eight-year-old grandson are out for a ride. A cabdriver swerves in front of their car, and the grandson yells out to the cabbie, "You schmuck!"

Grandfather: "Don't ever use that word again, and don't tell Grandma."

When they get home, the grandmother asks her grandson to tell her about their day.

Grandson: "Well, Grandma, I used a word I shouldn't have used, and I promise I'll never use it again, but it rhymes with *f****."

•

A teenager says to the doctor, "My friend has a problem. He thinks he's got VD. What should he do?"

Doctor: "Take out your friend, and let's have a look at him."

•

A kid walks into his schoolroom with a shiner.

Teacher: "What happened? How did you get that black eye?"

Kid: "I was hit with a sexual object; it was a f***ing rock."

•

Teacher: "Who said, 'Give me liberty or give me death'?"
    A voice: "Mexican-Americans."
    Another voice: "*F*** the Mexicans.*"
    Teacher: "Who said that?"
    A voice: "General Sam Houston at the Battle of the Alamo."

•

A man and a woman were driving down the road arguing about his deplorable infidelity. Suddenly the woman reaches over and slices off the man's pecker.

Angrily, the woman tosses the pecker out the window of the car.

Driving behind the car is a fellow in a pickup truck with his ten-year-old daughter chatting away beside him.

All of a sudden, the pecker smacks the pickup in the windshield and flies off.

Surprised, the daughter asks her father, "Daddy, what in the heck was that?"

Not wanting to expose his ten-year-old daughter to sex at such a tender age, the father replies, "It was only a bug, honey."

The daughter gets a confused look on her face, and after a minute she says, "Sure had a big dick!"

•

A young teenager runs into the house and asks her mother, "Is it true what Mandy just told me? Babies come out the same place that boys' thingies go in?"

"Yes," replies her mother, pleased that the embarrassing subject has finally come up, and she doesn't have to explain.

"Oh, gosh!" shrieked the panic-stricken girl. "When I have a baby, will it knock my teeth out?"

•

A little girl was leading her dog through the park when an old man stopped her, saying, "That's sure a pretty dress you're wearing."

The little girl smiled. "Thank you, sir. My mama bought it for me. This is my dog, Porky."

The old man chuckled. "I'll bet a nickel I can guess why you called him that."

She shook her head. "I'll bet you can't."

He laughed. "You called him Porky because he's so fat."

She shook her head. "No, sir, we call him that because he f***s pigs."

•

Two poor kids go to a birthday party at a rich kid's house.

The kid is so rich that he has his own swimming pool and all the kids go in.

As they're changing afterward, one of the poor kids says to the other one, "Did you notice how small the rich kids' penises were?"

"Yeah," says his friend. "It's probably because they've got toys to play with."

•

When Little Johnny grew out of diapers, his dad had to teach him how to pee like an adult.

"See here, Son, this is how you do it," says the old man.

"One. Unzip your pants.

"Two. Pull out your equipment.

"Three. Pull back your foreskin.

"Four. Relax your muscle that's holding in the pee.

"Five. Push back your foreskin.

"Six. Put your equipment back.

"Seven. Zip back up."

Later that day Johnny's sister, Little Jane, runs up to

Daddy, exasperated. "Daddy, Daddy! Johnny's hogging the bathroom!"

"That's fine," responds Daddy, "he's learning how to pee like an adult."

"No, he's not!" yells Jane. "He's just in there shouting, 'Three, five; three, five; three, five . . .'"

•

According to a radio report, a middle school in Oregon was faced with a unique problem. A number of girls were beginning to use lipstick and would put it on in the bathroom.

That was fine, but after they put on their lipstick they would press their lips to the mirrors, leaving dozens of little lip prints.

Finally, the principal decided that something had to be done. She called all the girls to the bathroom and met them there with the maintenance man. She explained that all these lip prints were causing a major problem for the custodian, who had to clean the mirrors every night. To demonstrate how difficult it was to clean the mirrors, she asked the maintenance guy to clean one.

He took out a long-handled squeegee, dipped it in the toilet, then cleaned the mirror with it.

Since then there have been no lip prints on the mirror.

•

A little girl and her mother are out shopping. The girl asks her mother, "Mommy, how old are you?"

The mother responds, "Honey, women don't talk about their age. You'll learn this as you get older."

The girl then asks, "Mommy, how much do you weigh?"

"That's another thing women don't talk about. You'll learn this, too, as you grow up."

The girl, still wanting to know about her mother, then fires off another question: "Mommy, why did you and Daddy get a divorce?"

The mother, a little annoyed by the questions, responds, "Honey, that is a subject that hurts me very much, and I don't want to talk about it now."

The little girl, frustrated, sulks until she is dropped off at a friend's house to play. She consults with her girlfriend about her and her mother's conversation.

The girlfriend says, "All you have to do is sneak a look at your mother's driver's license. It's just like a report card from school. It tells you everything."

Later, the little girl and her mother are out and about again. The little girl starts off, "Mommy, Mommy, I know how old you are. I know how old you are. You're thirty-two years old."

The mother is shocked. "Sweetheart, how do you know that?"

The little girl shrugs. "I just know. And I know how much you weigh. You weigh 130 pounds."

"Where did you learn that?"

The little girl says, "I just know. And I know why you and Daddy got a divorce. You got an F in sex."

•

A young boy on his way home from school must pass by a group of hookers. Every day as he passes them, the hookers wave at him with their pinkies and say, "Hi there, little boy!"

One day the boy stops and asks one of the hookers why they always wave at him with their pinkies. She replies, "Well . . . that's what size we imagine your penis to be. It's just a joke!"

The next day on his way home, the hookers repeat the tradition. The young boy stops and drops his schoolbooks on the ground, sticks all his fingers in his mouth to stretch his lips wide, and says, *"Hi there, ladies!"*

•

A little boy went to the bathroom at school, but when he went to wipe his ass, there was no toilet paper so he used his hands. When he got back to class, his teacher asked him what he had in his hands.

"A little leprechaun, and if I open my hands, he'll get scared away," the boy said. He was then sent to the principal's office, and the principal asked him what he had in his hands.

"A little leprechaun, and if I open my hands, he'll get scared away."

He was sent home and his mom asked him what he had in his hands.

"A little leprechaun, and if I open my hands, he'll get scared away."

He was sent to his room and his dad came in and asked him what he had in his hands.

"A little leprechaun, and if I open my hands, he'll get scared away."

Then his dad got really mad and yelled, "Open your hands!"

"Look, Dad. You scared the crap out of him."

•

Little Gregory wakes up in the middle of the night feeling alone and scared. He goes into his mother's room for comfort, and he sees his mom standing naked in front of the mirror. She is rubbing her chest and groaning, "I want a man, I want a man."

Shaking his head in bewilderment, Gregory takes off to his bed.

Next night the same thing happens. On the third night,

Gregory wakes up and goes into his mom's room, but this time a man is in bed with his mom.

Gregory hoofs back to his room and whips off his pajamas, rubs his chest, and groans, "I want a bike, I want a bike."

•

One day a teacher walks into her classroom and announces to the class that each Friday she will ask a question, and anyone who answers correctly doesn't have to go to school the following Monday.

On the first Friday, the teacher asks, "How many grains of sand are on the beach?" Needless to say, no one knows.

The following Friday, the teacher asks, "How many stars are in the sky?"

Again no one can answer.

Frustrated, little Johnny decides that the next Friday he will somehow answer the question and get a three-day weekend.

So Thursday night, Johnny takes two Ping-Pong balls and paints them black.

The next day he brings them to school in a paper bag. At the end of the day, just when the teacher says, "Here's this week's question," Johnny empties the bag on the floor, sending the Ping-Pong balls rolling to the front of the room.

Finding the disruption amusing, the entire class starts laughing.

The teacher says, "Okay, who's the comedian with the black balls?"

Immediately little Johnny stands up and says, "Bill Cosby. See ya on Tuesday!"

•

Little Johnny was sitting in class one day. All of a sudden he needed to go to the bathroom. He yelled out, "Miss Jones, I need to take a piss."

The teacher replied, "Now Johnny, that is *not* the proper word to use in this situation. The correct word you want to use is *urinate*. Please use the word *urinate* in a sentence correctly, and I will allow you to go."

Little Johnny thinks for a bit, then says, "You're an eight, but if you had bigger tits, you'd be a ten!"

•

A little girl is in line to see Santa. When it's her turn, she climbs up on Santa's lap. Santa asks, "What would you like Santa to bring you for Christmas?"

The little girl replies, "I want a Barbie and G.I. Joe."

Santa looks at the little girl for a moment and says, "I thought Barbie comes with Ken."

"No," said the little girl. "She comes with G.I. Joe. She fakes it with Ken."

•

A boy came home from school one day. His father asked him how his day was and the boy said, "Well, Dad, I looked stupid because I did not know the difference between potential and reality."

His dad says, "Well, Son, go ask your mother if she would sleep with our next-door neighbor for a million dollars."

The boy came back with a shocked look on his face and said, "Dad, she said yes!"

"Okay, Son, now go and ask your sister the same question."

A few minutes later the boy came back, shocked again. "Dad, she said yes, also."

His dad told him, "There you go."

His son looked at him, puzzled. "Dad, I still don't understand."

"Look, Son, *potentially* we are multimillionaires, but in *reality* we are dead broke living with a couple of whores."

•

The mom of an eight-year-old boy was awaiting her son's arrival from school.

As he ran in, he said he needed to talk to her about making babies. He claimed he knew about the development of a fetus but didn't understand the answer to that "million-dollar question."

The mom asked the boy what he thought the answer was.

The boy said that the sperm is manufactured in the man's stomach; it rises up to his chest, then throat, and into his mouth, whereupon he kisses the woman and deposits the sperm into her mouth.

The mom told her boy that that was a good guess, but wrong. She said that she would give him a hint . . . that the sperm came out of the man's penis.

Suddenly the boy's face became quite red and he said, *"You mean you put your mouth on that thing?!"*

•

One day a teacher went into her classroom and saw the word *penis* written in small letters on the chalkboard. She erased it and went on with the day's lesson.

The next day she came in and saw the same word on the chalkboard, but a little bigger. She erased it and went on with her lesson.

Each of the next several days, the teacher would come in to find *penis* on the board, a little larger each time. She went in one morning expecting to see it again, but instead the chalkboard read, *The more you rub it, the bigger it gets.*

•

This teacher was teaching young kids the different types of animals. She showed them a picture of a giraffe and asked them what it was.

Nobody answered, so she gave them a clue: "It has a long neck."

One kid answered, "Giraffe!"

Pleased, the teacher next showed a picture of a zebra. Nobody answered again, so she gave them a clue: "This animal has stripes."

"Zebra!" one kid answered.

So she put up another picture, of a deer. The teacher could not think of a clue . . . but suddenly she came up with one. She asked, "What does your mother call your father?"

Suddenly one child answered, "Horny bastard!"

•

A teacher walks in and finds an apple on her desk with the letters *I-L-U* written on it.

The teacher asks who left it.

A little white girl raises her hand.

"Well, sweetie, what does *I-L-U* mean?"

The little girl replies, "'I love you.'"

The teacher says, "Isn't that sweet," and continues with her class.

The next day the teacher finds a banana on her desk with the letters *Y-A-S* on it.

The teacher asks who left it and what it means.

A little white boy raises his hand and says, "It means 'you are special.' "

"Thank you, sweetheart," the teacher says.

The following day, the teacher walks in to find a watermelon with the letters *F-U-C-K* on it.

The enraged teacher asks who left it and if they know what that means.

A little black girl raises her hand and cheerfully says, "Yes, ma'am, I left it. It means *'from us colored kids'*!"

•

A little girl was playing in the garden when she spotted two spiders mating.

"Daddy, what are those two spiders doing?" she asked.

"They're mating," her father replied.

"What do you call the spider on top, Daddy?"

"That's a daddy longlegs."

"So the other one is a mommy longlegs?" the little girl asked.

"No. Both of them are daddy longlegs."

The little girl thought for a moment, then took her foot and stamped them flat. "Well, we're not having *that* sort of shit in our garden!"

•

One day, during a lesson on proper grammar, the teacher asked for a show of hands for who could use the word *beautiful* in the same sentence twice. First, she called on little Suzy, who responded, "My father bought my mother a beautiful dress and she looked beautiful in it."

"Very good, Suzy," replied the teacher. She then called on little Michael.

"My mommy planned a beautiful banquet and it turned out beautifully," he said.

"Excellent, Michael." Then, the teacher called on little Johnny.

"Last night, at dinner, my sister told my father that she was pregnant, and he said, 'Beautiful, f***ing beautiful!'"

•

Johnny came running into the house and asked, "Mommy, can little girls have babies?"

"No," said his mom, "of course not."

Johnny then ran back outside and his mom heard him yell to his friends, "It's okay, we can play that game again!"

•

Little Billy returned home from school one day and announced that he had received an F in arithmetic.

"How did that happen?" his father demanded.

"Well," said Billy, "the teacher asked how much is two times three and I said six."

"But that's the right answer," retorted Dad.

"Then she asked me how much is three times two."

"What's the f***ing difference?" asked the boy's father.

"That's exactly what I said!"

•

Little Billy's teacher made the mistake of calling on him on another occasion, when she was teaching her students multi-syllabic words. Little Billy waved his hand wildly after Miss Jones asked for students to cite an example of a multisyllabic word. At length and in spite of her better judgment, she relented and called on him.

"Mas-tur-bate," he announced proudly.

Miss Jones blushed and tried to control the smile that was curling up the corners of her mouth. "Well, gee, Billy, that's really a mouthful."

Little Billy replied, "No, ma'am. You're thinking of a blow job."

•

Little Willie had a gambling problem. He'd bet on anything. One day, Willie's father consulted his teacher. The teacher said, "Mr. Gaines, I think I know how to teach Willie a real lesson. We'll trap him into a big wager that he'll lose."

The next day at school, the teacher watched Willie making wagers with the other children, and she said, "Willie, I want you to remain after class."

When the others had left the classroom, Willie walked up to the teacher. Before she could say a word, he said, "Don't say it, Miss Brown. I know what you're going to say, but you're a liar!"

"Willie!" the startled teacher said. "What are you talking about?"

"You're a fake!" Willie continued. "How can I believe anything you tell me? You've got this blond hair on top but I've seen your bush and it's pitch-black."

Trying to keep her cool, the teacher said, "Willie, that isn't true."

"I'll bet a dollar it is!" Willie challenged.

The teacher saw her chance to teach Willie his lesson. "Make it five dollars and you have a bet," she said.

"You're on!" Willie whipped out a $5 bill. Before anyone could come into the room, Miss Brown dropped her panties, spread her legs, and showed Willie that her pubic hair was as blond as the hair on top of her head.

Willie hung his head. "You win," he said, handing her the $5. Miss Brown couldn't wait for him to leave so she could get to a phone to call his father. She reported what had happened. "Mr. Gaines," she said, "I think we've finally taught him his lesson."

"The hell we have," the father muttered. "This morning Willie bet me ten dollars that he'd see your pussy before the day was over."

•

Little Johnny asked his mother, "Ma, is it true that people can be taken apart like machines?"

"Of course not, where did you hear such nonsense?" replied his mother.

Little Johnny answered, "The other day, Daddy was talking to someone on the phone, and he said that he screwed the ass off his secretary."

•

A little girl wants to walk her dog, but her father says that she can't because the dog is in heat. After a moment's thought, he finally says, "Well, I guess if we pour gas on the dog's rear end, it will kill the scent." So he does.

Half an hour later, the girl returns. The father says, "Where's the dog?"

The girl replies, "She ran out of gas half a block down the street, and the neighbor's dog is pushing her home."

•

A cop was on his horse waiting to cross the road when a little boy on his shiny new bike stopped beside him.

"Nice bike," the cop said. "Did Santa bring it to you?"

"Yep," the little boy said, "he sure did."

The cop looked at the bike, then handed the boy a $20 ticket, saying, "Next year tell Santa to put a license plate on the back of it."

Going along with the cop, the little boy said, "Nice horse you got there, sir. Did Santa bring it to you?"

"Yes, he sure did."

The little boy looked up at the cop and said, "Next year tell Santa to put the dick underneath the horse instead of on top."

•

A little boy about ten years old was walking down the sidewalk, dragging a flattened frog on a string behind him. He came up to the doorstep of a whorehouse and knocked on the door. When the madam answered, she saw the little boy and asked what he wanted.

He said, "I want to have sex with one of the women inside. I have the money to buy it, and I'm not leaving until I get it."

The madam figured, why not? So she told him to come in. Once in, she told him to pick any of the girls he liked.

He asked, "Do any of the girls have any diseases?"

Of course, the madam said, "No!"

"I heard all the men talking about having to get shots after making love with Amber. *That's* the girl I want."

Since the little boy was so adamant and had the money to pay for it, the madam told him to go to the first room on the right. He headed down the hall dragging the squashed frog behind him. Ten minutes later he came back, still dragging the frog, paid the madam, and headed out the door.

The madam stopped him and asked, "Why did you pick the only girl in the place with a disease, instead of one of the others?"

He said, "Well, if you must know, tonight when I get home, my parents are going out to a restaurant to eat, leaving me at home with the babysitter. After they leave, my babysitter will have sex with me because she just happens to be very fond of cute little boys. She will then get the disease that I just caught. When Mom and Dad get back, Dad will take the babysitter home. On the way, he'll jump her bones, and he'll catch the disease. Then when Dad gets home from the babysitter's, he and Mom will go to bed and have sex, and Mom will catch it. In the morning when Dad goes to work, the milkman will deliver the milk, have a quickie with Mom, and catch the disease, and *he's* the son of a bitch who ran over my *frog!*"

Animals

A man feeling depressed walked into a bar and ordered a triple scotch whiskey. As the bartender poured him the drink, he remarked, "That's quite a heavy drink. Is something wrong?"

After quickly downing his drink the man replied, "I got home and found my wife in bed with my best friend."

"Wow," exclaimed the bartender as he poured the man a second triple scotch, "no wonder you needed a stiff drink. This one's on the house."

As the man finished the second scotch, the bartender asked him, "So what did you do?"

"I walked over to my wife, looked her straight in the eye, and told her that we were through. I told her to pack her stuff and to get the hell out."

"That makes sense," said the bartender, "but what about your best friend?"

"I walked over to him, looked him right in the eye, and said, 'Bad dog!' "

•

Two hunters went moose hunting every winter without success. Finally they came up with a foolproof plan.

They got a very authentic female-moose costume and learned the mating call of a female moose. The plan was to hide in the costume, lure the bull, then throw off the costume and shoot the bull.

They set themselves up on the edge of a clearing, donned their costume, and began to give the moose love call.

Before long, their call was answered as a bull moose came crashing out of the forest and into the clearing. When the bull was close enough, the guy in front said, "Okay, let's get out and get him."

After a moment that seemed like an eternity, the guy in the back shouted, "The zipper is stuck! What are we going to do?"

The guy in the front says, "Well, I'm going to start nibbling grass, but you'd better brace yourself."

•

A wealthy man decides to go on a safari in Africa. He takes his faithful pet dog along for company. One day the dog starts chasing butterflies, and before long the dog discovers that he is lost. So, wandering about, he notices a leopard heading rapidly in his direction with the obvious intention of having lunch.

The dog says, "Oh, boy, I'm in big trouble now."

Then he notices some bones on the ground close by and immediately settles down to chew on the bones with his back to the approaching cat.

Just as the leopard is about to leap, the dog exclaims loudly, "Man, that was one delicious leopard. I wonder if there are any more cats around here?"

Hearing this, a look of terror comes over the leopard. He halts his attack in midstride and slinks away into the trees. "Phew," says the leopard. "That was close. That dog nearly had me."

Meanwhile, a monkey who had been watching the whole scene from a nearby tree figures he can put this knowledge to good use. He decides to trade news of the deception for protection from the leopard. Off goes the monkey in hot pursuit. But the dog hears the commotion and notices the monkey heading after the leopard with great speed. He figures that something must be up and begins to analyze the possibilities.

Meanwhile the monkey soon catches up with the leopard and reveals how the dog tricked the cat. Then he strikes a deal for himself with the leopard.

The cat is furious at being made a fool of. He wants revenge! The leopard says, "Here, monkey, hop on my back and come with me to watch what's going to happen to that conniving canine!"

Angry and impatient, the leopard doesn't even bother with stealth. He just comes roaring through the jungle with the finesse of an elephant.

The dog hears the leopard coming with the monkey on his back. He has decided on his plan. Instead of running, the dog sits down with his back to his attackers and pretends he hasn't a clue as to their presence.

Just when they get close enough to hear, the dog says, "Where is that damn monkey! I am so *hungry*! He takes too long. I sent him off half an hour ago to bring me another leopard, and he's still not back yet!"

•

A blind man was walking down the street with his dog. They stopped at the corner to wait for the passing traffic. The dog, at this point, started pissing on the man's leg. As the dog finished, the man reached into his coat pocket and pulled out a doggie treat and started waving it at the dog. A passerby saw all this happening and was shocked. He approached the blind man and asked how he could possibly reward the dog for such a nasty deed.

The blind man replied, "Oh, I'm not rewarding him. I'm just trying to find his head so I can kick his f***ing ass."

•

An army camp in India received a new commander. During the new commander's first inspection, everything checked out except one thing: a camel was tied to a tree on the edge of the camp.

The commander asked what it was for. One of the soldiers who had been stationed there for a while explained that the men sometimes got lonely for sex since no women were there, so that was why they had the camel. The commander just let that go, but after a few weeks he was feeling lonely so he ordered the men to bring the camel into his tent. The men did, and he went to work on it. After about an hour the commander came out, zipped up his pants, and said, "So is that how the other men do it?"

One of the men responded, "No, we usually just use the camel to ride into town."

•

Being a virgin, Bob was nervous about his upcoming wedding night, so he decided to talk it over with his friend Fred, who was quite a man-about-town—a true cocksman.

"Relax, Bob," counseled Fred. "You grew up on a farm; so do like the dogs do."

After the honeymoon was over and the couple returned to town, the new bride stormed over to her mother's house and announced that she was never going to live with Bob again. "He's totally disgusting," she wailed to her mother.

Her mother asked what the problem was, what exactly he did that was so disgusting.

The bride blushed and refused to tell, but finally gave in. "Ma, he doesn't know how to make love. All he does is keep smelling my ass and pissing on the bedpost!"

•

A group of prisoners are in their rehabilitation meeting. Their task for today is to each stand up in turn, speak his name, and admit to his fellow inmates what crime he committed.

The first prisoner stands and says, "My name is Daniel, and I'm in for murder."

Everyone gives him approving looks and pats on the back for admitting his wrongdoing.

The next guy stands up and says, "My name is Mike, and I'm in for armed robbery."

Again, there is a round of approving looks.

They go around the circle until it gets to the last guy.

He stands up and says, "My name is Melvin, but I'm not telling you what I'm in for."

The group leader says, "Now, come on, Melvin, you have to admit it to us to make any progress. Tell us what you did."

"Okay then. I'm in for screwing dogs."

Everyone is disgusted. They all shout, "Oh, that's disgusting! How *low* can you go?!"

"Chihuahuas," Melvin replies.

•

Three mice are sitting at a bar in a pretty rough neighborhood late at night trying to impress each other with how tough they are.

The first mouse throws down a shot of bourbon, slams the empty glass onto the bar, turns to the second mouse, and says, "When I see a mousetrap, I lie on my back and set it off with my foot. When the bar comes down, I catch it in my teeth, bench-press it twenty times to work up an appetite, then make off with the cheese."

The second mouse orders two shots of tequila, drinks them down one after the other, slams both glasses onto the bar, turns to the first mouse, and replies, "Oh, yeah? When I see rat poison, I collect as much as I can, take it home, grind it up to a powder, and add it to my coffee each morning so I can get a good buzz going for the rest of the day."

The first mouse and the second mouse then turn to the

third mouse. The third mouse finishes the beer he has in front of him, lets out a long sigh, and says to the first two, "I don't have time for this bullshit. Gotta go home and f*** the cat."

•

Two whales, a male and a female, are swimming side by side in the ocean. Suddenly, the male whale spots a ship in the distance. He recognizes it as the whaling ship that killed his father. Filled with anger, he says to his female companion, "That's the ship that killed my father! Let's swim closer."

When they are close enough, the male says, "Why don't we swim under the ship and blow air through our blowholes and break the ship into a million pieces? That will be sweet revenge."

The female agrees to this. So they each take a deep breath of air, swim under the ship, and blow enormous amounts of air under the ship. The ship flies into the air and crashes back to the sea and breaks into a million pieces.

As the pair of whales start to swim off, they realize that the sailors are floating in the ocean. The male whale is furious and says to the female whale, "They're still alive, but I've got another idea! Let's swim around and gulp up all the sailors!"

That's when the female stops swimming, looks at the male, and says, "Oh, no . . . I agreed to the blow job, but I'm *not* swallowing the seamen."

•

This guy sees a sign in front of a house: TALKING DOG FOR SALE.

He rings the bell and the owner tells him the dog is in the backyard. The guy goes into the backyard and sees a black mutt just sitting there.

"You talk?" he asks.

"Yep," the mutt replies.

"So, what's your story?"

The mutt looks up. "Well, I discovered this gift pretty young and I wanted to help the government, so I told the CIA about my gift, and in no time they had me jetting from country to country, sitting in rooms with spies and world leaders, because no one figured a dog would be eavesdropping. I was one of their most valuable spies eight years running. The jetting around really tired me out, and I knew I wasn't getting any younger and I wanted to settle down. So I signed up for a job at the airport to do some undercover security work, mostly wandering near suspicious characters and listening in. I uncovered some incredible dealings there and was awarded a batch of medals. Had a wife, a mess of puppies, and now I'm just retired."

The guy is amazed. He goes back in and asks the owner what he wants for the dog.

The owner says, "Ten dollars."

The guy says, "This dog is amazing. Why on earth are you selling him, and so cheaply, too?"

The owner replies, "He's such a liar. He didn't do any of that stuff."

•

A guy named David received a parrot for his birthday. The parrot was fully grown, with a bad attitude and worse vocabulary. Every other word was an expletive. Those that weren't expletives were, to say the least, rude.

David tried hard to change the bird's attitude and was constantly saying polite words, playing soft music, anything he could think of to set a good example. Nothing worked. He yelled at the bird and the bird yelled back. He shook the bird and the bird just got angrier and more rude.

Finally, in a moment of desperation, David put the parrot in the freezer. For a few moments he heard the bird squawk and kick and scream. Then suddenly there was quiet. Not a sound for half a minute. David was frightened that he might have hurt the bird and quickly opened the freezer door. The parrot calmly stepped out onto David's extended arm and said, "I believe I may have offended you with my rude language and actions. I will endeavor at once to correct my behavior. I really am truly sorry and beg your forgiveness."

David was astonished at the bird's change in attitude and was about to ask what had made such a dramatic change when the parrot continued, "May I ask what the chicken did?"

•

Two storks are sitting in their nest—a father stork and a baby stork. The baby stork is crying so the father stork is trying to calm him.

"Don't worry, Son. Your mother will come back. She's only bringing people babies and making them happy."

The next night it's the father's turn to do the job. Mother and son are sitting in the nest, and the baby stork is crying again.

The mother says, "Son, your father will be back as soon as possible, but now he's bringing joy to new mommies and daddies."

A few days later, the stork's parents are desperate because their son has been absent from the nest all night! Shortly before dawn he returns, and the parents ask him where he's been all night.

The baby stork says, "Nowhere. Just scaring the crap out of college students!"

•

One day, three dogs were sitting in the waiting room of a vet's office. The first dog noticed the other dogs and asked them why they were there.

"I ate my owner's shoe," said the first dog, "and I'm getting put to sleep."

"Me, too," said the second dog.

"What did you do?" the first dog asked the third.

"Well, you see, my owner likes to do her housework in the nude. So yesterday she was vacuuming—in the nude, of course—and I couldn't resist; I jumped on and had the ride of my life," responded the third dog.

"So you're getting put to sleep, too?"

"No, I'm getting my nails trimmed."

•

A bear and a rabbit were in the forest taking a shit. The bear looked over at the rabbit and said, "Do you ever have a problem with shit sticking to your fur?"

The rabbit said, "No, I don't."

The bear then picked up the rabbit and wiped his ass with it.

•

A woman went into a store to buy her husband a pet for his birthday. After looking around, she found that all the pets were expensive. She told the clerk she wanted to buy a pet, but she didn't want to spend a fortune.

"Well," said the clerk, "I have a very large bullfrog. They say it's been trained to give blow jobs!"

"Blow jobs!" the woman replied.

The woman thought it would be a great gag gift, and what if it was true? No more blow jobs for her! She bought the frog. When she explained froggy's ability to her husband, he was extremely skeptical and laughed it off.

The woman went to bed happy, thinking she might never need to perform this less-than-riveting act again.

In the middle of the night she was awakened by the noise of pots and pans flying everywhere, making hellacious banging and crashing sounds. She ran downstairs to the kitchen and found her husband and the frog reading cookbooks.

"What are you two doing at this hour?" she asked.

The husband replied, "If I can teach this frog to cook, your f***ing ass is gone."

•

A boy was meeting his girlfriend's parents for the first time for dinner. After dinner his girlfriend and her mother left the room to do the dishes, leaving him with the father and the dog, Duke, who was sitting underneath the boy's chair. Unfortunately, it was a large dinner and he really had to fart. He stealthily let out a quiet, but audible, fart.

"Duke!" the dad yelled.

This is great! the boy thought. *He thinks the dog is farting!* So he let out another one.

"Duke!" the father barked.

The boy thought he was home free so he let everything out at once in a really loud and smelly fart.

"Duke! Get out of there before the boy shits on you!"

•

A farmer is giving his wife last-minute instructions before heading to town to do errands.

"That fellow from the vet will be along this afternoon to inseminate one of the cows. I've hung a nail by the right stall so you'll know which one I want him to impregnate."

Satisfied that even his mentally challenged wife could understand the instructions, the farmer left for town.

That afternoon, the inseminator arrives and the wife dutifully takes him out to the barn and directly to the stall with the nail.

"This is the cow right here," she tells him.

"What's the nail for?" the guy asks.

Replies the wife, "I guess it's to hang up your pants."

•

A woman had a dog she just loved, but the dog had the bad habit of attacking anything that moved, including people. Her friends told her that if she had the dog neutered, he would lose his aggression and quit this behavior.

So the woman had her dog done and a few days later was in her front room when the postman came up the steps. The dog jumped up and went right out the door and attacked the postman.

The woman ran out and pulled the dog off and began apologizing to the postman.

She said, "I am so sorry, I don't know what to do or say. My friends told me he would quit attacking people if I had him neutered. I just don't know what to do."

The postman picked himself up and said, "You should have had his teeth pulled. I knew when he came out of the door he didn't want to f*** me."

•

A bear walks into a bar in Billings, Montana, and sits down. He bangs on the bar with his paw and demands a beer. The bartender approaches and says, "We don't serve beer to bears in bars in Billings."

The bear, becoming angry, demands again that he be served a beer. The bartender tells him again, more forcefully, "We don't serve beer to belligerent bears in bars in Billings."

The bear, very angry now, says, "If you don't serve me a beer, I'm going to eat that lady sitting at the end of the bar."

The bartender says, "Sorry, we don't serve beer to belligerent, bully bears in bars in Billings."

The bear goes to the end of the bar and, as promised, eats the woman. He comes back to his seat and again demands a beer.

The bartender states, "Sorry, we don't serve beer to belligerent, bully bears in bars in Billings who are on drugs."

The bear says, "I'm *not* on drugs."

The bartender says, "You are now. That was a barbitch-youate."

•

A guy decides that maybe he'd like to have a pet and goes to a pet shop.

After looking around he spots a parrot sitting on a little perch; it doesn't have any feet or legs.

The guy says out loud, "Jeez, I wonder what happened to this parrot?"

"I was born this way," says the parrot. "I'm a defective parrot."

"Ha, ha," the guy laughs. "It sounded like this parrot actually understood what I said and answered me."

"I understand every word," says the parrot. "I am a highly intelligent and thoroughly educated bird."

"Yeah? Then answer this: how do you hang on to your perch without any feet?"

"Well," the parrot says, "this is a little embarrassing, but since you asked, I will tell you. I wrap my little parrot penis around this wooden bar, kind of like a little hook. You can't see it because of my feathers."

"Wow," says the guy, "you really can understand and answer, can't you?"

"Of course. I speak both Spanish and English. I can converse with reasonable competence on almost any subject: politics, religion, sports, physics, and philosophy. And I am especially good at ornithology. You should buy me; I am a great companion."

The guy looks at the $200 price tag. He says, "I can't afford that."

"Pssst," the parrot hisses, motioning the guy over with one

wing. "Nobody wants me because I don't have any feet. You can get me for twenty dollars; just make an offer."

The guy offers $20 and walks out with the parrot. Weeks go by and the parrot is sensational. He's fun, he's interesting, he's a great pal, he understands everything, sympathizes, and gives good advice. The guy is delighted.

One day the guy comes home from work and the parrot says, "Pssst," and motions him over with one wing. The guy goes up close to the cage. "I don't know if I should tell you this or not," says the parrot, "but it's about your wife and the mailman."

"What?"

"Well, when the mailman came to the door today, your wife greeted him in a pair of panties that showed everything and kissed him on the mouth."

"What happened then?"

"Then the mailman came into the house and put his hand on her crotch and began petting her all over."

"My God!" the guy says. "Then what?"

"Then he pulled down her panties, got down on his knees, and began to lick her, starting with her chest, slowly going down and down." The parrot pauses for a long time.

"What happened? What happened?" says the frantic guy.

"That's what pisses me off. I don't know. I got a hard-on and fell off my f***ing perch."

•

Joe goes to the doctor and says, "Doc, I'm having trouble getting my penis erect. Can you help me?"

After a complete examination the doctor tells him, "Well, the problem is that the muscles around the base of your penis are damaged. There's really nothing I can do for you unless you're willing to try an experimental treatment."

Joe asks sadly, "And that would be?"

"Well," the doctor explains, "what we would do is take the muscles from the trunk of a baby elephant and implant them in your penis."

Joe thinks about it silently, then says, "Well, the thought of going through life without ever having sex again is too much; let's go for it."

So he went under the knife and, after a period of recovery and healing, returned to the doc for his blessing. Following the examination, the doc pronounced Joe "healed and ready for action."

Eager to use his experimentally enhanced equipment, Joe planned a romantic evening for his girlfriend and took her to one of the nicest restaurants in town, anticipating a happy conclusion to the evening.

In the middle of dinner he felt a stirring between his legs that continued to the point of being painful.

To release the pressure, Joe placed his napkin on his lap and unzipped his fly. His penis immediately sprang from his pants, flipped the napkin on the floor, went to the top of the table, grabbed a bread roll, and then returned to his pants!

His girlfriend was stunned at first, but then, imagining the possibilities, said with a sly smile and a gleam in her eye, "That was incredible! Can you do it again?"

Joe groaned, "Probably, but I don't think I can fit another roll in my ass."

•

A man wants to buy a camel. He finally finds a dealer with extraordinarily large camels.

Buyer: "How do you get them so big?"

Dealer: "We castrate them."

Buyer: "How?"

Dealer: "A man stands behind the camel with two bricks and smashes the bricks against the testicles."

Buyer: "Doesn't it hurt?"

Dealer: "No, come see for yourself."

They watch the worker. He smashes the bricks together and the camel yelps and screams and runs into the desert.

Buyer: "I thought you said it doesn't hurt."

Dealer: "It doesn't, unless you get your finger in between the two bricks."

•

Marilyn had a parrot for a pet, but the parrot would embarrass her whenever she came into the apartment with a man. It would shout all kinds of obscenities, always leading off with "Somebody's gonna get it tonight!"

In desperation, Marilyn went to her local pet shop and explained her parrot problem to the pet shop proprietor.

"What you need," he said, "is a female parrot, too. I don't have one on hand, but I'll order one. Meanwhile, you could borrow this female owl until the female parrot arrives."

Marilyn took the owl home and put it near her parrot. It was immediately obvious that the parrot didn't care for the owl. He glared at it. That night, Marilyn wasn't her usual nervous self as she opened the door to bring her gentleman friend in for a nightcap. Then suddenly she heard the parrot screech and she knew that things hadn't changed.

"Somebody's gonna get it tonight! Somebody's gonna get it tonight!" the parrot said.

The owl said, "Whoo? Whoo?"

And the parrot said, "Not you, you big-eyed son of a bitch!"

•

Early-afternoon opening time at a bar. The bartender is polishing glasses when a mouse walks in, jumps up on a stool, and orders a beer. Pretty soon, in walks the second customer of the day, a lady giraffe. The little mouse starts eyeing her, and soon he gets a little bolder and asks the bartender to serve up two martinis at her end of the bar. The bartender does this and soon notices the mouse on the stool next to the giraffe. The afternoon crowd starts coming in and the bartender gets busy and doesn't really notice when the mouse and the giraffe leave together.

The next day, the bartender is setting up, polishing glasses as he has just unlocked the door for the day's business. In comes the same little mouse, just barely dragging his ass across the floor and struggling up onto a stool. The bartender looks at him and says, "Damn, Mr. Mouse, you look like you've had it!"

The mouse snaps back, "Had it . . . had it. Between the f***ing and the kissing I must have run two hundred miles!"

•

A farmer wanted to have his hens serviced, so he went to the market looking for a rooster. He was hoping he could get a special rooster—one that could service all of his many hens.

When he told this to the market vendor, the vendor replied, "I have just the rooster for you. Randy here is the horniest rooster you will ever see!"

So the farmer took Randy back to the farm. Before setting him loose in the henhouse, though, he gave Randy a little pep talk. "Randy," he said, "I'm counting on you to do your stuff."

Without a word, Randy strutted into the henhouse and set to work.

Randy was as fast as he was furious, mounting each hen like a thunderbolt. There was much squawking and many feathers flying, till Randy had finished having his way with each hen.

But Randy didn't stop there; he went into the barn and mounted all the horses, one by one and still at the same frantic pace. Then he went to the pig house, where he did the same.

The farmer, watching all of this with disbelief, cried out, "Stop, Randy, you'll kill yourself!" But Randy continued, seeking out each farm animal in the same manner.

Well, the next morning, the farmer looked out and saw Randy lying on the lawn. His legs were up in the air, his eyes were rolled back, and his long tongue was hanging out. A buzzard was already circling above him.

The farmer walked up to Randy saying, "Oh, you poor thing, look what you did, you've gone and killed yourself. I warned you, my little buddy."

"Shhhhh," Randy whispered, "the buzzard's getting closer."

•

One day a farmer was bragging to his neighbor that his dog was so smart he could count. The other farmer didn't believe him, so the first farmer ordered his dog to count the geese in the pond out back. The dog took off, came back, and barked four times.

Both farmers went out back to check if the dog was right, and sure enough four geese were in sight.

Back at the farmhouse the neighbor said that the dog was just lucky and he wanted more proof, so the farmer set the dog off again.

This time the dog came back and barked six times, and when they went to check, sure enough, there were six geese.

But the neighbor was still unsatisfied and demanded another demonstration, so the first farmer agreed to send the dog out one more time. On the dog's return he started humping his master's leg, then picked up a stick and started shaking it.

"I knew that fool dog couldn't count," said the neighbor triumphantly.

"Oh, yes, he can," said the farmer, "you just can't understand him. He just said there are more f***ing geese than you can shake a stick at."

•

This lady goes to a vet and learns that if you put a ribbon around a snoring dog's penis, he'll roll over and stop snoring. The next night, her dog is snoring, so she goes to the kitchen and gets a red ribbon and ties it around her dog's penis. His snoring stops.

Later on that night her husband is snoring, so she goes to the kitchen and gets a blue ribbon and ties it around her husband's penis, and he stops snoring.

The next morning her husband wakes up and looks at his dog and looks down at himself. "I don't know what happened last night, but we came in first and second."

•

A zoo had acquired a rare species of gorilla. Within a few weeks, the female gorilla became ornery and difficult to handle. Upon examination, the zoo veterinarian determined the problem: the gorilla was in heat. To make matters worse, no male gorillas were available.

While reflecting on their problem, the zoo administrators noticed Mike, an employee responsible for cleaning the animals' cages. Mike, it was rumored, possessed ample ability to satisfy any female, but he wasn't very bright. So, the zoo administrators thought they might have a solution.

Mike was approached with a proposition: would he be willing to have sex with the gorilla for five hundred bucks? He showed some interest, but he said he would have to think the matter over carefully.

The following day Mike announced that he would accept their offer, but only under three conditions. "First," he said, "I don't want to have to kiss her. Secondly, I want nothing to do with any offspring that may result from this union."

The zoo administration quickly agreed to these conditions, so they asked what his third condition was.

"Well," said Mike, "you've gotta give me another week to come up with the five hundred bucks."

•

A lady approached her priest one day and said, "Father, I have a problem. I have two female parrots that only know how to say one thing."

"What do they say?" the priest inquired.

"They say, 'Hi, we're prostitutes. Do you want to have some fun?' "

"That's obscene!" the priest exclaimed. "You know, I may have a solution to your problem. I have two male talking parrots that I have taught to pray and read the Bible. Bring your two parrots over to my house and we will put them in the cage with Francis and Job. My parrots can teach your parrots to pray and worship. Then your parrots are sure to stop saying that phrase in no time."

"Thank you," the woman responded, "this may very well be the solution."

The next day she brought her female parrots to the priest's house. As he ushered her in, she noticed his two male parrots inside their cage, holding rosary beads and praying. Impressed, she walked over and placed her parrots inside the cage with them. After a few minutes the female parrots cried out in unison, "Hi, we're prostitutes. Do you want to have some fun?"

There was stunned silence. Finally, one male parrot looked over at the other male parrot and exclaimed, "Put those damn beads away, Francis, our prayers have been answered!"

Man/Woman

Jack had been dating Jill for over a year now and was finally ready to pop the question. He decided to do it over dinner and invited Jill out to a restaurant.

After dinner, Jack said to Jill, "Honey, I've got something rather important to ask you, but first, there is something else I want to ask you."

Jill, a little surprised, said, "Well, sure, what is it?"

"Well, I wanted to know how you feel about sex."

"Oh, it's fine, as long as it is infrequent."

Jack paused for a second, then asked, "Is that one word, or two?"

•

Three old men are discussing their sex lives. The Italian man says, "Last week, my wife and I had great sex. I rubbed her body all over with olive oil, we made passionate love, and she screamed for five minutes at the end."

The Frenchman boasts, "Last week when my wife and I had sex, I rubbed her body all over with butter. We then made passionate love and she screamed for fifteen minutes."

The old Jewish man says, "Well, last week my wife and I had sex, too. I rubbed her body all over with chicken *shmalts* [kosher chicken fat], we made love, and she screamed for six hours."

The Italian and Frenchman were stunned. They replied, "What could you have possibly done to make your wife scream for six hours?"

"I wiped my hands on the drapes."

•

A guy has been asking the prettiest girl in town for a date, and finally she agrees to go out with him.

He takes her to a nice restaurant and buys her a fancy dinner with expensive wine. On the way home, he pulls over to the side of the road in a secluded spot. They start necking and he's getting pretty excited. He starts to reach under her skirt, and she stops him, saying she's a virgin and wants to stay that way.

"Well, okay," he says, "how about a blow job?"

"Yuck!" she screams. "I'm not putting that thing in my mouth!"

"Well, then, how about a hand job?"

"I've never done that. What do I have to do?"

"Well," he answers, "remember when you were a kid and you used to shake up a Coke bottle and spray your brother with it?"

She nods.

"Well, it's just like that."

So, he pulls it out and she grabs hold of it and starts shaking it. A few seconds later, his head flops back on the headrest, his eyes close, snot starts to run out of his nose, wax blows out of his ears, and he screams out in pain.

"What's wrong?" she cries out.

"Take your thumb off the end!"

•

Giorgio is in this country for about six months. He walks to work every day and passes a shoe store. Each day he stops and looks in the window and admires a certain pair of Bocelli leather shoes. After about two months he saves $300 and purchases the shoes.

Each Friday night the Italian community gets together at a

dance in the church basement, so Giorgio seizes the opportunity to wear his new Bocelli leather shoes to the dance.

He asks Sophia to dance, and as they dance, he asks her, "Sophia, do you weara red panties tonight?"

Sophia, startled, says, "Yes, Giorgio, I do wear red panties tonight, but how do you know?"

"I see the reflection in my new $300 Bocelli leather shoes. How do you like them?"

Next he asks Rosa to dance, and after a few minutes he says to her, "Rosa, do you weara white panties tonight?"

Rosa answers, "Yes, Giorgio, I do, but how do you know that?"

"I see the reflection in my new $300 Bocelli leather shoes. How do you like them?"

Now the evening is almost over and the last song is being played, so Giorgio asks Carmella to dance. Midway through the dance his face turns red. He says, "Carmella, stilla my heart, pleasa, pleasa tell me you weara no panties tonight, pleasa, pleasa, tella me this isa true?"

Carmella answers, "Yes, Giorgio, I wear no panties tonight."

Giorgio gasps. "Thanka God . . . I thought I had a *crack* in my $300 Bocelli leather shoes."

●

They made an engaging-looking couple in the swank restaurant. The man was handsome, graying, and obviously well-off; the woman was a joy to any eye—very young, ravishing, and delectable.

As they read their menus, the gentleman asked his date what she would like to eat. She scanned the menu yet again, then said, "To begin, I'll have two champagne cocktails, then a dozen oysters on the half shell, and a tureen of turtle soup.

As entrées I'll have the fillet of English sole followed by pheasant under glass, plus an à la carte order of asparagus tips. For dessert, they can just bring the cart."

Somewhat surprised not only by her appetite, but also by the cost of all of this, he asked, "Tell me, do you eat this well at home, too?"

"Well, no," she admitted. "But no one at home wants to screw me."

•

A midget went into a whorehouse. None of the girls really wanted to serve him, so finally they drew lots, and Mitzi was unlucky and went up to the room with him. A minute later, there was a loud scream. The madam and all of the girls charged up the staircase and into the room. Mitzi lay on the floor in a dead faint. Standing next to the bed was the midget, nude and with a three-foot cock hanging down and almost touching the floor. The girls were dumbfounded by the sight.

Finally, one of them regained her composure to say, "Sir, would you mind if we felt it? We've never seen anything like that before."

The midget sighed. "Okay, honey, but only touching. No sucking. I used to be six feet tall."

•

"Melissa, I don't know what to do," Janice said to her friend at work. "That good-looking Mike in accounting asked me out for Saturday night. Should I go?"

"Oh, my gosh," her friend exclaimed, "he'll wine you, dine you, and then use any ruse to get you up to his apartment. Then he'll rip off your dress and you'll have fantastic sex!"

"What should I do?"

"Wear an old dress."

•

A New York woman was at her Upper East Side hairdresser's getting her hair styled prior to a trip to Rome with her boyfriend.

She mentioned the trip to the hairdresser, who responded, "Rome? Why would anyone want to go to Rome? It's crowded and dirty and worse yet, full of Italians. You're crazy to go to Rome! So, how are you getting there?"

"We're flying on Continental. We've got a great rate!"

"Continental!" exclaimed the hairdresser. "That's a terrible airline. Their planes are old, their flight attendants are ugly, and they're always late. So, where are you staying in Rome?"

"We'll be at this exclusive little place over on Rome's west side called Teste—"

"Don't go any further. I know that place. Everybody thinks it's gonna be something special and exclusive. But it's really a dump, the worst hotel in the whole city! The rooms are small, the service is surly, and they're way overpriced. So, what will you do when you get there?"

"We're going to go see the Vatican and we hope to see the pope."

"That's rich." The hairdresser laughed. "You and a million other people trying to see him. He'll look the size of an ant. Boy, good luck on this lousy trip of yours. You're sure going to need it."

A month later, the woman, all smiling, went in for her hair appointment. The hairdresser asked her about her trip to Rome.

"It was absolutely wonderful," explained the woman. "Not only did we arrive on time in one of Continental's brand-new jets, but it was overbooked and they bumped us up to first class. The food and wine were wonderful, and I had a handsome twenty-eight-year-old steward who waited on me hand and foot. And the hotel—it was fabulous! They'd just finished a five-million-dollar remodeling job, and now it's just a jewel, the finest hotel in the city. They, too, were overbooked, so they gave us their owner's suite at no extra charge!"

"Well," muttered the hairdresser, "I know you didn't get to see the pope."

"Actually, we were quite lucky—as we toured the Vatican, a Swiss Guard tapped me on the shoulder and explained that the pope likes to personally meet some of the visitors, and if I'd be so kind as to step into his private room and wait, the pope would personally greet me. Five minutes later, the Holy Father walked through the door and shook my hand! I knelt down and he spoke a few words to me."

"Really?" asked the hairdresser. "What'd he say?"

"He said, 'I hope you didn't get that haircut in *my* country.' "

•

A lady wakes up one morning to find a gorilla in her tree. She looks in the phone book and finds a gorilla-removal service. When she asks if they can remove the gorilla, the service guy asks, "Is it a male or female?"

"Male," she replies.

"Oh, yeah, we can do it. I'll be right there."

An hour later, the service guy arrives with a stick, a Chihuahua, a shotgun, and a pair of handcuffs. He then gives the following instructions:

"I'm going to climb this tree and poke the gorilla with the stick until he falls out of the tree. When he does, the trained Chihuahua will go to bite the gorilla's testicles. The gorilla will then cross his hands to protect himself, allowing you to put the handcuffs on him."

The woman asks, "What do I do with the shotgun?"

The service guy replies, "If I fall out of the tree before the gorilla does, shoot the Chihuahua."

•

Two men are in a pub discussing their latest sexual conquests. The first man says he met this girl last week and they agreed to go back to his house and have sex. Once in the house the girl stripped down, lay down on the bed with her legs apart, and panted, "I want you to give me twelve inches and make me bleed."

The second man, not for one moment believing his friend is that well hung, asks what he did.

"Well," he says, "what could I do? I f***ed her twice and smacked her in the face!"

•

The hostess of a bridge club got a last-minute call from one of the players that she was sick. Unable to get a replacement on such short notice, the hostess drafted her husband, a mediocre player with a bad attitude. During the game, he got up and went to the bathroom, leaving the door ajar. Everyone listened as he peed.

Embarrassed, his wife called out, "John, would you please close the door!"

John's partner said, "Never mind, it's the first time since we started playing that I've known what the man has in his hand."

•

How to Shower Like a Woman

1. Take off clothing and place it in sectioned laundry hamper according to lights and darks.
2. Walk to bathroom wearing long dressing gown. If you see husband along the way, cover up any exposed areas.
3. Look at your womanly physique in the mirror—make mental note to do more sit-ups.
4. Get in the shower. Use facecloth, arm cloth, leg cloth, long loofah, wide loofah, and pumice stone.

5. Wash your hair once with cucumber-and-sage shampoo with forty-three added vitamins.

6. Wash your hair again to make sure it's clean.

7. Condition your hair with grapefruit-mint conditioner enhanced with natural avocado oil. Leave on hair for fifteen minutes.

8. Wash your face with crushed-apricot facial scrub for ten minutes until red.

9. Wash entire rest of body with ginger-nut and Jaffa-cake body wash.

10. Rinse conditioner off hair.

11. Shave armpits and legs.

12. Turn off shower.

13. Squeegee off all wet surfaces in shower. Spray mold spots with Tilex.

14. Get out of shower. Dry with towel the size of a small country. Wrap hair in superabsorbent towel.

15. Check entire body for zits; tweeze hairs.

16. Return to bedroom wearing long dressing gown and towel on head.

17. If you see husband along the way, cover up any exposed areas.

And Now . . .
How to Shower Like a Man

1. Take off clothes while sitting on the edge of the bed and leave them in a pile.

2. Walk naked to the bathroom. If you see wife along the way, shake penis at her, making the *woo-woo* sound.

3. Look in the mirror, look at your penis, and scratch your butt.

4. Get in the shower.

5. Wash your face.

6. Wash your armpits.
7. Blow your nose in your hands and let the water rinse them.
8. Make fart noises (real or artificial) and laugh at how loud they sound in the shower.
9. Spend majority of time washing privates and surrounding area.
10. Wash your butt, leaving those coarse hairs stuck on the soap.
11. Shampoo your hair.
12. Make a shampoo Mohawk.
13. Pee.
14. Rinse off and get out of shower.
15. Partially dry off. Fail to notice water on the floor because curtain was hanging out of tub the whole time.
16. Admire penis size in mirror again.
17. Leave shower curtain open, wet mat on floor, light on.
18. Return to bedroom with towel around your waist. If you pass wife, pull off towel, shake penis at her, and make the *woo-woo* sound again.
19. Throw wet towel on bed.

•

A man and a woman started to have sex in the middle of a dark forest. After about fifteen minutes of it, the man finally gets up and says, "Damn, I wish I had a flashlight!"

The woman says, "Me, too! You've been eating grass for the past ten minutes!"

•

As an airplane is about to crash, a female passenger jumps up frantically and announces, "If I'm going to die, I want to die feeling like a woman." She removes all her clothing and asks, "Is there someone on this plane who is man enough to make me feel like a woman?"

A man stands up, removes his shirt, and says, "Here, iron this!"

•

A guy walks into a sperm-donor bank wearing a ski mask and holding a gun. He goes up to the nurse and demands that she open the sperm-bank vault.

She says, "But, sir, it's just a sperm bank!"

"I don't care, open it now!" he replies.

So she opens the door to the vault, and inside are all the sperm samples.

The guy says, "Take one of those sperm samples and drink it!"

She looks at him. "But they are sperm samples!"

"Do it!"

So the nurse sucks it back.

"That one there, drink that one as well." So the nurse drinks that one as well. Finally after four samples the man takes off his ski mask and says, "See, honey—it's not that hard."

•

An old man stops by a café for breakfast. After paying the tab, he checks his pockets and leaves three pennies for a tip.

As he strides toward the door, his waitress muses, only half to herself, "You know, you can tell a lot about a man by the tip he leaves."

The old man turns around, curiosity getting the better of him. "Oh, really? Tell me, what does my tip say?"

"Well, this penny tells me you're a thrifty man.

"And this penny, it tells me you're a bachelor."

Surprised at her perception, he says, "Well, that's true, too."

"And the third penny tells me that your father was also a bachelor."

•

An elderly gentleman went to see his doctor and asked for a prescription of Viagra. The doctor said, "That's no problem. How many do you want?"

The man answered, "Just a few, maybe four, but cut each one in four pieces."

"That won't do you any good."

The old gentleman said, "That's all right. I don't need them for sex anymore, I'm ninety years old. I just want it to stick out far enough so I don't pee on my shoes."

•

A grandson goes to visit his grandfather in the nursing home. He asks the elderly gentleman how he has been sleeping at night.

The grandfather replies that they give him a cup of hot chocolate and a Viagra tablet every night before he goes to bed and he sleeps like a baby.

The grandson is curious about the Viagra so he finds his grandfather's nurse to ask why.

The nurse replies that the hot chocolate makes him sleepy and the Viagra tablet keeps him from rolling out of bed.

•

A man and a lady walk into the local sex-therapy center and demand an appointment with the doctor. After ten minutes, the doctor starts watching the couple have sex. A half hour later, after the vigorous action, the couple leave with an "all clear" from the doctor.

The next day the couple return and have sex in front of the doctor again. The doctor tells them all is okay, and they leave.

The very next day, they come in and start getting undressed, but the doctor says, "You're both all right, there is nothing wrong with you two."

The man says, "I know, but we're both married, so we can't do it at our houses. It costs $75 at the local motel, $100 at the Hilton, and $250 at the Waldorf. It costs $25 here and we get fifty percent back from health insurance."

•

A young couple with a box of condoms had sex. When they finished, she discovered that only six condoms remained in the box of twelve, so she asked him, "What happened to the other five condoms?"

He nervously replied, "Er, I masturbated with them."

Later she approached her male confidant, told him the story, then asked him, "Have you ever done that?"

"Yeah, once or twice," he told her.

"You mean you've actually masturbated with a condom before?"

"Oh," he said, "I thought you were asking if I'd ever lied to my girlfriend."

•

House Sex—when you are newly married and have sex all over the house in every room.

Bedroom Sex—after you have been married for a while, you only have sex in the bedroom.

Hall Sex—after you've been married for many years, you just pass each other in the hall and say, "F*** you."

Courtroom Sex—when your wife and her lawyer f*** you in divorce court in front of many people for every penny you've got.

•

While purchasing some condoms, Johnny remarked with a smile, "I'm giving my girl a birthday present tonight."

"Yes, sir." The drugstore clerk smiled, then added, forcing a straight face, "Would you perhaps like these gift wrapped?"

"That wouldn't make much sense," said Johnny. "They *are* the gift wrapping."

•

A guy's talking to a girl in a bar.

He says, "What's your name?"

She says, "Carmen."

"That's a nice name, who named you, your mother?"

"No, I named myself."

He says, "Why Carmen?"

"Because I like cars and I like men. What's your name?"

He says, "Beerf***."

•

"How about us spending a romantic weekend in a nice quiet hotel?" he whispered in the beautiful lady's ear.

"I'm afraid," she said, "that my awareness of your proclivities in the esoteric aspects of sexual behavior precludes you from such erotic confrontation."

"Err . . . sorry . . . I don't get it."

"Exactly!"

•

An Amish boy and his father were visiting a mall. They were amazed by almost everything they saw, but especially by two shiny, silver walls that could move apart and back together again.

The boy asked his father, "What is this, Father?"

The father, never having seen an elevator, responded, "Son, I have never seen anything like this in my life; I don't know what it is."

While the boy and his father were watching wide-eyed, an old lady limping slightly with a cane slowly walked up to the moving walls and pressed a button. The walls opened and the lady walked between them and into a small room. The walls closed, and as the boy and his father watched, small circles of light with numbers lit up above the wall. They continued to watch the circles light up in the reverse direction, then the walls opened up again and a beautiful twenty-four-year-old woman stepped out.

The father said to his son, "Go get your mother."

•

This old guy had never done a 69 before. So he goes down to the local whorehouse and tells the madam his problem. The madam says she can fix him up for fifty bucks. The old guy gives her fifty bucks, and she tells him to go upstairs to the second door on the right. He gets there and opens the door, and here is the most beautiful blonde he has ever seen. He tells her he wants to do a 69 with her but that he is not quite sure how to do it. The blonde says, "All we do is both get naked, and I put my head between your legs and suck you off while you have your head between my legs licking my pussy."

They both strip down and are going to town when all of a sudden she lets out a big, nasty-smelling fart. He jumps up and says, "What the f*** was that all about?"

She said she was sorry and it would not happen again. So they start going at it again, and sure enough she lets another one rip.

The old guy jumps again and starts putting his clothes back on. She asks him where he is going, and he says, "If you think I'm sticking around for sixty-seven more of those, you're crazy."

•

Two car salesmen were sitting at the bar. One complained to the other, "Boy, business sucks. If I don't sell more cars this month, I'm going to lose my f***ing ass."

Too late, he noticed a beautiful blonde sitting two stools away. Immediately he apologized for his language.

"That's okay," the blonde replied. "If I don't sell more ass this month, I'm going to lose my f***ing car."

•

A woman meets a gorgeous man in a bar. They talk, they connect, and they end up leaving together.

They get back to his place, and as he shows her around his apartment, she notices that his bedroom is completely packed with sweet, cuddly teddy bears. Hundreds of cute, small bears are on a shelf all the way along the floor, with cuddly, medium-size ones on a shelf a little higher, and huge, enormous bears on the top shelf.

The woman is surprised that this guy would have a collection of teddy bears, especially one that's so extensive, but she decides not to mention this to him and is actually quite impressed by his sensitive side.

She turns to him . . . they kiss . . . and then they rip each other's clothes off and make hot, steamy love.

After an intense night of passion with this sensitive guy, as they are lying together in the afterglow, the woman rolls over and asks, smiling, "Well, how was it?"

The guy says, "Help yourself to any prize from the bottom shelf."

•

A man once had a permanent erection. Try as he could, he couldn't get it to go down. Finally, he went to his local pharmacy, where he encountered a female pharmacist.

"I'd like to speak to the male pharmacist," he said.

She said, "I'm a professional. I run this pharmacy with my sister, who is also a professional. Anything you can tell a man, you can tell us."

"Okay," he said. "I have a permanent erection. What can you give me for it?"

"Hmmmm. I'll go into the back and confer with my sister."

After a minute, she returned and said, "We'll give you $25,000 and half the business."

•

A young couple were on their way to Vegas to get married. Before getting there, the girl said to the guy that she had a confession. The reason that they had not been too intimate was because she was flat chested.

"If you want to cancel the wedding, then I'll understand," she said.

The guy remarked, "I don't mind that you're flat, and sex is not the most important thing in a marriage anyway."

Several miles down the road, the guy turned to the girl and said that he also had a confession. The reason that they had not been too intimate was because he was just like a baby below the waist. The girl remarked, "I don't mind that you're like a baby below the waist, and sex is not the most important thing in a marriage anyway."

And so, the happy couple went on to Vegas and got married. On their wedding night, the girl took off her clothes. True to her word, she was as flat as a washboard. Then, the guy took off his clothes. After one glance at his naked body, the girl fainted and fell to the floor.

When she regained consciousness, the guy said, "I told you before we got married, so why were you so surprised?"

"You told me it was just like a baby."

The guy replied, "It is! Eight pounds and twenty-one inches long!"

•

James Bond walks into a bar and takes a seat next to an attractive woman. He gives her a quick glance, then casually looks at his watch. The woman notices this and asks, "Is your date running late?"

"No," he replies. "Q's just given me this state-of-the-art watch and I was just testing it."

The intrigued woman says, "A state-of-the-art watch? What's so special about it?"

"It uses alpha waves to talk to me telepathically."

"What's it telling you now?"

"Well, it says you're not wearing any panties."

The woman giggles. "Well, it must be broken because I am wearing panties!"

Bond tuts, taps his watch, and says, "Damn thing's an hour fast."

•

The Sunday before Christmas, a pastor told his congregation that the church needed some extra money. He asked the people to consider donating a little more than usual in the offering plate. He said that whoever gave the most would be able to pick out three hymns. After the offering plates were passed, the pastor glanced down and noticed that someone had placed a $1,000 bill in the offering. He was so excited that he immediately shared his joy with his congregation and said he'd like to personally thank the person who placed the money in the plate.

A quiet, elderly, saintly-looking lady all the way in the back shyly raised her hand. The pastor asked her to come to the front. Slowly she made her way to the pastor. He told her how wonderful it was that she gave so much and in thanks asked her to pick out three hymns. Her eyes brightened as she looked over the congregation, pointed to the three most handsome men in the building, and said, "I'll take him and him and him."

•

A woman married and had thirteen children. Her husband died. She soon married again and had seven more children.

Again, her husband died. She remarried and had five more children. Alas, she finally died.

Standing before her coffin, the preacher prayed to the Lord thanking Him for this loving woman who fulfilled His commandment to "go forth and multiply." In his eulogy the preacher said, "Lord, they're finally together."

Leaning over to a neighbor, one mourner quietly asked, "Do you think he means her first, second, or third husband?"

The neighbor replied, "I think he means her legs."

•

A man and a woman are sitting beside each other in the first-class section of the plane. The woman sneezes, takes a tissue, gently wipes her nose, and shudders quite violently in her seat. The man isn't sure why she is shuddering and goes back to reading.

A few minutes pass; the woman sneezes again. She takes a tissue, gently wipes her nose, and shudders again.

The man is becoming more and more curious about the shuddering. A few more minutes pass. The woman sneezes yet again. She takes a tissue, gently wipes her nose, and shudders violently again.

The man has finally had all he can handle. He turns to the woman and says, "Three times you've sneezed and three times you've taken a tissue and wiped your nose, then shuddered violently! Are you sending me signals, or are you going crazy?"

The woman replies, "I'm sorry if I disturbed you. I have a rare condition: when I sneeze, I have an orgasm."

The man, now feeling a little embarrassed but even more curious, says, "I've never heard of that before. What are you taking for it?"

The woman looks at him. "Pepper."

•

Her blind date hadn't been all that great, and the young lady was relieved the evening was finally over. At her apartment door, he suddenly said, "Hey! You wanna see my underwear?"

Before she could respond, he dropped his pants, right there in the hall, revealing that he wasn't wearing any underwear.

She glanced down and said, "Nice design. Does it also come in men's sizes?"

•

Her Diary

Sunday night I thought he was acting weird. We had made plans to meet at a bar to have a drink. I was shopping with my friends all day long, so I thought he was upset that I was a bit late, but he made no comment.

Conversation wasn't flowing so I suggested that we go somewhere quiet so we could talk. He agreed but kept quiet and absent.

I asked him what was wrong—he said, "Nothing."

I asked him if it was my fault that he was upset. He said it had nothing to do with me and not to worry.

On the way home I told him that I loved him; he simply smiled and kept driving. I can't explain his behavior; I don't know why he didn't say, "I love you, too."

When we got home, I felt as if I had lost him, as if he wanted nothing to do with me anymore. He just sat there and watched TV; he seemed distant and absent.

Finally I decided to go to bed. About ten minutes later he came to bed, and to my surprise he responded to my caress and we made love, but I still felt that he was distracted and his thoughts were somewhere else.

I could not take it anymore and decided to confront him with the situation, but he had fallen asleep.

I started crying and cried until I, too, fell asleep.

I don't know what to do. I'm almost sure that his thoughts are with someone else.

My life is a disaster.

His Diary

Today the Yankees lost, but at least I got laid!

•

Arriving home unexpectedly early from a business trip, the tired executive was shocked to discover his wife in bed with his next-door neighbor.

"Since you are in bed with my wife," the furious man shouted, "I'm going over to sleep with yours!"

"Go right ahead," was the reply. "The rest will do you good."

•

A man is about to have sex with a really fat woman, so he climbs on top of her.

"Can I turn the ceiling light off?" he asks.

"Why?" she replies. "Are you feeling a bit shy?"

"No," he says, "because it's burning my ass!"

•

This guy has been sitting in a bar all night, staring at a blonde wearing the tightest pants he's ever seen. Finally his curiosity gets the best of him, so he walks over and asks, "How do you get into those pants?"

The young woman looks him over and replies, "Well, you could start by buying me a drink."

•

A man walks out into the street and hails a taxi just going by. He gets into the taxi, and the cabbie says, "Perfect timing. You're just like Moishe."

"Who?"

"Moishe Cohen. There's a guy who did everything right. Like my coming along when you needed a cab. It would have happened like that to Moishe every single time."

"There are always a few clouds over everybody."

"Not Moishe. He was a terrific athlete. He could have gone on the pro tour in tennis. He could golf with the pros. He sang like an opera baritone and danced like a Broadway star. He was something. He had a memory like a trap. Could remember everybody's birthday. He knew all about wine, which fork to eat with. He could fix anything. Not like me. I change a fuse, and the whole neighborhood blacks out."

"No wonder you remember him."

"Well, I never actually met Moishe."

"Then how do you know so much about him?"

"I married his widow."

•

A woman walks into a pharmacy and up to the prescription ORDER HERE counter.

"I need some cyanide or some chemical like it, to kill my husband," she says.

"Ma'am, you can't just walk in here and order chemicals like that, and it's against the law to kill your husband," answers the pharmacist.

She searches around in her purse and produces a manila folder and pulls out something and hands it to the pharmacist. It's a photo of her husband having sex with the pharmacist's wife.

The pharmacist replies, "Oh, I didn't realize you had a prescription."

•

A saleswoman is driving toward home in northern Arizona when she sees a Native American woman hitchhiking. Because the trip had been long and quiet, she stops the car and the woman gets in.

After a bit of small talk, the hitchhiker notices a brown bag on the front seat. "What's in the bag?"

"It's a bottle of wine. I got it for my husband," says the saleswoman.

The other woman is silent for a while, nods several times, then says, "Good trade."

•

A mortician was working late one night. His job was to examine the dead bodies before they were sent off to be buried or cremated. As he examined the body of Mr. Schwartz, who was about to be cremated, he made an amazing discovery: Schwartz had the longest penis he had ever seen!

"I'm sorry, Mr. Schwartz," said the mortician, "but I can't send you off to be cremated with a tremendously huge penis like this. It has to be saved for posterity."

The coroner cut off the dead man's privates, stuffed his prize into a briefcase, and took it home. The first person he showed it to was his wife.

"I have something to show you that you won't believe," he said, and opened his briefcase.

"Oh, my God!" she screamed. "Schwartz is dead!"

•

While the bar patron savored a double martini, an attractive woman sat down next to him. The bartender served her a glass of orange juice, and the man turned to her and said, "This is a special day. I'm celebrating."

"I'm celebrating, too." She clinked glasses with him.

"What are you celebrating?" he asked.

"For years I've been trying to have a child, and today my gynecologist told me I'm pregnant!"

"Congratulations," the man said, lifting his glass. "As it happens, I'm a chicken farmer, and for years all my hens were infertile. But today they're finally fertile."

"How did it happen?"

"I switched cocks."

"What a coincidence," she said, smiling.

•

A woman tells her friend she's received a bunch of flowers from her husband.

"I suppose now I'll have to spend the entire weekend on my back with my legs in the air," she says.

The friend replies, "Why? Don't you have a vase?"

•

A salesman on business in Vegas is in a bar. He has been talking to a pretty woman for about a half hour when he realizes she is a hooker.

"I'll give you $200 for a mediocre blow job," he says.

"Honey," she replies, "for $200 I'll give you the blow job of a lifetime!"

"You don't understand. I'm not horny, just homesick."

•

A guy gets on a bus and sits in the front seat. He spits on the floor and says, "*F***!* What a driver!" After he does this a few times, the driver orders him off the bus.

Another guy gets off at the same time. He says, "I didn't think that guy was a bad driver. What's your problem with him?"

The man says, "I wasn't talking about the bus driver. When I was walking to the bus stop, I saw a really ugly fat broad trying to park a pink 1979 Cadillac Eldorado convertible in a space that was about a foot longer than the car. I yelled, 'Lady, if you can get that car into that space, I'll eat your snatch.' Ptui! *F***!* What a driver!"

•

One day the toilet stopped up. When her husband got home, his wife said sweetly, "Honey, the toilet is clogged. Would you look at it?"

Her husband snarled, "What do I look like? The Ty-D-Bol man?" and sat down on the sofa.

The next day, the garbage disposal wouldn't work. When her husband got home, she said nicely, "Honey, the disposal won't work. Would you try to fix it for me?"

He growled, "What do I look like? Mr. Plumber?"

The next day, the washing machine broke. When her husband got home, she steeled her courage and said, "Honey, the washer isn't running. Would you check on it?"

Again she was met with a snarl: "What do I look like? The Maytag repairman?"

Finally, she had had enough. The next morning, the woman called three repairmen to fix the toilet, the garbage disposal, and the washer. When her husband got home, she said, "Honey, I had the repairmen out today."

He frowned. "Well, how much is that going to cost?"

"Well, honey, they all said I could pay them by baking them a cake or having sex with them."

"Well, what kind of cakes did you bake them?"

She smiled. "What do I look like? Betty Crocker?"

•

An old lady tottered into a lawyer's office and asked for help in arranging a divorce.

"A divorce?" asked the unbelieving lawyer. "Tell me, how old are you?"

"I'm eighty-four," answered the old lady.

"Eighty-four! And how old is your husband?"

"My husband is eighty-seven."

"My, my," said the lawyer. "And how long have you been married?"

"Next September will be sixty-two years."

"Married sixty-two years? Why would you want a divorce now?"

"Because," the woman answered calmly, "enough is enough."

•

A guy's walking down the boardwalk in Atlantic City and he runs into a hooker.

He says, "How much?"

She says, "Twenty bucks."

He says, "All right."

They climb under the boardwalk, and he bangs her.

The next night he runs into the same hooker. They go under the boardwalk, only this time while he's banging her, she blasts two incredible farts.

When they get done, he hands her $25.

She says, "What's the extra five for?"

He says, "That's for blowing the sand off my balls."

•

The freshman and his date were naked in the motel bed, when the girl had a change of heart.

"I suppose you're going to tell me now that you're waiting for Mr. Right," he said dejectedly.

"That's a silly romantic notion," said the coed, laughing. "I'm just waiting for Mr. Big."

•

A couple visiting Mexico were mystified by a restaurant's menu and were deeply absorbed trying to translate and understand it when suddenly they heard a resounding trumpet fanfare.

Out of the kitchen burst a great procession of cooks and waiters and waitresses brightly dressed in native costume. In the center of the phalanx strode the chief chef, proudly adorned in his spectacular, tall white hat and regally bearing a huge, shining silver platter.

Ceremoniously, at a table near theirs, he swept off the lid

to reveal a glorious display of food: two large, round, and juicy pieces of meat bedded in a luscious mix of steaming vegetables, all accented by a magnificent garnish!

Excited, the couple asked their waiter what the magnificent meal was, and why it was accompanied by such ceremony. The waiter explained that they had just witnessed the serving of the house's daily specialty—the testicles of a bull from the day's bullfight.

Elated, the couple promptly decided that they, too, should like such a repast. Alas, the waiter explained, there was only one bullfight each day, so obviously they could not serve another this same night—but, if they liked, they could arrange to be the persons so honored the next evening. Delighted, they made the appropriate arrangements with the maître d'.

Next evening they returned, excited, anticipating a meal to be remembered and recounted for years. First they had cocktails and appetizers and salad and soup.

Then there sounded the great trumpet fanfare with, as before, the magnificent procession, and finally, with a grand flourish, the platter was revealed before them . . . a bed of vegetables accompanying two measly, wee, round morsels. The couple was shocked. Indignantly, the husband protested, "Yesterday's special was really impressive; how can you dare to serve us such small ones?"

"Well, señor"—the waiter shrugged—"you must understand: some days . . . the bull wins."

•

An elderly Italian man who lived on the outskirts of Monte Cassino went to the local church for confession.

When the priest slid open the panel in the confessional, the man said, "Father . . . during World War Two, a beautiful woman knocked on my door and asked me to hide her from the enemy. So I hid her in my attic."

The priest replied, "That was a wonderful thing you did, my son! And you have no need to confess that."

"It's worse than that, Father. She started to repay me with sexual favors."

The priest said, "By doing that you were both in great danger. However, two people under those circumstances can be very tempted to act that way. But if you are truly sorry for your actions, you are indeed forgiven."

"Thank you, Father. That's a great load off my mind. But I do have one more question."

"And what is that?"

"Should I tell her the war is over?"

•

Some *really, really true* facts about men:

- Men like to barbecue. Men will cook if danger is involved.
- If you buy your husband or boyfriend a video camera, for the first few weeks he has it, lock the door when you go to the bathroom. Most of my husband's early films ended with a scream and a flush.
- Men are confident people. My husband is so confident that when he watches sports on television, he thinks that if he concentrates, he can help his team. If the team is in trouble, he coaches the players from our living room, and if they're really in trouble, I have to get off the phone in case they call him.
- Men love watches with multiple functions. My husband has one that is a combination address book, telescope, and piano.
- Men are brave enough to go to war, but they are not brave enough to get a bikini wax.
- Most men hate to shop. That's why the men's department is usually on the first floor of a department store, two inches from the door.

- Men hate to lose. I once beat my husband at tennis. I asked him, "Are we going to have sex again?" He said, "Yes, but not with each other."

- Getting rid of a man without hurting his masculinity is a problem. "Get out" and "I never want to see you again" might sound like a challenge. If you want to get rid of a man, I suggest saying, "I love you . . . I want to marry you . . . I want to have your children."

- Sometimes they leave skid marks.

- When a woman tries on clothing from her closet that feels tight, she will assume she has gained weight. When a man tries something from his closet that feels tight, he will assume the clothing has shrunk.

- Male menopause is a lot more fun than female menopause. With female menopause you gain weight and get hot flashes. Male menopause—you get to date young girls and drive motorcycles.

- Men forget everything, women remember everything. That's why men need instant replays in sports. They've already forgotten what happened.

•

Jeff walks into a bar and sees his friend Paul slumped over the bar. He walks over and asks Paul what's wrong.

"Well," replies Paul, "you know that beautiful girl at work that I wanted to ask out, but I got an erection every time I saw her?"

"Yes," replies Jeff with a laugh.

"Well," says Paul, straightening up, "I finally plucked up the courage to ask her out, and she agreed."

"That's great!" says Jeff. "When are you going out?"

"I went to meet her this evening, but I was worried I'd get an erection. So I got some duct tape and taped my penis to my leg, so if I did, it wouldn't show."

"Sensible."

"I got to her door," says Paul, "and I rang her doorbell. She answered it in the sheerest, tiniest dress you ever saw."

"And what happened then?"

"I kicked her in the face."

•

Female Prayer

Before I lay me down to sleep,
I pray for a man who's not a creep.
One who's handsome, smart. and strong,
One who loves to listen long.
One who thinks before he speaks,
One who'll call, not wait for weeks.
I pray he's gainfully employed,
When I spend his cash, he won't be annoyed.
Pulls out my chair and opens my door,
Massages my back and begs to do more.
Oh! Send me a man who'll make love to my mind,
Knows what to answer to "How big is my behind?"
I pray that this man will love me to no end,
And always be my very best friend. Amen.

Male Prayer

I pray for a deaf-mute nymphomaniac with huge boobs who
owns a liquor store and a bass boat. Amen.

•

A man and a woman who have never met before find themselves assigned to the same sleeping room on a transcontinental train. After the initial embarrassment and uneasiness, they both go to sleep, the man in the upper berth and the woman in the lower berth.

In the middle of the night the man leans over, wakes the woman, and says, "I'm sorry to bother you, but I'm awfully

cold, and I was wondering if you could possibly get me another blanket?"

The woman leans out and with a glint in her eye says, "I
have a better idea. Just for tonight let's pretend that we are
married."

The man happily says, "Okay! Awesome!"

The woman says, "Good . . . get your own f***ing blanket."

•

The boss persuades the beautiful, cultivated, intellectual female assistant to visit his apartment. He offers her a choice
of wine.

She: "When I drink port, I become romantic, I think of
soft, perfumed breezes, trees and flowers; but on the other
hand, when I drink sherry, I fart."

•

The couple is in the backseat making love.

He: "If I knew you were a virgin, I would have been more
gentle."

She: "If you weren't in such a hurry, I could have removed
my panty hose."

•

A couple was engaged. One evening he got "hot pants" and
wanted to take his fiancée to bed.

She: "Oh, no, I couldn't, not right now. Wait till after we're
married, and besides, it gives me a headache."

The man brings his fiancée two aspirins.

She: "I don't have a headache."

He: "Okay, then let's go upstairs and f***."

•

Three guys were sitting in a bar talking. One was a doctor, one
was a lawyer, and one was a biker.

After a sip of his martini, the doctor said, "You know, tomorrow is my anniversary. I got my wife a diamond ring and a new Mercedes. I figure that if she doesn't like the diamond ring, she will at least like the Mercedes, and she will know that I love her."

After finishing his scotch, the lawyer replied, "Well, on my last anniversary, I got my wife a string of pearls and a trip to the Bahamas. I figured if she didn't like the pearls, she would at least like the trip, and she would know that I love her."

The biker took a big swig from his beer, then said, "Yeah, well, for my anniversary, I got my old lady a T-shirt and a vibrator. I figured if she didn't like the T-shirt, she could go f*** herself."

•

Three guys are discussing women.

"I like to watch a woman's breasts best," the first guy says.

The second guy says, "I like to look at a woman's butt." He asks the third guy, "What about you?"

"Me? The only thing I would really enjoy seeing is the top of her head."

•

A Frenchman, an Italian, and an American were discussing lovemaking.

"Last night I made love to my wife three times," boasted the Frenchman. "She was in sheer ecstasy this morning."

"Ah, last night I made love to my wife six times," the Italian responded, "and this morning she made me a wonderful omelet and told me she could never love another man."

When the American remained silent, the Frenchman smugly asked, "And how many times did you make love to your wife last night?"

"Once," he replied.

"Only once?" the Italian arrogantly snorted. "And what did she say to you this morning?"

"'Don't stop.'"

•

One night this guy and his girlfriend are about to go into his apartment, and before he can open his door, his girlfriend says, "Wait a minute. I can tell how a man makes love by how he unlocks his door."

So the guy says, "Well, give me some examples."

The girlfriend tells him, "Well, the first way is, if a guy shoves his key in the lock and opens the door hard, that means he is a rough lover and that isn't for me.

"The second way is, if a man fumbles around and can't seem to find the hole, that means he is inexperienced, and that isn't for me either." Then she says, "Honey, how do you unlock your door?"

He says, "Well, first, before I do anything else, I lick the lock."

•

A wealthy socialite had a night out on the town with her friends.

She awoke the next morning, totally naked and with a monster of a hangover, so she rang for the butler and asked for a cup of strong black coffee.

"Jeeves," she said, "I can't remember a thing about last night. How did I get to bed?"

"Well, madam, I carried you upstairs and put you to bed."

"But my dress?"

"It seemed a pity to crumple it, so I took it off and hung it up."

"But what about my underwear?"

"I thought the elastic might stop the circulation, so I took the liberty of removing them."

"What a night!" she said. "I must have been tight!"

"Only the first time, madam."

•

Three buddies decided to take their wives on vacation for a week in Las Vegas.

The week flew by and they all had a great time.

After they returned home and the men went back to work, they sat around at break and discussed their vacation.

The first guy says, "I don't think I'll ever do that again! Ever since we got back, my old lady flings her arms and hollers, 'Seven come eleven,' all night, and I haven't had a wink of sleep!"

The second guy says, "I know what you mean. My old lady played blackjack the whole time we were there, and now she slaps the bed all night and hollers, 'Hit me light or hit me hard,' and I haven't had a wink of sleep either!"

The third guy says, "You guys think you have it bad! My old lady played the slots the whole time we were there, and I wake up each morning with a sore dick and an ass full of quarters."

•

A shy but handsome fellow is at a club and sees a beautiful woman seated alone at the bar.

After an hour of screwing up his courage he heads over to her and asks tentatively, "Uh, would you mind if I chatted with you for a while?"

She responds by yelling at the top of her lungs, "No, I won't sleep with you tonight!"

Everyone in the bar is now staring at them. Naturally, the poor guy is hopelessly and completely embarrassed, and he meanders back to his table.

After a few minutes, the woman walks over to him, smiles, and says, "I'm sorry if I embarrassed you. You see, I'm a graduate student in psychology, and I'm studying how people respond to embarrassing situations."

To which he responds, at the top of his lungs, "What do you mean two hundred dollars an hour?!"

•

Two friends—a white guy and a black guy—work together. The white guy comes in late one morning, and his black friend asks where he has been.

The white guy replies, "My wife gives me good sex every night, and she kept me up really late last night."

The black guy says, "I can't get my wife to have sex with me, no matter what! How do you do it?"

"I read her poetry every night."

"What kind of poetry?"

The white guy replies, "Blondie, blondie, eyes so blue, how I want to make love to you." Then he tells his friend to go home and try it—it's a sure thing!

The next morning the black guy is about two hours late. When he comes in, he has a black eye and his arm is in a sling.

The white guy asks, "What happened?"

"Man, don't ever speak to me again!"

"Well, what did you say to her?"

The black man replies, "Black beauty, black beauty, check out my log, bend over, bitch, and take it like a dog!"

•

A cowboy walked into a barbershop, sat on the barber's chair, and said, "I'll have a shave and a shoeshine."

The barber began to lather the cowboy's face while a woman with the biggest, firmest, most beautiful breasts he had ever seen knelt and began to shine his shoes.

The cowboy said, "Young lady, you and I should go and spend some time in a hotel room."

She replied, "I'm married and my husband wouldn't like that."

"Tell him you're working overtime and I'll pay you the difference."

She said, "You tell him. He's the one shaving you."

•

A sixteen-year-old girl finally had the opportunity to go to a party by herself. Since she was good-looking, she was a bit nervous about what to do if boys hit on her.

Her mom said, "It's easy! Whenever a boy starts hitting on you, you ask him, 'What will be the name of our baby?' That'll scare them off."

So off she went.

After a little while at the party, a boy started dancing with her, and little by little he started kissing her and touching her. She asked him, "What will our baby be called?"

The boy found some excuse and disappeared.

Sometime later, the same thing happened: a boy started to kiss her neck, her shoulders . . . She stopped him and asked about the baby's name, and he ran off.

Later on, another boy invited her for a walk. After a few minutes, he started kissing her, and she asked him, "What will our baby be called?"

He continued, now slowly taking her clothes off.

"What will our baby be called?" she asked once more.

He began to have sex with her.

"What will our baby be called?"

After he was done, he took off his "full" condom, gave it a knot, and said, "If he gets out of this one . . . David Copperfield!"

•

A woman finds out that her husband has been cheating on her while stationed in Iraq. So she sends him a care package.

He is excited to get a package from his wife back home. He finds that it contains a batch of homemade cookies and a VHS tape of his favorite TV shows. He invites a couple of his buddies over, and they're all sitting around having a great time eating the cookies and watching some episodes of *South Park*.

Right in the middle of one episode the tape cuts to a home video of his wife on her knees sucking his best friend's ding-dong. After a few seconds, he blows his load in her pie hole, and she turns and spits the load right into the mixing bowl of cookie dough.

She then looks at the camera and says, "By the way, I want a divorce."

•

Morris Goldberg was old and suffering from a rare disease and could drink only human milk.

"How can I get human milk?" Morris asked the doctor.

"Well, Ruby Schwartz just had a baby, maybe she'll help."

So every day Morris went to Ruby's house for his daily feed. Ruby, a dark-eyed, big-breasted lady, gradually, in spite of herself, became aroused as Morris lapped at her ripe breasts.

One day as he lay quietly sucking, she whispered to him, "Tell me, Mr. Goldberg, do you like it?"

"Mmmm, wonderful," he sighed.

"Is there . . ." She hesitated, her lips parted, eyes aglow. "Is there anything else you'd like?"

"As a matter of fact there is," murmured Morris.

"What?" Ruby asked breathlessly.

Morris licked his lips. "Maybe a little cookie?"

•

Bruce is driving over a bridge one day when he sees his girl-friend, Sheila, about to throw herself off.

Bruce slams on the brakes and yells, "Sheila, what the hell d'ya think you're doing?"

Sheila turns around with a tear in her eye and says, "Goodbye, Bruce. You got me pregnant and so now I'm gonna kill myself."

Bruce gets a lump in his throat when he hears this. He says, "Well, Sheila . . . not only are you a great f***, but you're a real sport, too," and drives off.

•

Two high school buddies were attending the senior prom.

"Suzie wants to go out to my car. She's really hot," one boy said. "I'm really nervous, I know I'll goof up!"

"Take it easy," his friend assured him. "All you gotta do is compliment her. Chicks love to be complimented. You'll have her in the palm of your hand."

About a half hour later the young man came back rubbing a black eye.

"Shit, man! What happened to you?" his buddy asked.

"I took your advice."

"Didn't you compliment her?"

"Sure I did. We got in my car and started kissing. I told her that for such full lips, hers sure tasted sweet. She liked that. After a while I started feeling her tits, and I told her that for such large breasts, they sure were firm. She liked that, too."

"It sounds like you were doing great," his friend said.

"Well, that's when everything went wrong. I got her dress up and her panties off, and I paid her another compliment."

"What did you say?"

"'For such a large snatch, it sure doesn't stink much.'"

•

Gary and Mary go on their honeymoon, and Gary spends six hours of the honeymoon night eating Mary's pussy.

The next afternoon, they go to an Italian restaurant. Suddenly, Gary starts to freak out. He screams, "Waiter! Waiter! Come over here!"

The waiter says, "Can I help you, sir?"

Gary yells, "There's a hair in my spaghetti! Get it the f*** out of here!"

The waiter apologizes up and down as he quickly takes the spaghetti away.

Mary looks over at Gary, and shaking her head, she whispers, "What a hypocrite you are. You spent most of last night with your face full of hair."

Gary says, "Yeah? Well, how long do you think I'd have stayed if I'd found a piece of spaghetti in there?"

•

A guy runs into an ex-girlfriend, with whom he didn't have the greatest relationship, and says, "You know, I was with another woman last night, but I was still thinking of you."

"Why, because you miss me?"

"No, because it keeps me from coming too fast."

•

A guy walks into a bar and sits down to have a drink. A good-looking woman is sitting nearby. She looks at him and gives him a wink.

He scoots over and offers her a drink, which she gratefully accepts. After a few mild pleasantries, the young lady mentions she is going through a divorce.

"You, too?" says the man. "Why are you getting a divorce?"

"My husband thinks I am too perverted."

"What a coincidence! My wife thinks I am too perverted also! I guess I'm too kinky when it comes to sex."

"Wow! My husband thinks the same of me—why don't we explore this kinkiness together?"

He agrees; they finish their drinks and leave the bar.

Knowing neither can go home because of their pending divorces, they drive to a remote location where they can be alone.

The woman, becoming quite aroused, jumps into the backseat and takes off her clothes in anticipation of what is to come. "Please hurry, I want to get kinky with you!" she moans from the backseat.

She hears him fumble with his belt, hears his zipper come down, then finally his pants. Hardly able to control herself, she is somewhat surprised when she hears him pull his pants back up, zip his zipper, and fasten his belt.

"Hey, I thought we were going to explore our kinkiness here!" she complained.

"We did!" he says. "I just crapped in your handbag!"

•

A couple have been dating for quite some time. He wants her really bad, but she won't sleep with him because she's saving herself for marriage. As they're kissing, and doing their thing, he's hot and bothered and says, "Oh, come on, just a feel."

She replies, "No, I'm saving myself for marriage."

They go back and forth. He says, "Just one feel, I promise, that's all, just one feel."

She finally agrees, "Okay, just one feel, but that's all, just one, I'm saving myself for marriage."

So he puts his hand down her panties and takes a little feel. He's getting a lot hotter and asks, "Can't we please?"

She, of course, states, *"No,* I'm saving myself for marriage."

"Please, please?"

"No, absolutely not, I'm saving myself for marriage."

He says, "How about if I agree to only just put the tip in?"

"No way, I'm saving myself for marriage."

He begs and pleads with her. "I promise, just the tip, no more, and we'll stop after that."

She finally gives in. "Okay, but just the tip, no more."

He says okay and pulls down her panties and puts the tip in. He's so hot and ready that he can't control himself and shoves it the whole way in and starts going to town.

She is meanwhile moaning and groaning and shouts, *"Okay, go ahead, put it the whole way in!"*

A little stunned, he says, *"No,* absolutely not, a deal's a deal!"

•

Joe worked in a pickle factory. Unfortunately, he had a powerful desire to put his penis in the pickle slicer. This went on for years, and Joe couldn't stand it anymore. So he decided to seek professional help for this odd infatuation of his.

He spent a few months with a shrink, who finally gave up and told him that since his desire was so powerful, the only way to get over it was to do it. Joe gladly agreed to do it the next day at work.

The next day he came home from work about 11 a.m. His wife was worried and asked why he was home so early. He explained to her for the first time the desire he had to put his penis in the pickle slicer. He explained that he couldn't take it anymore, and today he did it and got fired.

His wife gasped and ran over to him, yanked down his pants and briefs, only to see his penis perfectly normal and intact.

She looked back up and said, "I don't understand . . . what happened to the pickle slicer?"

"I think she got fired, too."

•

Bill rents an apartment in Chicago and goes to the lobby to put his name on the building mailbox. While he's there, an attractive young lady comes out of the apartment adjacent to the mailboxes wearing only a robe.

Bill smiles at the young girl. So she strikes up a conversation with him. As they talk, her robe slips open, and she has nothing on under the robe.

Poor Bill breaks out into a sweat trying to maintain eye contact. After a few minutes, she places her hand on his arm and says, "Let's go to my apartment. I hear someone coming."

Bill follows her into the apartment. Once inside, she leans against the wall allowing her robe to fall off completely. Now completely nude, she purrs, "What would you say is my best feature?"

The flustered and embarrassed Bill stammers, clears his throat several times, and finally squeaks out, "Oh, your best feature has to be your ears!"

She's astounded. "Why my ears? Look at these breasts! They're full, they don't sag, and they are one hundred percent natural! My butt is firm and doesn't sag, and I have no cellulite! So, why in the world would you say my ears are my best feature?"

Clearing his throat once again, Bill stammers, "Because when we were in the hallway and you said you heard someone coming . . . that was me!"

•

A man returned home from the night shift and went straight up to the bedroom. He found his wife with the sheet pulled over her head, fast asleep. Not to be denied, the horny husband crawled under the sheet and made love to her.

Afterward, he hurried downstairs for something to eat and was startled to find breakfast on the table and his wife pouring coffee.

"How'd you get down here so fast?" he asked. "We were just making love!"

"Oh my God," his wife gasped. "That's my mother up

there! She came over and complained of having a headache. I told her to lie down for a while."

Rushing upstairs, the wife ran to the bedroom. "Mother, I can't believe this happened. Why didn't you say something?"

The mother-in-law huffed, "I haven't spoken to that jerk for fifteen years and I wasn't about to start now!"

•

"Hello?" Hearing only heavy breathing on the line, the woman repeated, "Hello?"

"I'll bet you want me to come into your bedroom," a male voice whispered, "undress you, lick you from head to toe, and make love to you until morning."

The woman replied, "You can tell all that just from two *hello*s?"

•

One day a midget came into this really trendy bar. He was dressed in black-and-white shoes and a beautiful silk coat and designer tie. His hair was fashionably combed back and he had perfectly white, straight teeth. He came into the bar whistling to himself and swinging, in small circles, a watch-chain attached to his designer trousers. You could see a diamond ring flashing on his right hand as he swung the chain.

As he walked in, he seemed extremely confident, almost smug. He thought he was hot and obviously felt good about himself. As he scanned the crowded bar filled with the "beautiful" people, he noticed—sitting at the other end of the bar—a gorgeous, well-built redhead with long, flowing hair to her waist.

She had a plunging neckline, with a diamond necklace sparkling down toward her beautiful cleavage and a matching bracelet on her wrist. She had on a skintight, long, blue dress that shimmered. She was a fox, and she knew it.

The bar was packed, and cigarette smoke hung in the air. She was sitting at the bar and had a long cigarette holder in her hand as she sat nursing a martini in her other slinky hand with long, red fingernails. Her attitude said rich, sexy, sophisticated, and untouchable, as she drew on her cigarette and exhaled slowly and deliberately.

The midget ordered a drink, took a sip, and, swinging his chain with his other hand, surveyed the whole bar and moved toward the beautiful redhead sitting by herself. He walked over to a vacant spot right next to her as she made a point of ignoring his presence.

Standing, he looked her up and down, and she could feel his eyes checking her from head to toe. The macho little midget finally leaned over right next to her, actually making physical contact, brushing past her arm as it held her martini.

She glanced over her shoulder down at the floor at him. He nestled up close to her and, with the cockiness and self-confidence of someone who thought he was God's gift to women, looked at her cleavage and slowly followed it up to her eyes and said:

"What do you say to a little f***?"

She slowly took a drag off her cigarette and exhaled slowly. Looking him directly in the eye, she said:

"Hi, little f***."

•

Three women were sitting around talking about their husbands' performances as lovers.

The first woman said, "My husband works as a marriage counselor. He always buys me flowers and candy before we make love. I like that."

The second woman said, "My husband is a motorcycle mechanic. He likes to play rough and slaps me around sometimes. I kinda like that."

The third woman just shook her head and said, "My husband works for Microsoft. He just sits on the edge of the bed and tells me how great it's going to be when I get it."

•

The beautiful secretary of the president of a bank goes on a sightseeing tour with a rich African king who is an important client. The client, out of the blue, asks her to marry him.

Naturally, the secretary is quite taken aback. However, she remembers what her boss told her—don't reject the guy outright. So, she tries to think of a way to dissuade the king from wanting to marry her.

So, after a few minutes, the woman says to the man, "I will only marry you under three conditions. First, I want my engagement ring to be a seventy-five-carat diamond ring with a matching two-hundred-carat diamond tiara."

The African king pauses for a while. Then, he nods his head and says, "No problem! I have. I have."

Realizing her first condition was too easy, the woman says to the man, "I want you to build me a hundred-room mansion in New York. As a vacation home, I want a château built in the middle of the best wine country in France."

The African king pauses for a while. He whips out his cellular phone and calls some brokers in New York and in France. He looks at the woman, nods his head, and says, "Okay, okay. I build. I build."

Realizing that she only has one last condition, the secretary knows that she'd better make this a good one. She takes her time to think and finally gets an idea. A sure-to-work condition.

She squints her eyes, looks at the man, and says, rather coldly, "Since I like sex, I want the man I marry to have a fourteen-inch penis."

The king seems a bit disturbed. He cups his face with his hands and rests his elbows on the table, all the while muttering in an African dialect. Finally, after what seems like forever, he shakes his head, looking really sad, and says to the woman, "Okay, okay. I cut. I cut."

•

A man had a problem: a red ring around his dick. He was really worried so he went to the doctor.

The doctor took a good look at it, then after hemming and hawing, said, "Apply this on it and then come and see me in a few days."

The man was a bit relieved but still worried about what would happen to his pride and joy. So that night before bed, he applied the cream. Sure enough, by the morning the ring had disappeared.

He was so happy he went straight to the doctor to tell him the good news. He showed the doctor the ring was gone, and the doctor was pleased.

The man asked him what the cream was.

The doctor replied, "Just lipstick remover."

•

The young couple were holding hands in the local nudist camp.

"When I tell you I love you," he asked, "why do you always lower your eyes?"

"To see if it's true," she answered shyly.

•

A lady tells the pet-shop keeper, "I want an animal that can really satisfy me, if you know what I mean."

He says, "I've got a frog here that's been trained to please a woman with its tongue."

"It's not possible to train a frog to do such a thing!"

"You don't believe me? Well, take it in the back room, take off your clothes, put this frog between your legs. He'll go right to work."

She's fascinated with the idea, so she tries it . . . puts the frog there . . . nothing. She calls out, "He's not doing anything!"

The shopkeeper bursts into the room, points at the frog, and says, "This is the last time I'm going to show you this!"

•

A man leaned toward an attractive woman at a bar and asked her, "Haven't I seen you somewhere before?"

"Yes," she replied in a loud voice. "I'm the receptionist at the VD clinic."

•

Two women are having lunch together and discussing the merits of cosmetic surgery. The first woman says, "I need to be honest with you, I'm getting a boob job."

The second woman says, "Oh, that's nothing. I'm thinking of having my asshole bleached!"

To which the first replies, "Whoa, I just can't picture your husband as a blond!"

•

A married couple has been stranded on a deserted island for many years.

One day another man washes up onshore. He and the wife become attracted to each other right away, but they realize they must be creative if they are to engage in any hanky-panky.

The husband is glad to see the second man there. "Now we will be able to have three people doing eight-hour shifts in the tower rather than two people on twelve-hour shifts."

The newcomer is only too happy to help and volunteers

to do the first shift. He climbs up the tower to stand watch. Soon, the couple on the ground are placing stones in a circle to make a fire to cook supper. The second man yells down, "Hey, no screwing!"

"We're not screwing!"

A few minutes later they start to put driftwood into the stone circle. Again, the second man yells down, "Hey, no screwing!"

Again they yell back, "We're not screwing!"

Later they are putting palm leaves on the roof of their shack to patch leaks. Once again, the second man yells down, "Hey, I said no screwing!"

They yell back, "We're not screwing!"

Eventually the shift is over and the second man climbs down from the tower to be replaced by the husband. He's not even halfway up before the wife and her new friend are hard at it.

The husband looks out from the tower and says, "Son of a bitch. From up here it *does* look like they're screwing."

•

God was just about done creating the universe. The Lord had a couple of leftovers in his bag of creations, so he stopped by to visit Adam and Eve in the Garden. He told the couple that one of the things he had to give away was the ability to urinate while standing up. "It can be very handy," God explained to Adam and Eve. "Would either of you like that ability?"

Adam jumped up and begged, "Oh, give that to me! It seems the sort of thing a man should be able to do. Please, Lord, let me have that ability. I would be forever grateful."

Eve just smiled and shook her head at Adam's display. She told God that if Adam really wanted it so badly, then she wouldn't mind if he was given the ability to urinate while standing up.

And so, the Lord gave Adam the ability to urinate while standing up. Then, he looked back into his bag of leftover gifts. "Now, what have we here? Oh, yes, multiple orgasms . . ."

•

There was a man who wanted a pure wife. So he started to attend church to find a woman. He met a gal who seemed nice so he took her home. When they got there, he whipped out his manhood and asked, "What's this?"

She replied, "A cock."

He thought to himself that she was not pure enough.

A couple of weeks later he met another gal and took her home. Again, he pulled out his manhood and asked the question.

She replied, "A cock."

He was pissed because she had seemed more pure than the first one, but, oh, well.

A couple of weeks later he meets a gal who seems real pure. She won't go home with him for a long time, but eventually he gets her to his house. He whips it out and asks, "What is this?"

She giggles and says, "A pee-pee."

He thinks to himself that he has finally found his woman.

They get married after several months. Every time she sees his member, she giggles and says, "That's your pee-pee."

He finally breaks down and says, "Look, this is not a pee-pee, it is a cock!"

She laughs and says, "No, it's not, a cock is ten inches long and black."

•

A married man thought he would give his wife a birthday surprise by buying her a bra.

He entered a ladies' shop, rather intimidated, but the salesgirls took charge to help him.

"What color?" they asked. He settled for white.

"How much does it cost?" he asked.

"Twenty-four dollars."

"Expensive, but okay."

All that remained was the size, but he hadn't the faintest idea.

"Now, sir, are they the size of a pair of melons? Coconuts? Grapefruits? Oranges?"

"No," he said, "nothing like that."

"Come on, sir, think. There must be something your wife's bust resembles."

He thought long and hard and then looked up. "Have you ever seen a spaniel's ears?"

Drunks

A new guy in town walks into a bar and notices a large jar behind the counter, filled to the brim with $10 bills.

The man guesses there must be thousands of dollars in it and approaches the bartender.

Man: "What's up with the jar?"

Bartender: "Well, you pay ten dollars, and if you pass three tests, then you get all the money."

Man: "What are the three tests?"

Bartender: "Pay first. Those are the rules."

So the guy gives him the ten bucks and the bartender adds it to the jar.

Bartender: "Okay, here's what you have to do. First you have to drink that whole gallon of pepper tequila—the *whole* thing at once. Second, there's a pit bull chained up out back with a sore tooth. You have to remove the tooth with your bare hands. Third, there is a ninety-year-old woman upstairs who's never had an orgasm in her life. You gotta make things right for her."

Man: "Well, I know I've paid my ten bucks, but I'm not an idiot; I won't do it. You have to be nuts to drink a gallon of tequila and get crazier from there."

Bartender: "Okay. But your money stays in the jar."

Well, as time goes on and the man drinks a few, he asks, "Wherez zat teeqeela?" He grabs the gallon of tequila with both hands and downs it with a big slurp. Tears are streaming down his cheeks, but he doesn't make a face.

Next he staggers out back, and soon all the people inside hear a huge scuffle. They hear barking and screams, yelps and growling, then eventually silence.

Just when they think the man must surely be dead, he staggers back into the bar with his shirt ripped and big scratches all over his body.

"Now," he says, "where's that woman with the sore tooth?"

•

This guy goes to a bar to hang out with some friends. After a few drinks, he decides that he should start heading home because he doesn't want his wife to know he's been drinking and, more so, doesn't want to barf all over himself.

He tells his friends he's gonna go home, but they say, "No, man! Come on, just have one more. If you throw up, we'll give you ten bucks and you can just say it was the guy next to you."

So he takes one more drink and throws up all over himself. He goes home and sees his wife sitting on the couch, and she sees him with the puke all over his shirt.

Immediately he says, "Hey, don't worry. It was the guy next to me, and he gave me ten bucks to spend on a new shirt."

His wife reaches in his pocket and pulls out the money. "But this is a twenty-dollar bill. I thought he gave you ten dollars."

"I know. He crapped in my pants, too."

•

A man and his wife were sitting next to a drunk in a bar. Suddenly the drunk stands up and yells, *"Attention all,"* and farts loudly.

The wife is extremely embarrassed, and the husband looks at the drunk and says, "Excuse me, you just farted in front of my wife."

The drunk replies, "I'm sorry, I didn't know it was her turn."

•

A drunk walks into a crowded bar and takes the last barstool, next to an older woman. After a while, the woman starts to smell this horrible odor coming from the direction of the drunk.

She turns to him. "Excuse me, mister, but did you just shit yourself?"

The drunk replies, "Yes, ma'am, I have indeed shit myself."

"Well, why don't you go somewhere and clean yourself up?"

The drunk says, "Cuz I'm not finished yet."

•

A man enters a five-star restaurant, sits at the bar, and orders four expensive drinks. The bartender serves them on a silver tray, setting all four in front of the patron. The man then consumes all four drinks in minutes.

The bartender comments, "Wow, you sure must have a problem."

"If you had what I had," the man replies, "you'd drink them fast, too."

Leaning over, the sympathetic bartender asks, "What do you have?"

"Only three dollars."

•

An American tourist dropped into a sidewalk café in Paris late one night and, after a couple of drinks, realized he was the last person in the bar except for a guy sleeping at one of the tables.

The man called the proprietor over and asked for his bill.

"Would Monsieur care for another drink?" asked the Frenchman.

"No, thanks, I imagine you want to close up. Why don't you send that other fellow home?"

"Well, I should," said the proprietor. Then, with Gallic logic, he added, "But each time I wake him up, he asks for the bill and pays it again."

•

Two old drunks were really lapping them up at a bar one night.

The first old drunk says, "Ya know, when I was thirty years old and got a hard-on, I couldn't bend it with both hands. By the time I was forty, I could bend it about ten degrees if I tried really hard. By the time I was fifty, I could bend it about twenty degrees, no problem. I'm gonna be sixty next week, and now I can almost bend it in half with just one hand."

"So," says the second drunk, "what's your point?"

"Well," says the first, "I'm just wondering how much stronger I'm gonna get!"

•

A drunk gets up from the bar and heads for the bathroom. A few minutes later, a loud, bloodcurdling scream comes from the bathroom. A few minutes after that, another loud scream reverberates through the bar. The bartender goes back to the bathroom to investigate why the drunk is screaming.

"What's all the screaming about in there?" he yells. "You're scaring my customers!"

"I'm just sitting here on the toilet," slurs the drunk, "and every time I try to flush, something comes up and squeezes the hell out of my balls."

The bartender opens the door, looks in, and says, "You idiot! You're sitting on the mop bucket."

•

A routine police patrol parked outside a neighborhood bar late in the evening. The officer noticed a man leaving the bar so intoxicated that he could barely walk.

After what seemed an eternity, and trying his keys on five different vehicles, the man found his own car, which he fell into. He was there for a few minutes as a number of other patrons left the bar and drove off. Finally he started the car, switched the wipers on and off (it was a dry night), flicked the hazard flasher on and off, tooted the horn, then switched on the lights. He moved the vehicle forward a few inches, reversed a little, then remained stationary for a few minutes as more patrons started to drive slowly down the street.

The police officer, having patiently waited all this time, now started up his patrol car, put on the flashing lights, promptly pulled the man over, and carried out a Breathalyzer test. To his amazement the Breathalyzer indicated the man had consumed no alcohol at all!

Dumbfounded, the officer said, "I'll have to ask you to accompany me to the police station. This Breathalyzer equipment must be broken."

"I doubt it," said the man. "Tonight I'm the designated decoy."

●

The officer says, "You're drunk, for God's sake. I should arrest you for indecent exposure." Pointing to the man's crotch: "You have your dick hanging out of your pants!"

The man looks down. "Oh, shit!"

"Now what?"

"Someone stole my girlfriend!"

●

A man comes home late one night drunk.

"Where have you been?" asks his wife.

"In the Golden Bar! They have golden chairs, golden glasses, golden beer, and a golden urinal."

This sounds awfully suspicious to the wife, who calls the Golden Bar.

"Do you have golden chairs?"

"Yes."

"Do you have golden glasses?"

"Yes."

"Do you have golden beer?"

"Yes."

"Do you have a golden urinal?"

"Hold on."

On the other end she hears, "I think we have a line on the guy who pissed in your saxophone."

Political

President Bush and Condi Rice are sitting in a bar.

A guy walks in and asks the bartender, "Isn't that Bush and Condi Rice sitting over there?"

The bartender says, "Yep, that's them."

So the guy walks over and says, "Wow, this is a real honor. What are you guys doing in here?"

Bush says, "We're planning WWIII."

And the guy says, "Really? What's going to happen?"

Bush says, "Well, we're going to kill 140 million Iraqis this time and one blonde with big tits."

The guy exclaims, "A blonde with big tits? Why kill a blonde with big tits?"

Bush turns to Rice and says, "See, I told you no one would worry about the 140 million Iraqis!"

•

Ariel Sharon, the Israeli prime minister, comes to Washington for meetings with George W. For the state dinner, Laura decides to bring in a special kosher chef and have a truly Jewish meal.

At dinner that night, the first course is served: matzo ball soup. George W. looks at this and, after learning what it is called, tells an aide that he can't eat such a gross and strange-looking brew. The aide says that Mr. Sharon will be insulted if the president doesn't at least taste it. Not wanting to cause any trouble, George W. gingerly lowers his spoon into the bowl and retrieves a piece of matzo ball and some broth. He hesitates, then swallows, and a grin appears on his face. He digs right in and finishes the whole bowl.

"That was delicious," he says to Sharon. "Do the Jews eat any other parts of the matzo or just the balls?"

•

An Israeli doctor says, "Medicine in my country is so advanced that we can take a kidney out of one man, put it in another, and have him looking for work in six weeks."

A German doctor says, "That is nothing. We can take a lung out of one person, put it in another, and have him looking for work in four weeks."

A Russian doctor says, "In my country, medicine is so advanced that we can take half a heart out of one person, put it in another, and have them both looking for work in two weeks."

The Texas doctor, not to be outdone, says, "You guys are way behind. We recently took a man with no brain out of Texas, put him in the White House for eight years, and now half the country is looking for work."

•

One day in the future, George Bush has a heart attack and dies. He immediately goes to hell, where the devil is waiting for him.

"I don't know what to do here," says the devil. "You are on my list, but I have no room for you. You definitely have to stay here, so I'll tell you what I'm going to do. I've got a couple folks here who weren't quite as bad as you. I'll let one of them go, but you have to take their place. I'll even let *you* decide who leaves."

Bush thinks that sounds pretty good, so the devil opens the first room.

In it is Richard Nixon and a large pool of water. He keeps diving in and surfacing empty-handed. Over and over and over, such is his fate in hell.

"No," George says. "I don't think so. I'm not a good swimmer and I don't think I could do that all day long."

The devil leads him to the next room; in it is Ronald Reagan with a sledgehammer and many rocks. All he does is swing that hammer time after time after time.

"No, I've got this problem with my shoulder. I would be in constant agony if all I could do was break rocks all day," comments George.

The devil opens a third door, and Bush sees Bill Clinton, lying on the floor with his arms tied over his head, and his legs restrained spread-eagled. Bent over him is Monica Lewinsky, doing what she does best. Bush takes this in with disbelief and finally says, "Yeah, I can handle this."

The devil smiles and says, "Okay, Monica, you're free to go."

•

Hillary Clinton goes to her doctor for a physical, only to find out that she's pregnant. She is furious . . . here she is a New York senator and this has happened to her.

She calls home, gets Bill on the phone, and immediately starts screaming, "How could you have let this happen? With all that's going on right now, you go and get me pregnant! How could you? I can't believe this! I just found out I am five weeks pregnant, and it is all your fault! Your fault! Well, what have you got to say?"

There is nothing but dead silence on the phone. She screams again, "Did you hear me?"

Finally she hears Bill's very, very quiet voice. In a barely audible whisper, he says, "Who is this?"

•

While trying to escape through Pakistan, Osama bin Laden found a bottle on a beach and picked it up. Suddenly a female genie rose from the bottle and with a smile said, "Master, may I grant you one wish?"

"You ignorant, unworthy daughter of a dog! Don't you know who I am? I don't need any common woman giving me anything," barked bin Laden.

The shocked genie said, "Please, I must grant you a wish or I will be returned to that bottle forever."

Osama thought a moment. Then he grumbled about the impertinence of the woman and said, "Very well, I want to awaken with three American women in my bed in the morning. So just do it and be off with you!"

The annoyed genie said, "So be it!" and disappeared.

The next morning bin Laden woke up in bed with Lorena Bobbitt, Tonya Harding, and Hillary Clinton.

His penis was gone, his knee was broken, and he had no health insurance.

God is good.

Religious

A judge is presiding over the divorce of a Jewish couple. When the final papers have been signed and the divorce is complete, the woman thanks the judge and says, "Now I have to arrange for a *get*."

The judge inquires what she means by a *get*. So, the woman explains that a get is a religious ceremony required under the Jewish religion in order to receive a divorce.

The judge says, "You mean a religious ceremony like a bris?"

She replies, "Yes, very similar, only in this case you get rid of the entire schmuck."

•

In Jerusalem, a reporter heard about an old Jew who'd been going to the Wailing Wall to pray, twice a day, every day, for a long, long time. She watched him pray, and after about forty-five minutes, when he turned to leave, she approached him for an interview.

"Rebecca Smith, CNN News. Sir, how long have you been coming to the Wailing Wall and praying?"

"For about fifty years."

"What do you pray for?"

"For peace between the Jews and the Arabs. For all the hatred to stop. For our children to grow up in safety and friendship."

"How do you feel after doing this for fifty years?"

"Like I'm talking to a f***ing wall."

•

A guy goes on vacation to the Holy Land with his wife and mother-in-law.

The mother-in-law dies.

They go to an undertaker, who explains that they can ship the body home, but that it'll cost over $5,000, whereas they can bury her in the Holy Land for only $150.

The guy says, "We'll ship her home."

The undertaker asks, "Are you sure? That's an awfully big expense, and we can do a very nice burial here."

The guy says, "Look, two thousand years ago they buried a guy here and three days later he rose from the dead. I just can't take that chance."

•

A rabbi and a priest get into a bad car accident. Both cars are totally demolished, but, amazingly, neither of the clerics is hurt.

After they crawl out of their cars, the rabbi sees the priest's collar and says, "So you're a priest. I'm a rabbi. Just look at our cars. There's nothing left, but we are unhurt. This must be a sign from God. God must have meant that we should meet and be friends and live together in peace."

The priest replies, "I agree with you completely. This must be a sign from God."

The rabbi continues, "And look at this. Here's another miracle. My car is completely demolished, but this bottle of Mogen David wine didn't break. Surely God wants us to drink this wine and celebrate our good fortune." Then he hands the bottle to the priest.

The priest agrees, takes a few big swigs, and hands the bottle back to the rabbi. The rabbi takes the bottle, puts the cap on, and hands it back to the priest. The priest asks, "Aren't you having any?"

"No," the rabbi replies, "I think I'll wait for the police."

•

O'Leary showed up at Mass one Sunday, and the priest almost fell down when he saw him. O'Leary had never been seen in church in his life.

After Mass, the priest caught him and said, "O'Leary, I am so glad you decided to come to Mass. What made you come?"

O'Leary said, "I got to be honest with you, Father. A while back, I misplaced my hat, and I really, really love that hat. I know that Shaunassy had one just like mine, and I knew that Shaunassy came to church every Sunday. I also knew that Shaunassy had to take off his hat during Mass, and I figured he would leave it in the back of the church. So, I was going to leave after Communion and steal his hat."

The priest said, "Well, O'Leary, I notice that you didn't steal Shaunassy's hat. What changed your mind?"

"Well, after I heard your sermon on the Ten Commandments, I decided that I didn't need to steal Shaunassy's hat."

The priest gave O'Leary a big smile and said, "After I talked about 'Thou shalt not steal,' you decided you would rather do without your hat than burn in hell, right?"

O'Leary shook his head. "No, Father, after you talked about 'Thou shalt not commit adultery,' I remembered where I left my hat."

•

A priest, a rabbi, and a Baptist minister are on a cruise ship. All of a sudden it hits a rock and starts going down like the *Titanic*. The Baptist ministers screams, "O Lord, what do we do? We must first save the children!"

The rabbi looks at him and yells, "Are you kidding? *F**** the children!"

The priest turns around and says, "You guys think we have time for that?"

•

A synagogue honors its rabbi for a quarter century of service by sending him to Hawaii on a well-deserved vacation, all expenses paid. The president of the temple decides that in addition to the trip, the rabbi should really have some fun, and the president makes arrangements to have a call girl be available at the rabbi's beck and call.

When the rabbi walks into his hotel room, a nude girl lying on the bed informs him that she's his at any time during his vacation.

The rabbi, stunned and extremely embarrassed, demands to know who arranged this, and, of course, the girl is compelled to tell him.

He picks up the phone, calls the temple, and gets through to the president of the congregation.

"Where is your respect?" the rabbi growls. "How could you do something like this? I must be held in high esteem by each and every member of the congregation. As your rabbi, I am very, very angry with you!"

As he continues to berate the president, the girl rises sheepishly from the bed, not wanting to further embarrass the rabbi.

As she stands, the rabbi says, "Where are you going? I'm not mad at you."

●

One morning a man came into the church on crutches. He stopped in front of the holy water, put some on both legs, then threw away his crutches.

An altar boy witnessed the scene, then ran into the rectory to tell the priest what he'd just seen.

"Son, you've just witnessed a miracle," the priest said. "Tell me, where is this man now?"

"Flat on his ass over by the holy water."

●

The Harvard School of Medicine conducted a study about why Jewish women like Chinese food so much. The study revealed that this is because *won ton* spelled backward is *not now*.

•

During the gold rush in the Yukon Territory, Harry packed a bag, grabbed his Bible, and started out of the tent he shared with Joe.

Joe asked, "Where are you going?"

"I'm heading into Fort Dawson. I hear it's the wildest town anybody's ever seen. There's booze you could take a bath in, gambling, and women who'll drive you crazy with their favors."

"Why are you taking your Bible?"

"Well, if it's as good as they say, I'm planning to stay over Sunday!"

•

Back in the time of the samurai, a powerful emperor needed a new head samurai, so he sent out a declaration throughout the country that he was searching for one.

A year passed and only three people showed up: a Japanese samurai, a Chinese samurai, and a Jewish samurai. The emperor asked the Japanese samurai to come in and demonstrate why he should be head samurai. The Japanese samurai opened a matchbox and out popped a little fly. Whoosh goes his sword, and the fly drops dead on the ground in two pieces.

The emperor exclaimed, "That is very impressive!"

The emperor then asked the Chinese samurai to come in and demonstrate. The Chinese samurai also opened a matchbox, and out popped a fly. Whoosh, whoosh goes his sword. The fly drops dead on the ground in four pieces.

The emperor exclaimed, "That is really very impressive!"

The emperor then had the Jewish samurai demonstrate

why he should be head samurai. The Jewish samurai also opened a matchbox and out popped a fly. His flashing sword went whooossshhh, whooossshhh, whooossshhh. A gust of wind filled the room, but the fly was still alive and buzzing around.

The emperor, obviously disappointed, asked, "After all of that, why is the fly not dead?"

The Jewish samurai smiled. "Well, circumcision is not intended to kill."

•

Q: Hear about the enterprising rabbi that's offering circumcision via the internet?
A: The service is called E-MOYL.

•

There's a big controversy on the Jewish view of when life begins. In Jewish tradition, the fetus is not considered viable until after it graduates from medical school.

•

Q: Why don't Jewish mothers drink?
A: Alcohol interferes with their suffering.

•

Q: Have you seen the newest Jewish American Princess horror movie?
A: It's called *Debbie Does Dishes*.

•

Q: Why do Jewish mothers make great parole officers?
A: They never let anyone finish a sentence.

•

Q: What's a Jewish American Princess's favorite position?
A: Facing Bloomingdale's.

•

A man calls his mother in Florida.
  "Mom, how are you?"

"Not too good," says the mother. "I've been very weak."

"Why are you so weak?"

"Because I haven't eaten in thirty-eight days."

The son says, "Why haven't you eaten?"

"Because I didn't want my mouth to be filled with food if you should call."

•

A Jewish boy comes home from school and tells his mother he's been given a part in the school play.

"Wonderful. What part is it?"

The boy says, "I play the part of the Jewish husband."

The mother scowls and says, "Go back and tell the teacher you want a speaking part."

•

Q: Where does a Jewish husband hide money from his wife?
A: Under the vacuum cleaner.

•

Q: How many Jewish mothers does it take to change a light-bulb?
A: (Sigh) Don't bother, I'll sit in the dark, I don't want to be a nuisance to anybody.

•

Short summary of every Jewish holiday: They tried to kill us, we won, let's eat.

•

Did you hear about the bum who walked up to the Jewish mother on the street and said, "Lady, I haven't eaten in three days."

She replied, "Force yourself."

•

Q: What's the difference between a rottweiler and a Jewish mother?
A: Eventually, the rottweiler lets go.

•

Jewish telegram: "Begin worrying. Details to follow."

•

A young Jewish man calls his mother and says, "Mom, I'm bringing home a wonderful woman I want to marry. She's a Native American and her name is Shooting Star."

"How nice," says his mother.

"I have a Native American name, too. It's Running Deer, and I want you to call me that from now on."

"How nice."

"You should have such a name, too, Mom."

"I already do," says the mother. "You can call me Sitting Shiva."

•

A rabbi was opening his mail one morning. Taking a single sheet of paper from an envelope, he found written on it only one word: *Schmuck.*

The next Friday night he announced, "I have known many people who have written letters and forgot to sign their names. But this week, I received a letter from someone who signed his name and forgot to write a letter."

•

An elderly Jewish man is sitting on a park bench reading the Reverend Louis Farrakhan's newspaper. His best friend walks by, sees the paper, and stops—in shock.

"What are you doing reading that paper?" he says. "You should be reading the *Jewish Journal*!"

The elderly man replies, "The *Jewish Journal* has stories about anti-Semitism, problems in Israel—all kinds of troubles of the Jewish people. I like to read about good news. Farrakhan's paper says the Jews have all the money . . . the Jews control the banks . . . the Jews control the press . . . the Jews control Hollywood . . . it's all good news!"

•

"In honor of this holy season," Saint Peter said, "you must each possess something that symbolizes Christmas to get into heaven."

The first man fumbled through his pockets and pulled out a lighter. He flicked it on. "This represents a candle."

"You may pass through the pearly gates," Saint Peter said.

The second man reached into his pocket and pulled out a set of keys. He shook them and said, "They're bells."

Saint Peter said, "You may pass through the pearly gates."

The third man started searching desperately through his pockets and finally pulled out a pair of women's panties. Saint Peter looked at the man with a raised eyebrow and asked, "And just what do those symbolize?"

The man replied, "They're Carol's."

•

Two nuns, Sister Marilyn and Sister Helen, are traveling through Europe in their car. They get to Transylvania and are stopped at a traffic light.

Suddenly, out of nowhere, a tiny little Dracula jumps onto the hood of the car and hisses through the windshield.

"Quick, quick!" shouts Sister Marilyn. "What shall we do?"

"Turn the windshield wipers on. That will get rid of the abomination," says Sister Helen.

Sister Marilyn switches them on, knocking Dracula about, but he clings on and continues hissing at the nuns.

"What shall I do now?" she shouts.

"Switch on the windshield washer. I filled it up with holy water at the Vatican," says Sister Helen.

Sister Marilyn turns on the windshield washer. Dracula screams as the water burns his skin, but he clings on and continues hissing at the nuns.

"Now what?" shouts Sister Marilyn.

"Show him your cross," says Sister Helen.

"Now you're talking." Sister Marilyn opens the window, waves the cross in front of Dracula, and shouts, "Get the f*** off our car!"

•

A modern Orthodox Jewish couple, preparing for their religious wedding, meet with their rabbi for counseling. The rabbi asks if they have any last questions before they leave.

The man asks, "Rabbi, we realize it's tradition for men to dance with men, and women to dance with women at the reception, but we'd like your permission to dance together."

"Absolutely not," says the rabbi. "It's immodest. Men and women always dance separately."

"So after the ceremony I can't even dance with my own wife?"

"*No!*" answered the rabbi. "It's absolutely forbidden."

"Well, okay," says the man. "What about sex? Can we finally have sex?"

"Of course!" replies the rabbi. "Sex is a mitzvah within marriage, to have children."

"What about different positions?" asks the man.

"No problem. It's a mitzvah."

"With the woman on top?"

"Sure. Go for it! It's a mitzvah."

"Can we do it doggie style?"

"Sure! Another mitzvah."

"On the kitchen table?"

"Yes, yes! A mitzvah!"

"Can we do it on rubber sheets with mirrors on the ceiling, a bottle of hot oil, a vibrator, a leather whip, a bucket of honey, and a porno video?"

"You may indeed. It's all a mitzvah."

"Can we do it standing up?"

"No! No! No!" cries the rabbi. "Absolutely *never* standing up!"

"Why not?" asks the man.

"Could lead to dancing."

•

A train hits a busload of Catholic schoolgirls and they all perish. They are all in heaven trying to enter the pearly gates past Saint Peter.

Saint Peter asks the first girl, "Jessica, have you ever had any contact with a penis?"

She giggles and shyly replies, "Well, I once touched the head of one with the tip of my finger."

Saint Peter says, "Okay, dip the tip of your finger in the holy water and pass through the gate."

Saint Peter asks the next girl, "Jennifer, have you ever had any contact with a penis?"

The girl is a little reluctant but replies, "Well, once I fondled and stroked one."

Saint Peter says, "Okay, dip your whole hand in the holy water and pass through the gate."

All of a sudden there is a lot of commotion as one girl is pushing her way to the front of the line of girls.

When she reaches the front of the line, Saint Peter says, "Lisa! What seems to be the rush?"

The girl replies, "If I'm going to have to gargle that holy water, I want to do it before Tiffany sticks her ass in it."

•

President Bush calls in the head of the CIA and asks, "How come the Jews know everything before we do?"

The CIA chief says, "The Jews have this expression, *'Vus tit-zuch?'* They just ask each other and they know everything."

The president decides to personally go undercover to determine if this is true. He gets dressed up as an Orthodox Jew (black hat, beard, long *payess*—side locks—etc.), is secretly flown in an unmarked plane to New York, picked up in an unmarked car, and dropped off in Brooklyn's most Jewish neighborhood.

Soon a little old man comes shuffling along. The president stops him and whispers, *"Vus titzuch?"*

The old guy whispers back, "Bush is in Brooklyn."

•

Q: What is the definition of a JAP (Jewish American Princess)?
A: A girl who thinks cooking and f***ing are two cities in China.

•

Three nuns were talking. The first nun said, "I was cleaning in the father's room the other day, and do you know what I found? A bunch of pornographic magazines."

"What did you do?" the other nuns asked.

"Well, of course I threw them in the trash."

The second nun said, "Well, I can top that. I was in the father's room putting away the laundry, and I found a bunch of condoms!"

"Oh my!" gasped the other nuns. "What did you do?"

"I poked holes in all of them!"

The third nun fainted.

•

An IRS auditor walks into a synagogue and asks to see the rabbi. He is shown into the rabbi's office and says, "Rabbi, a member of your synagogue, Mr. Katz, states on his tax return that he donated $100,000 to the synagogue. Is this correct?"

The rabbi answers, "Yes, he certainly will."

•

An older Jewish gentleman marries a younger lady and they are very much in love. However, no matter what the husband does sexually, the woman never achieves orgasm. Since a

Jewish wife is entitled to sexual pleasure, they decide to ask the rabbi.

The rabbi listens to their story, strokes his beard, and suggests, "Hire a strapping young man. While the two of you are making love, have the young man wave a towel over you. That will help the wife fantasize and should bring on an orgasm."

They go home and follow the rabbi's advice. They hire a handsome young man and he waves a towel over them as they make love. It doesn't help and the wife is still unsatisfied.

Perplexed, they go back to the rabbi.

"Okay," says the rabbi to the husband, "let's try it reversed. Have the young man make love to your wife and you wave the towel over them."

Once again, they follow the rabbi's advice. The young man gets into bed with the wife and the husband waves the towel. The young man gets to work with great enthusiasm, and the wife soon has an enormous, room-shaking, screaming orgasm.

The husband smiles, looks at the young man, and says to him triumphantly, "You see, schmuck? *That's* the way to wave a towel!"

•

Several years ago, the Catholic Church required women to wear a head covering to enter the sanctuary. One Sunday a lady arrived without her head covering. The priest informed her that she could not enter without it.

So she left, and a few moments later the lady came back wearing a brassiere tied to her head. And from the bouncing and jiggling, it was abundantly obvious where the brassiere came from. The shocked priest said, "Madam, I cannot allow you to enter this holy place without wearing a brassiere."

"But, Father, I have a divine right," she informed him.

"Yes, I see. And your left one isn't bad either, but you still cannot enter this church like that!"

•

A priest and a nun are traveling across the desert when, tragically, their camel dies of thirst.

The priest ponders the dilemma and finally says, "Our time is numbered here. Will you disrobe in front of me? I've never seen a naked woman."

Nun: "I've never seen a man nude before, will you also disrobe? What's that between your legs?"

Priest: "That's the staff of life. If I put it into you, it will bring a new life."

Nun: "Ah, so put it in the camel and let's go."

•

Sister Mary was raped by a gorilla. She's been in the hospital two weeks.

Sister Agnes is visiting and asks, "Does it hurt?"

Sister Mary says, "Does it hurt? He hasn't written, he hasn't called."

•

Two men are having a heated argument leading to:

#1: "God bless Golda."

#2: "*F**** Golda."

#1: "God bless Moshe Dayan."

#2: "*F**** Moshe."

#1: "Are you Jewish?"

#2: "No, Irish."

#1: "*F**** Ella Fitzgerald."

•

Sister Mary Katherine lived in a convent, a block away from Jack's Liquor Store. One day, in walked Sister Mary Katherine and she said, "Oh, Jack, give me a pint o' the brandy."

"Sister Mary Katherine," exclaimed Jack, "I could never do that! I've never sold alcohol to a nun in my life!"

"Oh, Jack, it's only for the mother superior." The nun's voice dropped. "It helps her constipation, you know."

So Jack sold her the brandy.

Later that night Jack closed the store and walked home. As he passed the convent, whom should he see but Sister Mary Katherine—and she was snookered. She was singing and dancing, whirling around and flapping her arms like a bird, right there on the sidewalk.

A crowd was gathering, so Jack pushed through and exclaimed, "Sister Mary Katherine! For shame! You told me this was for the mother superior's constipation!"

Sister Mary Katherine didn't miss a beat as she replied, "And so it is, me lad, so it is. When she sees me, she's going to shit!"

Golf

A husband and wife love to golf together, but neither of them is playing the way they want to, so they decide to take private lessons. The husband has his lesson first.

After the pro sees his swing, he says, "No, no, no, you're gripping the club way too hard!"

"Well, what should I do?"

"Hold the club gently, just like you'd hold your wife's breast."

The man takes the advice, takes a swing, and *wow*! He hits the ball 250 yards straight up the fairway. The man goes back to his wife with the good news, and the wife can't wait for her lesson.

The next day, the pro watches her swing and says, "No, no, no, you're gripping the club way too hard."

"What can I do?"

"Hold the club gently, just like you'd hold your husband's penis."

The wife listens carefully to the pro's advice, takes a swing, and *thump*. The ball goes straight down the fairway . . . about 15 feet.

"That was great," the pro says. "Now, take the club out of your mouth and swing the club like you're supposed to!"

•

A Catholic priest and a nun were playing a round of golf. The priest stepped up to the tee and took a mighty swing. He missed the ball entirely and said, "Shit, I missed."

Sister Marie told him to watch his language.

At the next swing he missed again. "Shit, I missed."

"Father, I am not going to play with you if you keep swearing."

The priest promises to do better. At the next tee he misses again, and out comes the usual reply: "Shit, I missed."

Sister Marie is really mad now. "Father John, God is going to strike you dead if you keep swearing like that."

At the next tee, the priest misses and swears, "Shit, I missed."

Out of the sky comes a gigantic bolt of lightning, which strikes Sister Marie dead in her tracks.

Then the skies open up and a big booming voice says, "Shit, I missed."

●

On a sunny Saturday morning on the first hole of a busy course, I was beginning my pre-shot routine, visualizing my upcoming shot, when a piercing voice came over the clubhouse speaker.

"Would the gentleman on the women's tee back up to the men's tee, please?!"

I could feel every eye on the course looking at me. I was still deep in my routine, impervious to the interruption. Again came the announcement from the clubhouse.

"Would the *man* on the *women's* tee kindly back up to the men's tee!"

I simply ignored the guy and kept concentrating, and once more the speaker blared out its message.

"Would the man on the women's tee back up to the men's tee, please!"

I finally stopped, turned, looked through the clubhouse window directly at the person with the microphone, cupped my hands over my mouth, and shouted back:

"Would the asshole in the clubhouse kindly shut the hell up and let me play my second shot!"

•

Toward the end of the golf course, Fred hit his ball into the woods. Harry, his partner, laughed and poked fun, but then he, too, hit his ball into the woods, just a few yards beyond.

Fred looked for a long time, getting angrier every minute. Finally, in a patch of pretty yellow buttercups, he found his ball. Instead of just continuing the game, he took his club and thrashed every single buttercup in that patch.

All of a sudden, in a flash and puff of smoke, a little old woman appeared.

She said, "I'm Mother Nature! Do you know how long it took me to make those buttercups? Just for that, you won't have any butter for your popcorn the rest of your life. Better still, you won't have any butter for your toast for the rest of your life. And as a matter of fact, you won't have any butter for anything for the rest of your life."

Then, *poof!* . . . she was gone.

After Fred got ahold of himself, he hollered for his friend. "Harry! . . . Harry! . . . Where are you?"

Harry yelled, "I'm over here, in the pussy willows."

Fred screamed back, *"Don't swing! For God's sake, don't swing!"*

•

A foursome is waiting at the men's tee while another foursome of ladies is hitting from the ladies' tee.

The ladies are taking their time, and when finally the last one is ready to hit the ball, she hacks it about ten feet, goes over to it, and hacks it another ten feet.

She looks up at the men, who are watching, and says apologetically, "I guess all those f***ing lessons I took this winter didn't help."

One of the men immediately replies, "Now, you see, that's your problem. You should have taken golf lessons instead."

•

A father, son, and grandfather go out to play a round of golf. On the way out to the first tee they are joking, boasting, and cursing. This is very much the men's day out.

Just before the son is ready to tee off, a fine-looking woman carrying her clubs approaches them. She explains that her partner didn't show and asks if she can join them.

Naturally the guys all agree. Soon afterward the son starts grumbling because now he can't curse in her presence.

The lady then turns to the three of them and says, "Listen, boys, I don't care what the three of you do or say out here. Go ahead, curse, smoke, chew, spit, or whatever, just don't try to coach me on my game."

She then proceeds to tee off.

All eyes are on her butt as she bends over to place the ball on the tee. She then knocks the hell out of the ball, right up the middle of the fairway. She continues to amaze the three guys, shooting for at least par on every hole. When they get to the eighteenth green, she has a twelve-foot putt for par.

She turns around and says, "I want to thank you guys for not trying to coach my game. But I have never shot par before and I want your opinions on this putt. If any of your opinions help me make par, then I'll give you a night of hot sex that you'll never forget."

The son jumps at the thought. He strolls onto the green, eyes up the putt for a couple of minutes, and finally says, "Lady, aim that putt six inches to the right of the hole. The ball will break left twelve inches from the hole and will go in the cup."

Then the father says, "Don't listen to the youngster. Aim

twelve inches to the right and the ball will break left two feet from the hole and fall into the cup."

The grandfather walks over to her ball on the green, picks it up, and says, "That's a 'gimme.' "

•

One day this guy, who has been stranded on a desert island all alone for ten years, sees an unusual speck on the horizon. *It's certainly not a ship,* he thinks to himself. And as the speck gets closer and closer, he begins to rule out the possibilities of a small boat, then even a raft.

Suddenly, emerging from the surf comes this drop-dead-gorgeous brunette wearing a wet suit and scuba gear.

She approaches the stunned guy and asks, "How long has it been since you've had a cigar?"

"Ten years!" he says.

She reaches over and unzips a waterproof pocket on her left sleeve and pulls out matches, stainless clippers, and a packet of fresh cigars.

He takes one, clips it, sits back, lights it, takes a puff, and says, "Man, oh, man! Is that ever good!"

She then asks, "How long has it been since you've had a sip of scotch?"

Trembling, he replies, "Ten years!"

She reaches over, unzips her waterproof pocket on her right sleeve, pulls out a stainless flask, and gives it to him.

He opens the flask, takes a long swig, and says, "Wow, that's absolutely fantastic!"

Then she starts slowly unzipping the long zipper that runs down the front of her wet suit, looks at him seductively, and asks, "And how long has it been since you've played around?"

The guy, with tears in his eyes, replies, "O sweet Lord! Don't tell me you've got golf clubs in there!"

•

David and John were teeing off on the long par 5 seventh hole. John decided he was going to reach the green in two and took such a cut at the ball that he almost fell over. The ball skimmed out over the course about five feet above the ground, slicing into a tree and bouncing into the fairway about 150 yards out.

David said, "Nice condom shot."

John said, "What's a condom shot?"

David said, "Safe, but doesn't feel good."

•

A fellow is getting ready to tee off on the first hole when a second fellow approaches and asks if he can join him. The first man says that he usually plays alone, but agrees to let the second guy join him. Both are even after the first couple of holes.

The second guy says, "Say, we're about evenly matched. How about we play for five dollars a hole?"

The first fellow says that he usually plays alone and doesn't like to bet, but agrees to the terms. Well, the second guy wins the rest of the holes.

As they're walking off the eighteenth hole, and while counting his $80, the second guy confesses that he's the pro at a neighboring course and likes to pick on suckers.

The first fellow reveals that he's the parish priest at the local Catholic church, at which the second fellow gets all flustered and apologetic and offers to give the priest back his money.

The priest says, "No, no. You won fair and square and I was foolish to bet with you. You keep your winnings."

The pro says, "Well, is there anything I can do to make it up to you?"

"Well, you could come to Mass on Sunday and make a

donation. Then, if you bring your mother and father by after Mass, I'll marry them for you."

•

A nun is sitting with her mother superior, chatting.

"I used some horrible language this week and I feel absolutely terrible about it."

"When did you use this awful language?" asks the elder.

"Well, I was golfing and hit an incredible drive that looked like it was going to go over 280 yards, but it struck a phone line that was hanging over the fairway and fell straight down to the ground after going only about 100 yards."

"Is that when you swore?"

"No, Mother," says the nun. "After that, a squirrel ran out of the bushes and grabbed my ball in its mouth and began to run away."

"Is *that* when you swore?"

"Well, no. You see, as the squirrel was running, an eagle came down out of the sky, grabbed the squirrel in his talons, and began to fly away!"

"Is *that* when you swore?" asks the amazed elder.

"No, no yet. As the eagle carried the squirrel away in its claws, it flew near the green and the squirrel dropped my ball."

"Did you swear *then*?" asks the mother superior, becoming impatient.

"No, because the ball fell on a big rock, bounced over the sand trap, rolled onto the green, and stopped about six inches from the hole."

The two nuns are silent for a moment.

Then the mother superior sighs and says, "You missed the f***ing putt, didn't you?"

•

Three golfers, Bob, Max, and Ted, are looking for a fourth.

Bob mentions that his friend George is a pretty good golfer, so they decide to invite him for the following Saturday.

"Sure, I'd love to play," says George, "but I may be about ten minutes late, so wait for me."

So Saturday rolls around. Bob, Max, and Ted arrive promptly at 9 a.m. and find George already waiting for them. He plays right-handed and beats them all.

Quite pleased with their new fourth, they ask him if he'd like to play again the following Saturday.

"Yeah, sounds great," says George. "But I may be about ten minutes late, so wait for me."

The following Saturday, again, all four golfers show up on time, but this time George plays left-handed and beats them all.

As they're getting ready to leave, George says, "See you next Saturday, but I may be about ten minutes late, so wait for me."

Every week, George is right on time and plays great with whichever hand he decides to use. And every week, he departs with the same message.

After a couple of months, Ted is pretty tired of this routine, so he says, "Wait a minute, George. Every week you say you may be about ten minutes late, but you're right on time. You beat us either left-handed or right-handed. What's the story?"

"Well," George says, "I'm kind of superstitious. When I get up in the morning, I look at my wife. If she's sleeping on her left side, I play left-handed, and if she's sleeping on her right side, I play right-handed."

"So what do you do if she's sleeping on her back?"

"Well . . . that's when I'm about ten minutes late."

•

A golfer stands over his tee shot for what seems like an eternity to his partner. He looks up, he looks down, measures the distance, and figures the wind direction and speed. The longer he takes, the more his partner fidgets.

Finally, his exasperated partner says, "What's taking so long? Hit the blasted ball."

The guy answers, "My wife is up there watching me from the clubhouse. I want to make the perfect shot."

"Forget it, man," the partner says. "You'll never hit her from here."

•

A man constantly and continuously talked only about golf. His wife threatened to leave him if he did not talk about something else.

She: "Let's talk about sex."

He: "I wonder if Arnold Palmer got laid last night."

•

On the seventh tee at the golf club, a golfer drives five balls into the water and borrows three from a friend. Those three balls end up in the water, too.

Friend: "Hey, those balls cost money."

Golfer who lost the balls: "Look, if you can't afford the game, you shouldn't play."

•

A famous golfer is invited by a local female golf enthusiast for cocktails; he stays on and the couple make love.

Then she holds up two fingers to her cheek and says, "I know you are a great golfer, but as a lover . . . Gary played this course last year twice"—she then puts three fingers to her cheek—"and Julius played here two years ago"—she then puts four fingers to her cheek—"and Jack played here three years ago . . ."

Golfer: "Madam, tell me, what is par for this hole anyway?"

•

Four American engineers on a business trip to Paris decided to visit a brothel. This foursome worked for the same company. They played golf together and always seemed to be together.

At the brothel, each of the men paired off with a companion to go to their rooms upstairs.

Shortly, one of the young women came running to the madam, screaming hysterically, "Madame, what's a mulligan?"

•

Arnold Palmer agrees to a match with a blind golfer.

Blind golfer: "Mr. Palmer, you set the handicap and I'll set the tee-off time."

Palmer, deciding to be generous, says, "Yes, okay, I'll give you thirty-six strokes. What time shall we tee off?"

Blind golfer: "Let's start at ten thirty p.m."

•

A golfer hits a wicked slice off the tee that ricochets through the trees and into the next fairway, narrowly missing another golfer.

When the first golfer gets to his ball, his unintended victim angrily tells him of the near miss.

"I'm sorry, I didn't have time to yell *fore*," says the first golfer.

"That's funny," replies the second. "You had plenty of time to yell, '*Oh, shit!*' "

•

One day a man came home and was greeted by his wife dressed in a sexy nightie.

"Tie me up," she purred, "and you can do anything you want."

So he tied her up and went golfing.

•

A foursome was on the last hole, and when the last golfer drove off the tee, he hooked into a cow pasture. He advised his friends to play through and he would meet them at the clubhouse. They followed the plan and waited for their friend.

After a considerable time he appeared, disheveled, bloody, and badly beaten up. They all wanted to know what happened.

He explained that he went over to the cow pasture but could not find his ball. He noticed a cow wringing her tail in obvious pain. He went over and lifted her tail and saw a golf ball solidly embedded. It was a yellow ball so he knew it was not his. A woman came out of the bushes apparently searching for her lost golf ball. The helpful male golfer lifted the cow's tail and asked, "Does this look like yours?"

That was the last thing he could remember.

•

A Scot and an American were talking about playing golf during the various seasons of the year.

"In most parts of the USA we cannot play in the wintertime. We have to wait until spring," the Yank said.

"Why, in Scotland we can even play in the wintertime. Snow and cold are no object to us," said the Scot.

"Well, what do you do—paint your balls black?"

"No," said the Scot, "we just put on an extra sweater or two."

Lawyers

A man walks into a bar. He sees a good-looking lady sitting on a stool. He walks up to her and says, "Hi there, how's it going?"

She turns to him, looks him straight in the eyes, and says, "I'll screw anybody, anytime, anywhere—your place, my place, doesn't matter."

"No shit," he says. "What law firm do you work for?"

•

Two attorneys boarded a flight out of Seattle. One sat in the window seat, the other sat in the middle seat. Just before takeoff, a physician got on and took the aisle seat next to the two attorneys.

The physician kicked off his shoes, wiggled his toes, and was settling in when the attorney in the window seat said, "I think I'll get up and get a Coke."

"No problem," said the physician, "I'll get it for you."

While he was gone, one of the attorneys picked up the physician's shoe and spat in it.

When he returned with the Coke, the other attorney said, "That looks good, I think I'll have one, too."

Again, the physician obligingly went to fetch it, and while he was gone, the other attorney picked up the other shoe and spat in it.

The physician returned and they all sat back and enjoyed the flight. As the plane was landing, the physician slipped his feet into his shoes and knew immediately what happened.

"How long must this go on?" he asked. "This fighting between our professions? This hatred? This animosity? This spitting in shoes and pissing in Cokes?"

•

Two alligators are sitting on the edge of a swamp. The small one turns to the big one and says, "I don't understand how you can be so much bigger than me. We're the same age, we were the same size as kids . . . I just don't get it."

"Well," says the big alligator, "what have you been eating?"

"Lawyers, same as you."

"Hmmm. Well, where do you catch 'em?"

"Down at that law firm on the edge of the swamp."

"Same here. Hmmmm . . . how do you catch them?"

"Well, I crawl under a BMW and wait for someone to unlock the door. Then I jump out, grab 'em in my jaws, shake the crap out of 'em, and then I eat 'em!"

"Ah!" says the big alligator. "I think I see your problem. By the time you get done shakin' the crap out of a lawyer, there's nothin' left but lips and a briefcase."

•

The madam opened the brothel door to see a rather dignified, well-dressed, good-looking man in his late forties or early fifties.

"Can I help you?" she asked.

"I want to see Natalie," the man replied.

"Sir, Natalie is one of our most expensive ladies. Perhaps you would prefer someone else?"

"No. I must see Natalie."

Just then Natalie appeared and announced to the man that she charged $1,000 a visit.

Without hesitation, the man pulled out ten $100 bills and gave them to Natalie, and they went upstairs. After an hour, the man calmly left.

The next night, the same man appeared again, demanding

to see Natalie. Natalie explained that no one had ever come back two nights in a row—too expensive—and she didn't give discounts. The price was still $1,000.

Again the man peeled off ten $100 bills, gave them to Natalie, and they went upstairs. After an hour, he left.

The following night the man was there again. Everyone was astounded that he had come for a third consecutive night, but he paid Natalie the $1,000 and they went upstairs.

After their session, Natalie said, "No one has ever used me three nights in a row. Where are you from?"

The man replied, "South Carolina."

"Really. I have family in South Carolina."

"I know. Your father died. I'm your sister's attorney. She asked me to give you your $3,000 inheritance."

•

A man went to his lawyer and stated, "I would like to make a will, but I don't know exactly how to go about it."

The lawyer said, "No problem, leave it all to me."

The man looked somewhat upset as he said, "Well, I knew you were going to take the biggest slice, but I'd like to leave a little to my children, too!"

•

An elderly spinster called a lawyer's office and told the receptionist she wanted to see the lawyer about having a will prepared. The receptionist suggested they set up an appointment for a convenient time for the spinster to come into the office.

The woman replied, "You must understand, I've lived alone all my life, I rarely see anyone, and I don't like to go out. Would it be possible for the lawyer to come to my house?"

The receptionist checked with the attorney, who agreed, and he went to the spinster's home for the meeting to discuss her estate and the will.

The lawyer's first question was "Would you please tell me what you have in assets and how you'd like them to be distributed under your will?"

She replied, "Besides the furniture and accessories you see here, I have $40,000 in my savings account at the bank."

"Tell me, how would you like the $40,000 to be distributed?"

"Well, as I've told you, I've lived a reclusive life, people have hardly ever noticed me, so I'd like them to notice when I pass on. I'd like to provide $35,000 for my funeral."

The lawyer remarked, "Well, for $35,000 you will be able to have a funeral that will certainly be noticed and will leave a lasting impression on anyone who may not have taken much note of you! But tell me, what would you like to do with the remaining $5,000?"

"As you know, I've never married, I've lived alone almost my entire life, and in fact I've never slept with a man. Before I die, I'd like you to use the $5,000 to arrange for a man to sleep with me."

"This is a very unusual request, but I'll see what I can do to arrange it and get back to you."

That evening, the lawyer was at home telling his wife about the eccentric spinster and her weird request. After thinking about how much she could do around the house with $5,000, and with a bit of coaxing, she got her husband to agree to provide the service himself.

She said, "I'll drive you over tomorrow morning and wait in the car until you're finished."

The next morning, she drove him to the spinster's house and waited while he went in. She waited for over an hour, but her husband didn't come out. Finally, she blew the car horn. Shortly thereafter, the upstairs bedroom window opened, and the lawyer stuck his head out and yelled, "Pick me up tomorrow! She's going to let the county bury her!"

•

Three lawyers and three engineers are traveling by train to a conference. At the station, the three lawyers each buy tickets and watch as the engineers buy only a single ticket.

"How are three people going to travel on only one ticket?" asks one of the three lawyers.

"Watch and you'll see," answers one of the engineers.

They all board the train. The lawyers take their respective seats, but all three engineers cram into a restroom and close the door behind them.

Shortly after the train has departed, the conductor comes around collecting tickets. He knocks on the restroom door and says, "Ticket, please."

The door opens just a crack and a single hand emerges with a ticket. The conductor takes it and moves on. The lawyers see this and agree it is quite a clever idea.

So after the conference, the lawyers decide to copy the engineers on the return trip and save some money. When they get to the station, they buy a single ticket for the return trip. To their astonishment, the engineers don't buy a ticket at all.

"How are you going to travel without a ticket?" asks one perplexed lawyer.

"Watch and you'll see," says one of the engineers.

When they all board the train, the three lawyers cram into a restroom and the three engineers cram into another one nearby. The train departs. Shortly afterward, one of the engineers leaves his restroom and walks over to the restroom where the lawyers are hiding. He knocks on the door and says, "Ticket, please."

•

A doctor, a lawyer, and an architect were arguing about who had the smartest dog. They decided to settle the issue by getting all the dogs together and seeing whose could perform the most impressive feat.

"Okay, Rover," ordered the architect, and Rover trotted over to a table and, in four minutes, constructed a complete scale model of a cathedral out of toothpicks. The architect slipped Rover a cookie, and everyone agreed that it was a pretty impressive performance.

"Hit it, Spot," commanded the doctor. Spot lost no time in performing an emergency caesarean on a cow. Three minutes later the proud mother of a healthy little heifer was all sewed up and doing fine. "Not bad," conceded the onlookers, and Spot got a cookie from the doctor.

"Your turn, Fella," said the lawyer. Over went Fella, screwed the other two dogs, took their cookies, and went to lunch.

•

A young associate was romantically ambushed in a darkened room of the law firm. After months of the social isolation that comes from eighty-hour workweeks, the associate was happy to reciprocate. However, when asked by a friend to identify the lover, the associate was puzzled.

"All I know for sure is that it was a partner—I had to do all the work."

•

Two lawyers were walking down Rodeo Drive and saw a beautiful model walking toward them. "What a babe," one said. "I'd sure like to f*** her!"

"Really?" the other responded. "Out of what?"

•

A lawyer married a woman who had previously divorced ten husbands. On their wedding night, she told her new husband, "Please be gentle, I'm still a virgin."

"What?" said the puzzled groom. "How can that be if you have been married ten times?"

"Well, husband number one was a sales representative; he kept telling me how great it was going to be.

"Husband number two was in software services; he was never really sure how it was supposed to function, but he said he'd look into it and get back to me.

"Husband number three was from field services; he said everything checked out diagnostically but he just couldn't get the system up.

"Husband four was in telemarketing; even though he knew he had the order, he didn't know when he would be able to deliver.

"Husband five was an engineer; he understood the basic process but wanted three years to research, design, and implement a new state-of-the-art method.

"Husband six was from finance and administration; he thought he knew how, but he wasn't sure whether it was his job or not.

"Husband seven was in marketing; although he had a nice product, he was never sure how to position it.

"Husband eight was a psychologist; all he ever did was talk about it.

"Husband nine was a gynecologist; all he did was look at it.

"Husband ten was a stamp collector; all he ever did was . . . God! I miss him! But now that I've married you, I'm really excited! You're a lawyer. This time I know I'm gonna get screwed!"

Old Age

A little old lady in a nursing home stands and raises her fist in the rec center one day and says, "Whoever can guess what's in my hand can have sex with me tonight!"

A little old man in the back of the room yells, "An elephant!"

She says, "Close enough."

•

It seems that there is a computer virus, called the C-Nile virus, that even the most advanced antivirus programs cannot take care of, so be warned. It appears to affect those of us who were born before 1958. Symptoms of C-Nile virus (pronounced *senile*):

1. Causes you to send same email twice.
2. Causes you to send blank email.
3. Causes you to send to the wrong person.
4. Causes you to send back to person who sent it to you.
5. Causes you to forget to attach the attachment.
6. Causes you to wonder who all the people in your address book are.
7. Causes you to hit SEND before you've finished.

•

An old lady was standing at the railing of the cruise ship holding her hat on tightly so that it would not blow off in the wind.

A gentleman approached her and said, "Pardon me, madam, I do not intend to be forward, but did you know that your dress is blowing up in this high wind?"

"Yes, I know," said the lady. "I need both hands to hold on to this hat."

"But, madam, you must know that your privates are exposed!" said the gentleman in earnest.

The woman looked down, then back up at the man. "Sir, anything you see down there is eighty-five years old. I just bought this hat yesterday!"

•

Ethel and Mabel, two elderly widows, were watching the folks go by from their park bench.

Ethel said, "You know, Mabel, I've been reading this *Sex and Marriage* book, and all they talk about is 'mutual orgasm.' 'Mutual orgasm' here and 'mutual orgasm' there—that's all they talk about. Tell me, Mabel, when your husband was alive, did you two ever have mutual orgasm?"

Mabel thought for a long while. Finally, she shook her head and said, "No, I think we had State Farm."

•

An old farmer in Georgia had owned a large farm for several years. He had a pond in the back, fixed up nice—picnic tables, horseshoe courts, basketball court, etc. The pond was properly shaped and constructed for swimming.

One day the old farmer decided to go down to the pond, as he hadn't been there for a while, to look it over. As he neared the pond, he heard voices shouting and laughing. As he came closer, he saw it was a bunch of young women skinny-dipping. He made the women aware of his presence and they all went to the deep end of the pond.

One of the women shouted to him, "We're not coming out until you leave!"

The old man replied, "I didn't come down here to watch you ladies swim or make you get out of the pond naked. I'm here to feed the alligator."

Moral: Old age and cunning will triumph over youth and enthusiasm every time.

•

Two old ladies are outside their nursing home having a smoke when it starts to rain. One of the ladies pulls out a condom, cuts off the end, puts it over her cigarette, and continues smoking.

Lady 1: "What's that?"

Lady 2: "A condom. This way my cigarette doesn't get wet."

Lady 1: "Where did you get it?"

Lady 2: "You can get them at any drugstore."

The next day, Lady 1 hobbles herself into the local drugstore and announces to the pharmacist that she wants a box of condoms. The guy, obviously embarrassed, looks at her kind of strangely (she is, after all, over eighty), but delicately asks what brand she prefers.

Lady 1: "Doesn't matter, son, as long as it fits a Camel."

The pharmacist faints.

•

Two elderly ladies were playing cards when one looked at the other and said, "Now don't get mad at me . . . I know we've been friends for a long time . . . but I just can't think of your name! I've thought and thought, but I can't remember it. Please tell me what your name is."

Her friend glared at her. For at least three minutes she just stared and stared at her. Finally she said, "How soon do you need to know?"

•

Ethel was a bit of a demon in her wheelchair and loved to charge around the nursing home, taking corners on one wheel and getting up to maximum speed on the long corridors.

Because the poor woman was one sandwich short of a picnic, the other residents tolerated her, and some of the males actually joined in. One day, Ethel was speeding up one corridor when a door opened and Kooky Clarence stepped out with his arm outstretched. "Stop," he shouted in a firm voice. "Have you got a license for that thing?"

Ethel fished around in her handbag and pulled out a Kit Kat wrapper and held it up to him.

"Okay," he said, and away Ethel sped down the hall. As she took the corner near the TV lounge on one wheel, Weird Harold popped out in front of her and shouted, *"Stop! Have you got proof of insurance?"*

Ethel dug into her handbag, pulled out a drink coaster, and held it up to him.

Harold nodded. "Carry on, ma'am."

As Ethel neared the final corridor before the front door, Crazy Craig stepped out in front of her, stark naked, holding a sizable erection in his hand.

"Oh, good grief," said Ethel, "not the Breathalyzer again!"

•

The doctor that had been seeing an eighty-year-old woman for most of her life finally retired. At her next checkup, the new doctor told her to bring a list of all the medicines that had been prescribed for her.

As the young doctor was looking through these, his eyes grew wide as he realized she had a prescription for birth control pills.

"Mrs. Smith, do you realize these are *birth control* pills?"

"Yes, they help me sleep at night."

"Mrs. Smith, I assure you there is absolutely *nothing* in these that could possibly help you sleep!"

She reached out and patted the young doctor's knee. "Yes, dear, I know that. But every morning I grind one up and mix it in the glass of orange juice that my sixteen-year-old granddaughter drinks . . . and believe me, it helps me sleep at night!"

•

An elderly couple are vacationing in the West. Sam always wanted a pair of authentic cowboy boots. Seeing some on sale one day, he buys them and wears them home, walking proudly. He walks into their hotel room and says to his wife, "Notice anything different, Bessie?"

Bessie looks him over. "Nope."

Sam says excitedly, "Come on, Bessie, take a good look. Notice anything different about me?"

Bessie looks again. "Nope."

Frustrated, Sam storms off into the bathroom, undresses, and walks back into the room completely naked except for his boots. Again he asks, a little louder this time, "Notice anything *different*?"

Bessie looks up. "Sam, what's different? It's hanging down today, it was hanging down yesterday, and the damn thing will be hanging down again tomorrow."

Furious, Sam yells, *"And do you know why the son of a bitch is hanging down, Bessie? It's hanging down because it's looking at my new boots!"*

To which Bessie replies, "Shoulda bought a hat, Sam . . . shoulda bought a hat."

•

A woman's husband dies. He has only $20,000 to his name. After everything is paid at the funeral home and cemetery, she tells her closest friend that no money is left.

The friend says, "How can that be? You told me he still had $20,000 left a few days before he died. How could he be broke?"

The widow says, "Well, the funeral home cost me $6,000.

And of course, I had to make the obligatory donation to the temple, so that was another $2,000. The rest went for the memorial stone."

The friend says, "My God, $12,000 for the memorial stone? How big was it?"

Extending her left hand, the widow says, "Three carats."

•

On this man's thirty-third birthday, he has a package at the post office and goes to collect it.

At the counter the woman brings his package to him, and the man says, "It's my birthday today."

"Oh, happy birthday, how old are you?" asks the postal worker.

"Thirty-three."

"Well, have a good day."

"Thank you."

To get home, the man has to take the bus. At the bus stop an old lady walks up soon after he arrives. The man says to the old lady, "It's my birthday today."

"Oh, happy birthday," says the old lady.

"I'm—"

"No, don't tell me. I know a unique way of telling how old somebody is."

"Oh, yeah? What's that?"

"If I can feel your balls for about five minutes, I can tell exactly how many years old you are," says the old lady.

"I don't believe it."

"Well, let me prove it!"

"I'm not going to let you feel my balls!" says the man.

"Oh, well, I guess you'll never know then."

After a couple minutes, curiosity gets the better of the man. "Oh, okay then, you can do it."

After a good feel of the man's balls the woman finally takes her hands out of his pants. "You are thirty-three years old exactly!"

"How the f*** did you know that?" exclaims the man, impressed.

"I was behind you in the line at the post office."

•

An old man walks into a confessional and says, "I am eighty-two years old, have a wonderful wife of sixty years, many children, grandchildren, and great-grandchildren. Yesterday I picked up two teenage girls, hitchhiking. We went to a motel, where I had sex with each of them three times."

Priest: "Are you sorry for your sins?"

Man: "What sins?"

Priest: "What kind of a Catholic are you?"

Man: "I'm Jewish."

Priest: "Why are you telling me all this?"

Man: "I'm telling everybody."

•

An elderly couple is enjoying an anniversary dinner together in a small tavern.

The husband leans over and asks his wife, "Do you remember the first time we had sex together over fifty years ago? We went behind this tavern where you leaned against the fence and I made love to you."

"Yes," she says, "I remember it well."

"Okay. How about taking a stroll round there again and we can do it for old times' sake."

"Ooooooooh, Henry, you devil, that sounds like a good idea."

A police officer is sitting in the next booth listening to all this and having a chuckle to himself. He thinks, *I've got to see this . . . two old-timers having sex against a fence. I'll just keep an eye on them so there's no trouble.*

So he follows them. They walk haltingly along, leaning on each other for support, aided by walking sticks. Finally they get to the back of the tavern and make their way to the fence. The old lady lifts her skirt, takes her panties down, and the old man drops his trousers. She turns around, and as she hangs on to the fence, the old man moves in.

Suddenly they erupt into the most furious sex that the watching policeman has ever seen. They are bucking and jumping like crazy. This goes on for about twenty minutes!

She's yelling, "Ohhh, God!" He's hanging on to her hips for dear life. This is the most athletic sex imaginable.

Finally, they both collapse, panting, on the ground.

The policeman is amazed. He thinks he has learned something about life that he didn't know. He starts to think about his own aged parents and wonders whether they still have sex like this.

After about half an hour of lying on the ground recovering, the old couple struggle to their feet and put their clothes back on.

The policeman, still watching, thinks, *That was truly amazing; he was going like a train. I've got to ask him what his secret is.*

As the couple pass, he says to them, "That was something else, you must have been having sex for about twenty minutes. How do you manage it? You must have had a fantastic life together. Is there some sort of secret?"

"No, there's no secret," the old man says, "except that fifty years ago that dang fence wasn't electrified."

•

An old man and his daughter go to the doctor for his monthly checkup. During the examination, the doctor asks how his nightly incontinence is.

"It's fine," says the old man. "I just get up and go to the bathroom, and God turns on the light for me."

The doctor finishes up the examination, then calls in the daughter to tell her about the God-light thing.

"Oh, my God!" says the daughter. "He's been using the fridge again!"

•

One day poor old Mary decided she didn't want to be in this world any longer. She resolved to commit suicide. She figured the best way was to shoot herself in the heart . . . but she didn't know just where her heart was. She called a doctor for the information.

The doctor said that usually on a woman the heart is located about four inches below the left nipple.

Mary followed the directions perfectly and was therefore surprised to regain consciousness in a hospital.

"I should be dead!" she wailed.

"Don't worry, lady," the orderly answered, "your knee will mend before you know it!"

•

When I was sixteen, I got a boyfriend, but there was no passion. So I decided I needed a passionate guy with a zest for life.

In college, I dated a passionate guy, but he was too emotional. Everything was an emergency; he was a drama queen, cried all the time and threatened suicide. So I decided I needed a boy with stability.

When I was twenty-five, I found a stable guy, but he was boring. He was totally predictable and never got excited about anything. Life became so dull that I decided I needed a boy with some excitement.

When I was twenty-eight, I found an exciting boy, but I couldn't keep up with him. He rushed from one party to another, never settling on anything. He did mad, impetuous things and flirted with everyone he met. He made me miserable as often as happy. He was great fun initially and energetic, but directionless. So I decided to find a boy with some ambition.

When I turned thirty-one, I found a smart, ambitious boy with his feet planted firmly on the ground, so I moved in with him. He was so ambitious that he dumped me and took everything I owned.

I am older now and looking for a guy with a big dick.

•

The seventy-year-old groom and the twenty-five-year-old bride attracted raised eyebrows as they checked into the resort hotel. Next morning at eight sharp, the groom came into the dining room whistling a gay tune, sat down at a table, and ordered ham and eggs. The smile on his face and the twinkle in his eye told everybody present that he was happy and confident.

Fifteen minutes later the young bride slowly trudged into the dining room and seated herself across from her seventy-year-old. Her face was drawn and her voice weak as she ordered toast and coffee.

The groom, now finished, excused himself and strolled into the lobby for his morning cigar.

As the waitress approached with the bride's toast and coffee, she said, "Honey, I don't understand it. Here you are a young bride with an old husband, looking like you've encountered a buzz saw."

"That guy," said the bride, "double-crossed me. He told me he saved up for sixty years and I thought he was talking about money!"

•

A young man walking through a park looked over and saw an old man crying his heart out. The young man approached and asked the old man why he was crying.

He replied, "My wife is twenty years old and has sex with me every morning when I wake up. Then she brings me breakfast in bed."

The young man was amazed and asked what the problem was.

The old man replied, "After breakfast we have sex until noon, when she makes me lunch."

Again the young man asked what the problem was.

The old man replied, "After lunch she gives me a bath and we have sex until dinnertime, when she fixes me a four-course meal and then tucks me into bed."

The young man, still not seeing what the problem was, asked again why the old man was crying.

He replied, "Because I can't remember where I live."

•

This really old guy at an old-timers' dance hadn't had sex for a long time. He'd been dancing with all the grandmas all night, but still hadn't scored.

Frustrated, he approached an old grandma and said, "I'm having no luck scoring a woman. How about coming back to my place for a roll in the hay? I'll give you twenty bucks!"

She says, "I'm willing, let's go."

They get back to his place, and after a bit of foreplay, they head for the bedroom. He loves the sex and can't get over how tight she is for such an old woman. He thinks that she's got to be a virgin.

After the wonderful performance, he rolls off her and puffs, "Wow! Lady, if I had known you were a virgin, I would have given you fifty bucks."

Surprised, she says, "If I had known you were actually going to get a hard-on, I would have taken my panty hose off!"

•

The rescue squad was called to the home of an elderly couple for an apparent heart attack the gentleman had. When the squad got there, it was too late; the man had died.

While consoling the wife, one of the rescuers noticed that the bed was a mess. He asked the lady what symptoms the man had suffered and if anything had precipitated the heart attack.

The lady replied, "Well, we were in the bed making love, and he started moaning and groaning and thrashing around the bed, panting and sweating. I thought he was coming, but I guess he was going."

●

On hearing that her elderly grandfather had passed away, Jenny rushed to her grandmother's side. When she asked the particulars of her grandfather's death, her grandmother explained, "He had a heart attack during sex on Sunday morning."

Horrified, Jenny suggested sex at age ninety-four was surely asking for trouble.

"Oh, no," her grandmother replied, "we had sex every Sunday morning, in time with the church bells—in with the dings and out with the dongs." She paused and wiped away a tear. "If it hadn't been for that ice cream truck going past, he'd still be alive."

●

On Fred's eighty-sixth birthday one of his female neighbors from down the hall in the old folks' home came into his room and unzipped his pants. She then stripped him of his trousers. She sat down on the bed with him and grasped his withered schlong and held him for an hour.

She did this routine of undressing him and holding his dick for an hour every birthday morning. On Fred's ninety-third birthday she disrobed him, but he told her to stop.

"What do you mean, you don't want me to do it any-more?" she said, baffled.

"I just don't want you to hold me anymore."

"Why, is there someone else?"

"Actually there is," Fred shamefully admitted.

"Well, what does she have that I don't?"

"Parkinson's."

•

Dear Middle School:

God blesses you for the beautiful radio I won at your recent senior citizens' luncheon. I am eighty-four years old and live at the Middletown Assisted Home for the Aged. All of my family has passed away. It's nice to know that someone really thinks of me. God blesses you for your kindness to an old, forgotten lady. My roommate is ninety-five and always had her own radio, but would never let me listen to it, even when she was napping.

The other day her radio fell off the nightstand and broke into a lot of pieces. It was awful and she was in tears. She asked if she could listen to mine, and I said F*** YOU!

Sincerely,

Mary Jones

•

Goldie, a recently widowed lady, was sitting on a Florida beach near Miami. She looked up and noticed that an elderly gentleman had walked up, placed his blanket on the sand nearby, and begun reading a book. Smiling, she attempted to strike up a conversation with him.

"Hello, sir. How are you today?"

"Fine, thank you." He turned back to his book.

"I love the beach. Do you come here often?"

"First time since my wife died last year," he replied.

"Do you live around here?"

"Yes." He continued to read.

Goldie persisted. "Do you like pussycats?"

With that, he threw his book down, jumped off his blanket onto hers, whipped off both their swimsuits, and gave her the ride of her life.

As the cloud of sand began to settle, Goldie gasped and asked, "How did you know what I wanted?"

The man replied, "How did you know my name was Katz?"

•

Seniors are the nation's leading carriers of AIDS!

Hearing AIDS
Band AIDS
Roll AIDS
Walking AIDS
Medical AIDS
Government AIDS

Most of all—monetary AIDS to their kids!

•

The golden years have come at last—I cannot see, I cannot pee, I cannot chew, I cannot screw.

My memory shrinks, my hearing stinks, no sense of smell, I look like hell!

My body is drooping, got trouble pooping.

The golden years have come at last—

The golden years can kiss my ass!

•

A man and a woman were celebrating their fiftieth anniversary. They were talking about how they should celebrate their big evening. The woman decided she would cook a big dinner for her husband. Then he said they should do what they did on their wedding night and eat at the dinner table naked. The woman agreed.

Later that night at the table, the woman said, "Honey, my nipples are as hot for you as they were fifty years ago."

The man replied, "That's because they are sitting in your soup."

•

In a tiny village lived an old maid. In spite of her age, she was still a virgin and was proud of it. She knew her last days were getting closer, so she told the local undertaker that she wanted the following inscription on her tombstone:

BORN AS A VIRGIN, LIVED AS A VIRGIN, DIED AS A VIRGIN.

Not long after, the old maid died peacefully, and the undertaker told his men what the lady had said. The men went to carve her words in, but the lazy no-goods thought the inscription was unnecessarily long. They simply wrote RETURNED UNOPENED.

•

A little old lady, well into her eighties, slowly enters the front door of a sex-toy shop. Obviously unstable on her feet, she shakily hobbles the few feet across the store to the counter. Grabbing the counter for support, she asks the salesclerk:

"Ddddooo youuuu hhhave dddddildoss?"

The clerk, politely trying not to burst out laughing, replies, "Yes, we do have dildos. Actually we carry many models."

"Dddddoooo yyyyouuu hhhave aaa pppinkk one, tttenn inchesses lllong aaandd aabboutt tttwo inches thththiiickkk?"

The clerk responds, "Yes, we do."

"Cccccannnn yyyouuutttelll mmmmmeeee hhhowwww tttooo tturrrnnn ttthe ffff*****inggg ttthinggg offffff?"

•

Mrs. Goldberg and Mrs. Murphy were friends for many years. After both their husbands died they each moved into a different retirement home. Sometime later, they met and chatted to get caught up on their current situations.

Mrs. Goldberg said that her residence was okay, but she now had a boyfriend. After lunch, they would go to her room, and "he touches me up here, then he touches me down here, and then we sing Jewish songs."

Mrs. Murphy responded that her home was also okay, and that she also had a boyfriend. After lunch they would go to her room, and "he touches me up here, then he touches me down there. We don't know any Jewish songs, so we just f***!"

•

This old man in his eighties got up and was putting on his coat. His wife said, "Where are you going?"

"I'm going to the doctor."

"Why? Are you sick?"

"No," he said. "I'm going to get me some of those new Viagra pills."

So his wife got up out of her rocker and was putting on her sweater and he said, "Where are you going?"

"I'm going to the doctor, too."

"Why?"

"If you're going to start using that rusty old thing again, I'm going to need a tetanus shot."

•

A senior couple goes to the doctor. The husband has become impotent and can't perform. The doctor examines him and explains that he can correct the man's condition by operating, but there is a $25,000 fee and suggests that the couple think it over.

The doctor calls in a few days to see what they have decided.

Husband: "We've talked it over, and we decided instead to remodel the kitchen."

•

A senior has decided to make a contribution to the sperm bank. The nurse gives him a bottle for his sperm.

After twenty minutes the nurse is worried and goes to see him.

Nurse: "Any problem?"

Senior: "Look, I did it with my left hand, I did it with my right hand, I tried it with both hands, and I still can't open the bottle."

•

An eighty-year-old man is dancing with an eighty-year-old lady at the senior citizens center. He blows in her ear and says, "How about having a little party?"

She: "I don't mind. Your place or mine?"

He: "Yours is okay."

Once there, they get undressed, and as he is about to get into bed, he says, "Wait, I'll be right back, I have to get a condom."

She: "Never mind the condom, I'm on the pill."

He: "You don't understand, the dampness bothers my arthritis."

•

The wife has just returned from a session with her psychiatrist. She tells her husband that the doctor says she should have intercourse ten times a month.

He: "Okay, put me down for three."

•

A senior has no employment records, but wants to apply for Social Security. After his meeting with the Social Security people, he explains to his wife what happened during the visit.

He: "Well, I was able to convince them that I'm eligible, even though I don't have any papers. I took off my shirt and showed them the gray hairs on my chest, and they decided I was old enough."

She: "You should have dropped your pants. You could have also collected disability payments."

•

A man was walking down the street when he noticed his grandpa sitting on the porch, in the rocking chair, with nothing on from the waist down.

"Grandpa, what are you doing?" he exclaimed.

The old man looked off in the distance and did not answer him.

"Grandpa, what are you doing sitting out here with no pants on?"

The old man looked slyly at him. "Well, last week I sat out here with no shirt on, and I got a stiff neck. This was your grandma's idea!"

•

A woman went to the doctor's office. She was seen by one of the new doctors, but after about four minutes in the examination room, she burst out, screaming as she ran down the hall. An older doctor stopped and asked her what the problem was, and she explained. So he had her sit down in another room while he talked to the intern.

The older doctor marched back to the first and demanded, "What's the matter with you? Mrs. Terry is sixty-three years old, she has four grown children and seven grandchildren, and you told her she was pregnant?"

The new doctor smiled smugly as he continued to write on his clipboard. "Cured her hiccups though, didn't it?"

•

Three advanced seniors are sitting in the doctor's waiting room, sharing their problems with one another.

#1: "I'm here because I can't pee."

#2: "I'm here because I can't crap."

#3: "Oh, I have no trouble—I'm like clockwork: at seven

thirty I pee, at eight I crap. The trouble is I don't get out of bed until eight thirty."

•

An old guy gets a hard-on for the first time in years. He runs into the living room and says to his wife, "I forget what I'm supposed to do with this."

She says, "Why don't you wash it while you've got the wrinkles out?"

•

An old man in a nursing home always fell out of his wheel-chair. Finally, the nurses decided to do something about it, so they appointed a nurse to watch him all the time. He started to lean forward, so the nurse stuck a pillow in front of him. Then he started to lean backward, so she stuck a pillow be-hind him. Then he started to lean to the left, so she stuck a pillow to the left of him. Then he leaned to the right, so she stuck a pillow to the right of him.

Later on that day, his son came to visit him. "Dad, why do you have all those pillows around you?"

"Well, the nurses around here won't let me fart!"

•

An old man goes to the doctor for his yearly physical, his wife tagging along. When the doctor enters the examination room, he tells the old man, "I need a urine sample, a stool sample, and a sperm sample."

The old man, being hard of hearing, looks at his wife and yells, "*What?* What did he say? What did he want?"

His wife yells back, "He needs your underwear!"

Prostitutes

The agent for a beautiful actress discovered one day that she had been selling her body at $100 a night. The agent, who had long lusted for her, hadn't dreamed that she could be so easily attainable. He approached her, told her how much she turned him on, and how much he wanted to make it with her.

She agreed to spend the night with him, but said he would have to pay her the same $100 that the other customers did. He scratched his head, considered it, then asked, "Don't I even get my agent's ten percent as a deduction?"

"No siree," she said. "If you want it, you're going to have to pay full price for it, just like the other johns."

The agent didn't like that at all, but he agreed. That night, she came to his apartment after her performance at a local nightclub. The agent screwed her at midnight, after turning out all the lights.

At 1 a.m. she was awakened. Again she was vigorously screwed. In a little while, she was awakened again, and again she was screwed. The actress was impressed with her lover's vitality.

"My God," she whispered in the dark, "you are virile. I never realized how lucky I was to have you for my agent."

"I'm not your agent, lady," a strange voice answered. "He's at the door taking tickets."

•

A husky foreigner, looking for sex, accepted a prostitute's terms. When she undressed, he noticed that she had no pubic hair.

The man shouted, "What, no wool? In my country all women have wool down there."

The prostitute snapped back, "What do you want to do, knit or f***?"

•

One day, after striking gold in the Yukon, a lonesome miner came down from the mountains and walked into a saloon in the nearest town.

"I'm lookin' for the meanest, roughest, and toughest whore in the Yukon!" he said to the bartender.

"Well, we got her!" replied the barkeep. "She's upstairs in the second room on the right."

The miner handed the bartender a gold nugget to pay for the whore and two beers. He grabbed the bottles, stomped up the stairs, kicked open the second door on the right, and yelled, "I'm lookin' for the meanest, roughest, and toughest whore in the Yukon!"

The woman inside the room looked at the miner and said, "You found her!"

Then she stripped naked, bent over, and grabbed her ankles.

"How do you know I want to do it in that position?" asked the miner.

"I don't," replied the whore, "but I thought you might like to open those beers first."

•

One day a man walks into a whorehouse. He goes to the madam and says, "I want something different."

The madam says, "Well, we have one girl that loves to take it up the ass."

"No, that's too common. I want something different."

"Well, have you ever tried a Hurricane Gussy?"

"I'll be damned, that is different. I'll try that."

The man goes up to the room and takes off his clothes. A minute later a huge Amazon-type woman comes in. She starts jumping up and down, blowing as hard as she can. The man says, "What the hell are you doing?"

"I'm Hurricane Gussy and that is the wind coming from the hurricane."

"Okay, I'll buy that."

Then she starts beating him over the head with her breasts.

"What the hell are you doing?"

"Those are the coconuts falling off the tree hitting you on the head."

The man says, "All right."

Then she stands over the top of him and starts pissing all over him.

"What the hell are you doing now?"

"Those are the warm rains coming from the hurricane."

The man gets up and starts to put on his clothes. Gussy says, "Where are you going?"

"I'm leaving! Who can f*** in this weather?"

•

The new hooker had just finished her first trick. When she came back down to the street, the seasoned veterans all gathered around to hear the details.

She said, "Well, he was a big, muscular, and handsome marine."

"Well, what did he want to do?" they all asked.

"I told him that a straight f*** was a hundred dollars, but he said he did not have that much. So, I told him a blow job would be seventy-five dollars, but he did not have that much either. Finally I said, 'Well, how much do you have?' He said he only had twenty-five dollars."

"So I told him, 'For twenty-five dollars all I can give you is a hand job.' He agreed, and after getting the finances straight, he pulled it out. I put one hand on it. Then, I put the other hand above that one." She paused, raised her eyebrow, then continued, "Then I put the first hand above the second hand . . ."

"Oh my God!" they all exclaimed. "It must have been huge! Then what did you do?"

"I loaned him seventy-five dollars!"

•

A man staying at a hotel removes a card offering sexual services from a nearby phone booth. Back at the hotel he rings the number, and a lady with a silky soft voice asks if she can be of assistance.

The guy says he wants a blow job plus regular plus doggie plus some bondage, finishing with a pearl necklace. Then he asks her, "What do you think?"

The lady says, "That sounds really good and I'd like to oblige, but if you press nine first, you'll get an outside line."

•

Two prostitutes are standing on a street corner. One says to the other, "I think it's gonna be a good night tonight, I can smell cock in the air!"

"Sorry," says the other, "I just burped!"

•

A man met a beautiful lady and decided he wanted to marry her right away.

She protested, "But we don't know anything about each other."

He replied, "That's all right; we'll learn about each other as we go along."

So she consented, and they were married. One morning

they were lying by the pool when he got up off his towel, climbed up to the ten-meter board, and did a two-and-a-half-tuck gainer, entering the water perfectly, almost without a ripple. This was followed by a dive with three rotations in jackknife position before he again straightened out and cut the water like a knife. After a few more demonstrations, he came back and lay down on his towel.

"That was incredible!" she said.

He said, "I used to be an Olympic diving champion."

She then got into the pool, did laps in freestyle, breaststroke, even butterfly! After about thirty laps, completed in mere minutes, she climbed back out and lay down on her towel, barely breathing hard.

He said, "That was incredible! Were you an Olympic endurance swimmer?"

"No. I was a hooker in Wheeling, West Virginia, and I worked both sides of the river."

●

A man meets a hooker on the street. He says, "Come on, let's go in the alley and f***. I've got fifteen dollars."

She says, "Fifteen dollars? You're crazy. For fifteen bucks, I'll let you look at it."

They go into the alley, she pulls down her pants, and he gets down on his knees. But he can't see anything because it's too dark, so he gets out his lighter and lights it. He says, "Wow, your pubic hair is so thick and curly, it's beautiful."

"Thank you."

"Do you mind if I ask you a personal question?"

"Sure."

He says, "Can you pee through all that hair?"

"Of course."

"Well, you better start, you're on fire!"

Stupid People

A stupid father says to his pregnant daughter, "Are you sure it's yours?"

•

Two dimwits are walking down the lonely country road, after being thrown out of the girl's car.

One says to the other, "From now on, don't say 'F*** or walk' unless we're in our own car."

•

Dimwit general tells his orderly, "Bring me my horse and my red battle uniform."

Orderly: "Red is dangerous, you'll be a target."

Dimwit general: "It's okay, I'm brave. If I get shot, my troops won't see the blood and will fight without a leader. Also, bring me my brown pants."

•

The hillbilly woman went to the hospital to have her first child. A year later she was back for a second child. The next year, almost like clockwork, she was back for her third child. The hospital staff naturally began to expect her, and she was there, just like clockwork.

In the twelfth year, she didn't show, and the staff wondered what had happened. A couple of years later she showed up, but she was not pregnant. The hospital staff wondered, did her husband die, or what?

When asked why she hadn't been there having a baby the

past couple of years, she replied, "No, no more. Found out what was causin' it."

•

Jenny was a knockout, but alas, she also was virtually brainless. Fortunately this was no drawback as far as Jack's plans for the evening were concerned. He was delighted when she agreed to come up to his apartment for a late-night cocktail.

As he prepared the drinks, full of anticipation, Jenny explored the apartment, stopping now and then to examine a painting or a book title that she didn't quite understand. At last she stopped dead in front of his fireplace.

"What on earth is that?" she asked, pointing to a carved wooden object lying on the mantel.

"Oh, that. It's African," he replied. "They use them in their fertility rites. It's a phallic symbol."

"Oh, I see," stated Jenny demurely. "I'd hate to tell you what it looks like!"

•

A hillbilly gets married, and on his wedding night he calls his father for advice on what to do since he had never been intimate with a woman before.

"We're in the bedroom, Pa. What do we do now?"

Thinking that nature would take its course, the father replies, "Take her clothes off and then you both get in bed."

The hillbilly calls his dad five minutes later and says, "She's nekid and we're in bed. What do I do now?"

Knowing his son wasn't the brightest crayon in the box, his dad asks, "Did you take your clothes off, too?"

"No."

"Well, take your clothes off and get back in bed with her."

The son calls back a few minutes later and says, "We're both nekid and in bed. What do I do now?"

The father's patience is quickly running out, and he growls, "Look, Son, do I have to spell everything out? Just stick the hardest thing on your body where she pees!"

The son calls again a minute later. "Okay, Pa. I've got my head in the toilet bowl. Now what?"

•

Three expectant mothers were sitting in the obstetrician's waiting room. Two of the ladies began to chat about their pregnancies, and their due dates and such.

One of the women said to the other, "I know that my baby is going to be a boy, because when my baby was conceived, my husband was on top."

Replied the other woman, "Oh! That must mean that I'm going to have a girl, because when my baby was conceived, I was on top."

The third woman suddenly burst into tears. Concerned, the other two ladies turned to her and asked, "My heavens, whatever is wrong?"

The third woman wailed tearfully, "I'm afraid that I may be having a puppy!"

•

Ray and Bubba, two old navy buddies, are on leave and decide to go to Bubba's house and get drunk. Lo and behold they run out of beer, so Bubba says that he will go for more.

As he is leaving, he tells his wife, Linda-Lou, to show Ray her best Southern hospitality. She agrees.

Bubba comes back with the beer and finds Ray and Linda-Lou screwing right on the kitchen floor. Bubba yells, "What are you doing, Linda-Lou?"

"You told me to show Ray my best Southern hospitality."

Bubba then says, "Well, girl, arch your back! Poor Ray's balls are on the floor!"

•

The young bride's mother had some old-fashioned ideas of marriage and passed them on to her daughter.

"Never let your husband see you in the nude," she advised. "You should always wear something."

"Yes, Mother," replied the obedient girl.

Two weeks after the wedding, the girl and her brand-new husband were preparing to retire when the guy asked, "Dear, has there ever been any insanity in your family?"

"Not that I know of. Why?"

"Well, we've been married for two weeks now and every night you've worn that silly hat to bed."

•

Mary went to the doctor complaining of body odor.

"Do you wash?" the doc asked the rank young girl.

"Oh, yes," Mary answered. "Each morning, I start at my head and wash down as far as possible. Then I start at my feet and wash up as far up as possible."

"Well, go home and wash possible."

•

This guy goes to a whorehouse and says to the madam, "I want to get screwed."

The madam tells him to go up to room 12 and knock on the door. The guy walks up to the door, knocks on it, and says, "I really want to get screwed, bad!"

A sexy voice replies, "Just slide twenty dollars under the door."

So the man slides the $20 under the door and waits . . . nothing happens! He knocks on the door again and yells out, "I want to get screwed!"

The sexy voice behind the door answers, "Again?"

•

A police officer stops a blonde for speeding and asks her nicely if he can see her license. She replies in a huff, "I wish you guys would get your act together. Just yesterday you take away my license, and then today you expect me to show it to you!"

•

A blonde is out for a walk. She comes to a river and sees another blonde on the opposite bank. "Yoo-hoo!" she shouts. "How can I get to the other side?"

The second blonde looks up the river, then down the river, and shouts back, "You *are* on the other side!"

•

This young couple got married and decided to honeymoon in Miami Beach, Florida. With limited resources, they opted to take a bus to Florida from New York City.

On the first day, the bus got as far as Delaware, then broke down. The bus company agreed to put the passengers up at a nearby motel. The young husband was most anxious to consummate the marriage during that evening.

But, the young wife said, "No. We must wait till we start our honeymoon in Miami Beach."

The next morning, they got back on the bus. But in South Carolina, the bus broke down again. Again, the bus company agreed to put the passengers up at a local motel. With more urgency, the young groom wanted to consummate the marriage, but the young wife said, "Not until we start our honeymoon in Miami Beach."

The next morning, they got back on the bus, and in Jacksonville, Florida, the bus broke down for the third time. Once again, the bus company paid for a motel. They were hardly in the room a minute when the young bride tore off her clothes and his and pent-up sex ran rampant.

After, as they lay in bed, the young groom asked, "How is it that after wanting to wait until the honeymoon starts in Miami Beach, you changed your mind?"

"I was listening to the two people sitting in back of us, and they said, 'By the time we get to Miami Beach, the f***ing season will be over.' "

•

Three Italian nuns died and went to heaven, where they were met at the pearly gates by Saint Peter.

He said, "Sisters, you all led such wonderful lives that I'm granting you six months to go back to earth and be anyone you want to be."

The first nun said, "I want to be Sophia Loren." *Poof*, she was gone.

The second said, "I want to be Madonna." *Poof*, she was gone.

The third said, "I want to be Sara Pipalini."

Saint Peter was perplexed. "Who?"

"Sara Pipalini."

Saint Peter shook his head. "I'm sorry, but that name just doesn't ring a bell."

The nun took a newspaper out of her habit and handed it to Saint Peter. He read the paper and started laughing.

"No, Sister, the paper says it was the 'Sahara Pipeline' that was laid by fourteen hundred men in six months."

•

A blond girl enters a store that sells curtains.

She tells the salesman, "I would like to buy a pink curtain the same size as my computer screen."

The surprised salesman replies, "But, madam, computers do not have curtains!"

And the blonde says, "Helloooo? I've got Windows!"

•

Three dead bodies turn up at the mortuary, all with big smiles on their faces. The coroner calls the police to tell them what has happened.

"First body: Frenchman, sixty, died of heart failure while making love to his mistress. Hence the enormous smile, Inspector," says the coroner.

"Second body: Scotsman, twenty-five, won a thousand pounds on the lottery, spent it all on whiskey. Died of alcohol poisoning, hence the smile."

The inspector asks, "What of the third body?"

"Ah, this is the most unusual one. Bill-Bob, the redneck from Alabama, thirty, struck by lightning."

"Why is he smiling then?"

"Thought he was having his picture taken."

•

Two Jewish women, Ruth and Golda, are walking along the street.

Ruth says to Golda, "My son, Irving, is finally getting married. He tells me he is engaged to a wonderful girl, but . . . he thinks she may have a disease called herpes."

Golda says to Ruth, "Do you have any idea what this herpes is, and can he catch it?"

"I don't know, but I am just so thrilled to hear about Irving's engagement. It's about time he's settled. As far as the herpes goes . . . who knows?"

"Well," Golda says, "I have a fine medical dictionary at home—I'll look it up and call you."

So Golda goes home, looks it up, and calls Ruth.

"Ruth, *keinahora* [thank goodness]! I found it. Not to worry! It says, 'Herpes is a disease of the gentiles'!"

•

One day, Jimmy Joe was walking down Main Street when he saw his buddy Bubba driving a brand-new pickup.

Bubba pulled up to him with a big, wide, toothless grin.

"Hey, Bubba, where'd you get that new truck?"

"Bobbie Sue gave it to me."

"She gave it to you? . . . I knew she was kinda sweet on ya, but a new truck?"

"Well, Jimmy Joe, let me tell you what happened. We were driving out on County Road 512, out past the falls, when Bobbie Sue pulled off the road. She put the truck in four-wheel drive and headed into the woods. She parked the truck, got out, threw off all her clothes, and said, 'Bubba, take whatever you want.'

"So, I took the truck!"

•

A young brunette goes into the doctor's office and says that her body hurts wherever she touches it.

"Impossible," says the doctor. "Show me."

She takes her finger and pushes her elbow and screams in agony. She pushes her knee and screams, pushes her ankle and screams, and so it goes.

The doctor says, "You're not really a brunette, are you?"

She says, "No, I'm really a blonde."

"I thought so. Your finger is broken."

•

Three hillbillies are settin' on a porch in Kansas.

One says, "Boy, my wife is so dumb. She's so stupid, she went to town today and bought an air conditioner. Hell, we ain't got no electricity!"

The second hillbilly says, "Hell, that ain't nothing, my wife's dumber than that! She went shoppin' yesterday and had a warshin' machine delivered."

They all laugh and laugh. "Why, nobody round here has any plum'in'!"

The third hillbilly says, "Well, I reckon my woman has to be the dumbest. Just this morning I was looking through her purse for some change and found six rubbers. Hell, she ain't got no pecker!"

•

A blonde got on an elevator and said, "T-G-I-F," to the man.

He smiled at her and replied, "S-H-I-T."

She looked puzzled and repeated, "T-G-I-F," more slowly.

He again answered, "S-H-I-T."

The blonde was trying to keep it friendly, so she smiled her biggest smile and said as sweetly as possibly, "T-G-I-F."

The man smiled back to her. "S-H-I-T."

The exasperated blonde finally decided to explain. "T-G-I-F means 'Thank goodness it's Friday.' Get it, duuuhhh?"

The man answered, "S-H-I-T means 'Sorry, honey, it's Thursday.'"

•

A young blonde went on a trip on an old steam train that took the passengers through mountains and tunnels.

As the train approached a tunnel, the conductor hurriedly walked through the coaches warning passengers, "Tunnel ahead. Look out!"

The blonde quickly stuck her head out the window, and her forehead met with the concrete entrance of the tunnel.

After being revived fifteen minutes later, the blonde's first words were "That stupid son of a bitch! He should have told me to look in!"

•

A couple of redneck hunters are out in the woods when one of them falls to the ground. He doesn't seem to be breathing and his eyes are rolled back in his head.

The other redneck starts to panic, then whips out his cell phone and calls 911.

He frantically blurts out to the operator, "Oh my Gawd! Help! My friend just died. He's dead! What can I do?"

The operator, trying to calm him, says, "Take it easy. I can help. Just listen to me and follow my instructions. First, let's make sure he's dead."

There's a short pause, then the operator hears a loud gunshot!

The redneck comes back on the line. "Okay, now what?"

•

The sheriff in a small town walks out in the street and sees a cowboy coming down the walk with nothing on but his cowboy hat, his gun, and his boots, so he arrests him for indecent exposure.

As he is locking him up, he asks, "Why in the world are you dressed like this?"

The cowboy says, "Well, it's like this, Sheriff. I was in the bar down the road, and this pretty little redhead asks me to go out to her motor home with her . . . so I did. We go inside and she pulls off her top and asks me to pull off my shirt . . . so I did. Then she pulls off her skirt and asks me to pull off my pants . . . so I did. Then she pulls off her panties and asks me to pull off my shorts . . . so I did. Then she gets on the bed and looks at me kind of sexy and says, 'Now go to town, cowboy.'

"And here I am."

•

The bride-to-be and her best friend were discussing her impending wedding.

"If you want an unforgettable wedding night," her friend said, "get him to eat a dozen oysters after the ceremony."

A week after, the new bride thanked her friend but said plaintively, "Only eight of the oysters worked."

•

The farmer's neglected wife steps behind the barn and sees the young hired hand taking a piss.

She stares in disbelief at his huge apparatus and says, "Boy, I'd sure like to have some of *that*!"

He says, "Well, you'd best run get you a cup. I'm 'bout through."

•

An innocent couple, one of the few in the world today, came to the doctor for sexual advice. The doctor had the woman undress, lie down on the table, then allow him to demonstrate the sex act.

When it was over, the doctor said, "That was the sex act. Do you understand?"

The man said, "Sure. How often do I have to bring her in?"

•

Somewhere in the Deep South, Bubba called an attorney and asked, "Is it true they're suing the cigarette companies for causing people to get cancer?"

"Yes, Bubba, that's true," answered the lawyer.

"And people are suing the fast-food restaurants for making them fat and clogging their arteries with all them burgers and fries? Is that true, mister lawyer?"

"Sure is, Bubba, but why do you ask?"

"Cuz I was thinkin' maybe I can sue Budweiser for all them ugly women I been wakin' up with."

•

A blonde pushes her BMW into a gas station.

She tells the mechanic, "It died."

After he works on it for a few minutes, it's idling smoothly.

She says, "What's the story?"

He replies, "Just crap in the carburetor."

"How often do I have to do that?"

•

A stupid girl called up her druggist and asked him what she could do for her boyfriend's dandruff. The druggist recommended Head & Shoulders.

She called back a week later and asked, "How do you give someone shoulders?"

•

After the excitement and the expense of Rosalie's wedding, and after Mama's bugging him about Rosalie's honeymoon, Papa got sick from exhaustion. The doctor told him he should take a nice vacation in Miami.

He didn't know what to do; he didn't want to leave the business, and someone had to run it.

So Mama said Papa should take a three-month vacation by himself; Mama would run the business. So, Papa went off to Miami.

After three months, it was time for him to come back. Mama met him at the airport. Papa got off the plane all tan and good-looking, and Mama was so happy to see him. But Mama noticed that Papa did not look happy. He looked healthy, but not happy.

"Papa, Papa," she said, "vot's the matter? You don't look so happy."

"Oh, Mama, it's something terrible!"

"Vot's so terrible? You look healthy. You had a nice vacation. You got back home safely. Vot's so terrible?"

Papa looked miserable. "Oh, Mama, you'll never guess vot I got. I'm so sorry, Mama. I got a case of syphilis!"

Mama shrugged her shoulders. "Don't vorry, Papa, I was getting very tired of dot Manischewitz, anyway."

•

A beautiful blonde goes into a bar and sits down next to a guy who's so homely he hasn't had a date in over a year. Also, he's so dumb that one night he slept with a ruler next to his head to see how long he slept. So he figures that he has absolutely no chance in the world to score a date with this ravishing, buxom blonde.

Then suddenly she strikes up a conversation with him, and soon they become rather chummy. It starts to get late and the bartender calls out for last drinks. The blonde leans over to the guy and says, "Let's have this last drink at my apartment."

Taken aback by her request, and trembling, the guy finally utters, "Okay."

They get up from their barstools, arm in arm, headed for the door, but the blonde stops him and says, "Before we go back to my apartment, there's one thing I have to tell you. I'm on my menstrual cycle."

"That's okay, I'll follow you in my Honda."

●

Bubba was fixing a door and found that he needed a new hinge, so he sent Betty Sue to the hardware store. There, Betty Sue saw a beautiful teapot on a top shelf while she was waiting for Joe Bob to finish helping a customer. When Joe Bob was finished, Betty Sue asked, "How much for the teapot?"

Joe Bob replied, "That's silver and it costs one hundred dollars!"

"My goodness, that sure is a lotta money!" Betty Sue said, then described the hinge that Bubba had sent her to buy, and Joe Bob went to the back room to find a hinge.

From the back room Joe Bob yelled, "Betty Sue, you wanna screw for that hinge?"

To which Betty Sue replied, "No, but I will for the teapot."

●

A redneck is sitting in a bar, drinking, when a woman slides up next to him and says, "You're cute. Do you want to go back to my place and have some nasty sex?"

The redneck gets excited, but admits to the hottie, "I've never done that before. To tell you the truth, I'm right scared to. My mama says that women have sharp teeth between their legs."

"Don't worry," the woman says, and the two head back to her place, where she strips down and shows the redneck her private parts. "Now, does it look like I have teeth down there?"

"How could you possibly have teeth down there? Look at the shape your gums are in!"

•

There was a contest to swim from Santa Monica to Catalina doing only the breaststroke, and the three women who entered the race were a brunette, a redhead, and a blonde.

After approximately fourteen hours, the brunette staggered up on the shore and was declared the fastest breaststroker. About forty minutes later, the redhead crawled onshore and was declared the second-place finisher.

Nearly four hours after that, the blonde finally came ashore and promptly collapsed in front of the worried onlookers.

When she was asked why it took her so long to complete the race, she replied, "I don't want to sound like a sore loser, but I think those two other girls were using their arms."

•

Mary decides to do something wild she hasn't done before, so she sets out to rent her first X-rated adult video. She goes to the video store and, after looking around for a while, selects a title that sounds stimulating. She drives home, lights some candles, slips into something comfortable, and puts the tape in the VCR. To her disappointment, there's nothing but static on the screen, so she calls the video store to complain.

Mary: "I just rented an adult movie from you and there's nothing on the tape but static."

Store clerk: "Sorry about that. We've had problems with some of those tapes. Which title did you rent?"

Mary: "It's called HEAD CLEANER."

Miscellaneous

A man doing market research knocked on a door and was greeted by a young woman with three small children running around at her feet.

He said, "I'm doing some research for Vaseline. Have you ever used the product?"

She said, "Yes, my husband and I use it all the time."

"If you don't mind me asking, what do you use it for?"

"We use it for sex."

The researcher was a little taken aback. "Usually people lie and say they use it on a bicycle chain or to lubricate a hinge, but, in fact, I know that most people do use it for sex. I admire your honesty. Since you've been so frank, can you tell me exactly how you use it for sex?"

"I don't mind telling you—we put it on the doorknob, and it keeps the kids out."

•

A woman was interested in getting a boob job, so she went to see Dr. Jones and questioned him about implants.

He explained, "Before you do anything too serious, there is a method that has worked for a lot of my patients. Every morning when you wake up, rub your breasts and say, 'Scoobie doobie doobie, give me bigger boobies.'"

She did this faithfully for weeks and noticed one day that they were actually getting bigger.

One morning she woke up late for work and was very

rushed. By the time she got on the bus, she realized she had forgotten to go through her routine. So, standing in the aisle while rubbing her boobs, she said, "Scoobie doobie doobie, give me bigger boobies."

The man next to her said, "You go to Dr. Jones?"

"Yes. How did you know?"

"Hickory dickory dock!"

•

For years 'n' years they told me,
  "Be careful of your breasts.
Don't ever squeeze or bruise them,
  And give them monthly tests."

So I heeded all their warnings,
  And protected them by law . . .
Guarded them very carefully,
  And always wore a bra.

After thirty years of careful care,
  The doctor found a lump.
She ordered up a mammogram,
  To look inside that clump.

"Stand up very close," she said,
  As she got my boob in line,
"And tell me when it hurts," she said,
  "Ah yes! There! That's just fine."

She stepped upon a pedal . . .
  I could not believe my eyes!
A plastic plate was pressing down.
  My boob was in a vise!

My skin was stretched 'n' stretched,
  From way up by my chin,

And my poor boob was being squashed
  To Swedish-pancake thin!

"Take a deep breath," she said to me.
  Whom does *she think she's kidding?*
My chest is smashed in her machine,
  I can't breathe and woozy I am getting.

"There, that was good," I heard her say,
  As the room was slowly swaying.
"Now let's get the other one."
  "Lord, have mercy," I was praying.

It squeezed me from the up and down,
  It squeezed me from both sides.
I'll bet she's *never had this done,*
  To her *tender little hide!*

If I had no problem when I came in,
  I'd surely have one now . . .
If there had been a cyst in there,
  It would have popped . . . Ker-Pow!

This machine was made by a man,
  Of this I have no doubt . . .
I'd like to get his balls in there,
  For months he'd go "without"!

•

Mystery of Women's Toilets

My mother was a fanatic about public toilets.

As a little girl, she'd bring me in the stall, teach me to wad up toilet paper, and wipe the seat. Then she'd carefully lay strips of toilet paper to cover the seat.

Finally, she'd instruct, "Never, never sit on a public toilet seat." And she'd demonstrate "the Stance," which consisted of balancing over the toilet in a sitting position without actually letting any of your flesh make contact with the toilet seat.

But by this time, I'd have wet down my leg. And we'd go home.

That was a long time ago. Even now in our more mature years, the Stance is excruciatingly difficult to maintain when one's bladder is especially full.

When you have to "go" in a public bathroom, you find a line of women that makes you think there's a half-price sale on Mel Gibson's underwear in there. So, you wait and smile politely at all the other ladies, also crossing their legs and smiling politely.

And you finally get closer. You check for feet under the stall doors. Every one is occupied. Finally, a stall door opens and you dash, nearly knocking down the woman leaving.

You get in to find the door won't latch. It doesn't matter. You hang your purse on the door hook, yank down your pants, and assume the Stance.

Relief. More relief. Then your thighs begin to shake. You'd love to sit down, but you certainly hadn't taken time to wipe the seat or lay toilet paper on it, so you hold the Stance as your thighs experience a quake that would register an eight on the Richter scale.

To take your mind off it, you reach for the toilet paper. The toilet-paper dispenser is empty. Your thighs shake more. You remember the tiny tissue that you blew your nose on that's in your purse. It will have to do. You crumple it in the puffiest way possible. It is still smaller than your thumbnail.

Someone pushes open your stall door because the latch doesn't work, and your purse whams you in the head.

"Occupied!" you scream as you reach out for the door, dropping your tissue in a puddle and falling backward, directly onto the toilet seat. You get up quickly, but it's too late. Your bare bottom has made contact with all the germs and life-forms on the bare seat because *you* never laid down toilet paper, not that there was any, even if you had had enough time to.

And your mother would be utterly ashamed of you if she knew, because her bare bottom never touched a public toilet seat because, frankly, "You don't know what kind of diseases you could get."

And by this time, the automatic sensor on the back of the toilet is so confused that it flushes, sending up a stream of water akin to a fountain, and then it suddenly sucks everything down with such force that you grab on to the toilet paper dispenser for fear of being dragged to China.

At that point, you give up. You're soaked by the splashing water. You're exhausted. You try to wipe with a Chiclets wrapper you found in your pocket, then slink out inconspicuously to the sinks.

You can't figure out how to operate the sinks with the automatic sensors, so you wipe your hands with spit and a dry paper towel and walk past a line of women, still waiting, cross-legged and unable to smile politely at this point.

One kind soul at the very end of the line points out that you are trailing a piece of toilet paper on your shoe as long as the Mississippi River!

You yank the paper from your shoe, plunk it in the woman's hand, and say warmly, "Here. You might need this."

At this time, you see your spouse, who has entered, used, and exited his bathroom and read a copy of *War and Peace* while waiting for you.

"What took you so long?" he asks, annoyed.

This is when you kick him sharply in the shin and go home.

This is dedicated to all women everywhere who have ever had to deal with a public toilet. And it finally explains to all you men what takes us so long.

•

Several men are sitting around in the locker room of a private club after golf. Suddenly a cell phone on one of the benches rings. One of the men picks it up.

"Hello?"

"Honey. It's me. Are you at the club?"

"Yes."

"Great! I am at the mall two blocks from where you are. I just saw a beautiful mink coat. It's absolutely gorgeous! Can I buy it?"

"What's the price?"

"Only $1,500."

"Well, okay, go ahead and get it if you like it that much."

"Ahhh, and I also stopped by the Mercedes dealership and saw the 2008 models. I saw one I really liked. I spoke with the salesman and he gave me a really good price . . . and since we need to exchange the BMW that we bought last year . . ."

"What price did he quote you?"

"Only $80,000."

"Okay, but for that price I want it with all the options."

"Great! But before we hang up, something else . . ."

"What?"

"It might look like a lot, but I stopped by the real estate agent this morning and saw the house we had looked at last year. It's on sale! Remember? The one with a pool, garden, beachfront property . . ."

"How much are they asking?"

"Only $850,000—a magnificent price . . . and I see that we have that much in the bank to cover . . ."

"Well, then go ahead and buy it, but just bid $820,000. Okay?"

"Okay, sweetie. Thanks! I'll see you later! I love you!"

"Bye . . . I do, too."

The man hangs up, closes the phone's flap, and raises it in his hand to ask all those present, "Does anyone know who this phone belongs to?"

•

Blow Job Etiquette

1. First and foremost, we are not obligated to do it.
2. Extension to rule #1—so if you get one, be grateful.
3. I don't care *what* they did in the porn video you saw: it is not standard practice to come on someone's face.
4. Extension to rule #3—no, I don't have to swallow.
5. My ears are *not* handles.
6. Extension to rule #5—do not push on the top of my head. Last I heard, deep throat had been done. And additionally, do you really *want* puke on your dick?
7. I don't care *how* relaxed you get; it is *never okay* to fart.
8. My having my period does not mean that it's "hummer week." Get it through your head, I'm bloated and I feel like shit so, no, I don't feel particularly obligated to blow you just because *you* can't have sex right now.
9. Extension to #8—"blue balls" might have worked on high school girls—if you're that desperate, go jerk off and leave me alone with my Midol.
10. If I have to pause to remove a pubic hair from my teeth, don't tell me I've just "wrecked it" for you.
11. Leaving me in bed while you go play video games immediately afterward is highly inadvisable if you would like my behavior to be repeated in the future.
12. If you like how we do it, it's probably best not to speculate about the origins of our talent. Just enjoy the mo-

ment and be happy that we're good at it. See also rule #2 about gratitude.

13. No, it doesn't particularly taste good. And I don't care about the protein content.

14. No, I will *not* do it while you watch TV.

15. When you hear your friends complain about how they don't get blow jobs often enough, keep your mouth shut. It is inappropriate to either sympathize or brag.

16. Just because "it's awake" when you get up does not mean I have to "kiss it good morning."

•

Why does a bride smile when she walks down the aisle?
    She knows she's given her last blow job.

•

A man walks into a bar and sits down and orders twelve shots of whiskey. The bartender, stunned by this order, asks, "What's the occasion?"

The man says, "I'm celebrating in a way."

The bartender asks the man what he's celebrating.

The man smiles. "Today I just had my first blow job."

"Well now, that sure is worth celebrating. Hell, I'll buy you another shot. It's on me!"

"No thanks. If twelve shots don't get the taste out of my mouth, nothing will."

•

A woman walked into a busy butcher shop. Looking at meats and poultry on display, she suddenly grabbed hold of a dressed chicken. She picked up one wing, sniffed it, picked up the other wing and sniffed it, picked up one leg, sniffed it, picked up the other leg, sniffed it. Just as she finished sniffing the second leg, the butcher walked up to her and said, "Madam, could you pass such a test?"

•

A shy man was preparing to board a plane when he heard that the pope was on the same flight. Imagine his surprise when the pope sat down in the seat next to him. He was too shy to speak to the pontiff; however, shortly after takeoff, the pope began a crossword puzzle.

This is fantastic, thought the man. *I'm very good at crosswords. Perhaps if the pope gets stuck, he'll ask me for assistance.*

Soon, the pope turned to the man and said, "Excuse me, but do you know a four-letter word referring to a woman that ends in *u-n-t*?"

Only one word leapt to mind. *My goodness,* thought the man, *I can't tell the pope that. There must be another word.* He thought for a while, then it hit him.

Turning to the pope, he said, "I think the word you're looking for is *aunt.*"

"Of course!" said the pope. "Do you have an eraser?"

•

The devil is showing a man his options down in hell. He takes him into three rooms. In room 1, people are standing in shit up to their head. In room 2, people are standing in shit up to their chest. In room 3, all are drinking coffee and standing in shit up to their knees.

Man: "I'll take room three." At that, the devil announces, "Coffee break is over, everyone back on his head."

•

A mother and daughter are talking.

"Mom, I'm getting married and I want some information on how to please my husband."

The mother begins to talk about sex.

"Mom, I know all about f***ing. It's cooking I don't know about."

•

The general calls the motor pool. "Send up the black Cadillac."

GI: "I can't, it belongs to the fat-ass general."

General: "Do you know who this is? It's the general."

GI: "Do you know who this is?"

General: "No."

GI: "Good-bye, fat-ass general."

•

An old Italian gentleman stops an Alfa Romeo on the road to Rome. The old man pulls a gun, escorts the driver into the woods, and makes him masturbate three times. When the driver looks totally worn-out, the old Italian gentleman calls out, "Hey, Angelina, this nice man is gonna drive you to Rome."

•

The furious husband calls home and asks the trusted butler, "Where is my wife?"

Butler: "She's in bed with her lover."

Husband: "This is an order. Get the rifle from the gun cabinet, shoot them both, and return to the phone."

When the butler returns, the husband says, "Throw them both in the swimming pool."

Butler: "But, sir, we have no swimming pool."

Husband: "What phone number is this?"

•

The stewardess on a plane asks the priest what he'd like to drink.

Priest: "A dry martini."

She turns to the Baptist minister to ask him what he'd like to drink. The minister indignantly says, "I'd rather fornicate than taste whiskey."

Priest: "I didn't know we had a choice."

•

A man is checking in at the hotel.

Clerk: "Will that be OV or BV?"

Patron: "What's that?"

Clerk: " 'Ocean view' or 'bay view.' "

In the restaurant the man orders juice.

Waiter: "Will that be OJ or TJ?"

Patron: "What's that?"

Waiter: " 'Orange juice' or 'tomato juice.' "

Later, while he's in his room, the maid walks in and he spells out, "F-*-*-*." The maid is indignant at the abusive language and complains to the manager. They both go to the patron's room for an apology. The patron responds, "All you people talk in abbreviations, so I did likewise."

Manager: "What did you want to say?"

Patron: "F*** means 'first you could knock'!"

●

Two men are seated at a bar.

As he looks admiringly at a beautiful woman nearby, one says, "I'd give $500 to kiss that woman's titties."

"That's my wife, I'll ask her," the other man says.

She agrees and the couple goes into the back room. She undresses and he nibbles.

Finally he says, "I have no money, but I sure meant what I said."

●

A guy from Louisiana went to the dentist and said he had a toothache.

The dentist went to give him a shot of Novocain and he said, "Oh, no, you don't, Doctor. I don't like needles so you'd better get that needle away from me."

The dentist said, "Okay, then how about some gas?"

"Oh, no, you don't, Doctor, I'm allergic to gas."

The dentist went into the back room and came back out with a blue pill and handed it to him.

"Doctor, I may be from Louisiana, but I know what this is, this is Viagra."

"Yeah, I know, but it will give you something to hold on to while I yank out your tooth."

•

This guy is eating this girl out and stops for a second and says, "Damn, this pussy's big. Damn, this pussy's big."

She looks at him and says, "I know, but why did you say it twice?"

"I didn't."

•

A woman walking past a shop sees an advertisement in the window: GOOD HOME WANTED FOR CLITORIS-LICKING FROG.

She goes inside and says to the guy behind the counter, "I've come about the clitoris-licking frog."

"*Oui, madame,*" the shopkeeper says.

•

A man took a woman to an X-rated movie, purchased some refreshments, and showed his date to her seat.

Soon after the on-screen action started, she put her hand on the man's lap.

Looking over at him, she remarked, "I see this is getting you excited, too. But how come it's so cold?"

"Because you're jerking off my ice lollipop."

•

A guy corners a girl at a party and whispers something in her ear.

"You filthy pervert!" she shrieks. "What makes you think I'd let you do a thing like that to me?"

Then her eyes narrow and she says, "Unless you're the son of a bitch that stole my diary."

•

A woman seated herself in the psychiatrist's office.

"What seems to be the problem?" the doctor asked.

"Well . . . I . . . uh," she stammered. "I think I . . . uh . . . might be a nymphomaniac."

"I see. I can help you, but I must advise you that my fee is $150 an hour."

"That's not bad," the woman replied. "How much for all night?"

•

A man bumps into a woman in a hotel lobby, and his elbow touches her breast. They are both quite startled. The man turns to her and says, "Miss, if your heart is as soft as your tits, I know you'll forgive me."

She replies, "If your dick is as hard as your elbow, I'm in room 221."

•

Two women from the South were conversing on the porch of a large, white-pillared mansion.

The first woman said, "When my first child was born, my husband built this beautiful mansion for me."

The second woman commented, "Well, isn't that nice."

"When my second child was born, my husband bought me that fine automobile you see parked in the driveway."

"Well, isn't that nice."

The first woman boasted, "Then, when my third child was born, my husband bought me this exquisite diamond bracelet."

Yet again, the second woman commented, "Well, isn't that nice."

The first woman then asked the second woman, "What did your husband buy for you when you had your first child?"

The second woman replied, "My husband sent me to charm school."

"Charm school!" the first woman shouted. "Land sakes, child, what on earth for?"

"So that instead of saying, 'Who gives a shit,' I learned to say, 'Well, isn't that nice!' "

•

Two dwarfs go into a bar, where they pick up two hookers and take them to their separate hotel rooms. The first dwarf, however, is unable to get an erection. His depression is enhanced because, from the next room, he hears nonstop cries of *"One, two, three . . . uuh!"*

In the morning, the second dwarf asks the first, "How did it go last night?"

The first whispered back, "It was so embarrassing. I simply couldn't get an erection."

The second dwarf shook his head. "You think that's embarrassing? I couldn't even get on the bed!"

•

Two men camping in the mountains have spent four days together, and they are getting a little testy with each other.

In the morning, the first friend says, "You know, we're starting to get on each other's nerves. Why don't we split up today, and I'll hike north and you hike south. Then we will share our experiences tonight when we have dinner."

The second man agrees and hikes south.

That night over dinner, the first man tells his story: "Today I hiked into a beautiful valley. I followed a stream up into a canyon and ate lunch there. Then I swam in a crystal-clear mountain lake. As I sat out to dry, I watched deer come and drink from the lake. The wildflowers were filled with butterflies, and the hawks floated all day overhead. So how was your day?"

The second friend says, "I went south and ran across a set of railroad tracks, and I followed them until I came across a young woman tied to the tracks. I cut off the ropes, gently lifted her off the tracks, and had sex with her in every imaginable way all afternoon. Finally, when I was so tired I could barely move, I came back to camp."

"Wow!" the first guy exclaims. "Your day was much better than mine. Did you get a blow job, too?"

"Nah, I couldn't find her head."

•

A young man goes into a drugstore to buy condoms. The pharmacist says the condoms come in packs of three, nine, or twelve and asks which the young man wants.

"Well," he says, "I've been seeing this girl for a while and she's really hot. I want the condoms because I think tonight's *the* night. We're having dinner at her parents' house, and then we're going out. I've got a feeling I'm gonna get lucky after that. Once she's had me, she'll want me all the time, so you better give me the twelve-pack."

The young man makes his purchase and leaves.

Later that evening, he sits down to have dinner with his girlfriend and her parents. He asks if he may give the blessing, and they agree. He begins the prayer but continues praying for several minutes.

The girl leans over and says, "You never told me that you were such a religious person."

He leans over to her and says, "You never told me that your father is a pharmacist."

•

A coroner came out of his lab to talk to his boss about the body he was attending to.

The coroner said to his boss, "In all my years working here, I've seen some pretty odd stuff, but nothing as weird as what I have in the lab."

"What's wrong?" asked the boss.

"There's this really obese woman with a shrimp stuck in her pussy."

"What? Are you sure?" the boss cried.

"Yeah! Go see for yourself."

After the boss checked the vagina, he shouted, "My God, you're an asshole. That wasn't a shrimp! It was her clitoris!"

"Oh, well, it tasted like shrimp."

•

A blind man walks into a restaurant and sits down.

The waiter, who is also the owner, walks up to the blind man and hands him a menu.

"I'm sorry, sir, but I am blind and can't read the menu. Just bring me a dirty fork from a previous customer; I'll smell it and order from there."

A little confused, the owner walks over to the dirty pile and picks up a greasy fork. He returns to the blind man's table and hands it to him. The blind man puts the fork to his nose and takes in a deep breath.

"Ah, yes, that's what I'll have, meat loaf and mashed potatoes."

"Unbelievable," the owner says to himself as he walks toward the kitchen. The cook is the owner's wife, and he tells her what just happened. The blind man eats his meal and leaves.

Several days later the blind man returns, and the owner mistakenly brings him a menu again.

"Sir, remember me? I'm the blind man."

"I'm sorry, I didn't recognize you. I'll go get you a dirty fork." The owner again retrieves a dirty fork and brings it to the blind man.

After another deep breath, the blind man says, "That smells great. I'll take the macaroni and cheese with broccoli."

Once again, walking away in disbelief, the owner thinks

the blind man is screwing around with him and tells his wife that the next time the blind man comes in, he's going to test him. The blind man eats and leaves.

He returns the following week, but this time the owner notices him coming and runs to the kitchen.

He tells his wife, "Mary, rub this fork on your panties before I take it to the blind man." Mary complies and hands the fork back to her husband.

As the blind man sits down, the owner is ready and waiting. "Good afternoon, sir. This time I remembered you and I already have the fork ready for you."

The blind man puts the fork to his nose, takes a whiff, and says, "Hey, I didn't know that Mary works here."

•

An American and a Scot are in a bar, each enjoying a drink. After a while the Scot approaches the American and says in a strong Scottish accent:

"You see that fence out there? I built that fence with my own two hands, but they don't call me Angus the fence-builder."

"Oh, really," mumbles the American.

"You know this bar we are sitting in? I built this bar with my own two hands, but they don't call me Angus the bar-builder."

"I see," mumbles the American.

"What hotel are you staying in?"

"Oh, the Loch Ness Inn."

"I built that hotel with my own two hands, but they don't call me Angus the hotel-builder. . . . But you f*** one sheep . . . !"

•

A wealthy couple had planned to go out for the evening. The woman of the house decided to give their butler, Jeeves, the rest of the night off. She said they would be home late, and that he should just enjoy his evening.

As it turned out, however, the wife wasn't having a good time at the party, so she came home early, alone. Her husband had to stay there, as several of his important clients were there.

As the woman walked into her house, she saw Jeeves sitting by himself in the dining room.

She called for him to follow her and led him into the master bedroom. She then closed and locked the door.

She looked at him and smiled. "Jeeves, take off my dress."

He did this carefully.

"Jeeves, take off my stockings and garters."

He silently obeyed her.

"Jeeves, remove my bra and panties."

As he did this, the tension continued to mount.

She looked at him and said, "Jeeves, if I ever catch you wearing my clothes again, you're fired."

•

An extremely ugly man is sitting in a bar having a drink with his friend, who is his polar opposite. In fact, he may be the most handsome man in town.

The two of them are discussing a beautiful blond girl sitting at the bar.

The handsome man says, "Boy, I sure would like to get some of that."

The ugly man says, "Go ahead, go for it."

"There's no way, she won't go with anybody. I've tried many times."

"I think I could go out with her if I wanted to."

The handsome man laughs. "If she won't go out with me, she sure as hell won't go out with you."

"I'll bet you fifty bucks she'll go with me."

"You're on!"

"Okay, just leave the money with the bartender and I'll pick it up later."

The ugly man walks up to the girl, starts talking, then turns around and walks out of the bar, with the girl right behind him.

The handsome man can't believe it. He goes over and asks the bartender, "What happened? What did he say to her?"

The bartender says, "Well, he didn't say much. He just said it's a nice night for a walk. And then he licked his eyebrows and left."

•

The supermarket had a sale on boneless chicken breasts, and I intended to stock up. At the store, however, I was disappointed to find only a few skimpy prepackaged portions of the poultry, so I complained to the butcher.

"Don't worry," she said, "I'll pack some more trays and have them ready for you by the time you finish shopping."

Several aisles later, I heard the lady butcher's voice boom over the public-address system, "Will the gentleman who wanted bigger breasts please meet me at the back of the store."

•

A guy walks into a pharmacy and says to the pharmacist, "Listen, I have three girls coming over tonight. I've never had three girls at once, I need something to keep me horny . . . keep me potent."

The pharmacist reaches under the counter, unlocks the bottom drawer, takes out a small cardboard box labeled VIAGRA EXTRA STRENGTH, and says, "Here, if you swallow this, you'll go nuts for twelve hours."

The guy says, "Gimme three boxes."

The next day, the guy walks into the same pharmacy, limps up to the pharmacist, and pulls down his pants.

The pharmacist looks in horror at the man's black-and-blue penis, the skin hanging off in some places.

The man moans, "Gimme a bottle of Deep Heat."

The pharmacist replies aghast, "You can't put Deep Heat on that."

"No, it's for my arms, the girls didn't show up."

•

Jerry's at the urinal in an airport restroom when a guy with no arms sidles up next to him and pleads, "Hey, buddy—can you help me out here?"

Though Jerry feels uneasy, he considers the guy's predicament and decides to help. He bravely unzips the man, takes a deep breath, reaches in, and pulls out the guy's penis. Much to his horror, it is hideous! It's moldy and bluish green, covered with pus-filled scabs, and it reeks something awful.

Imagining the kudos he'll get on Judgment Day for this selfless good deed, Jerry holds the man's unit while he urinates, then shakes it, puts it back in the man's pants, and zips him up.

The guy tells Jerry, "Thanks, man, I really appreciate it."

"No problem," says Jerry. "But I gotta ask—what the hell's wrong with your johnson?"

The guy pokes his arms back out of his sleeves and says, "I don't know, but I sure as hell ain't touching it."

•

A man walked into a restaurant and seated himself. Soon, the waitress came over to take his order.

"What would you like to drink?" she asked.

The man said he would like coffee.

The waitress promptly returned with a cup of coffee, but

spilled it on the man's lap when she stopped at the table. "Oh my God! I am so sorry!"

"That's okay," he said as he wiped his pants with a napkin. "But tell me, is this regular or decaf?"

"Regular."

"Oh, great . . . now this thing is gonna be up all night!"

•

On a Saturday afternoon a man walks into a posh and expensive fur salon with his girlfriend. They select a $12,000 fur coat, and she has a fitting and is told that the sleeves will be adjusted and that the coat will be ready by Monday noon.

On Monday, the gentleman stops into the fur salon to see the salesman. The salesman is irate and tells the customer that the coat is not ready and will never be ready for him because his credit is so awful.

The customer says, "Young man, calm yourself, no one was hurt. I haven't taken anything out of the store—I just stopped by to thank you for helping me have a wonderful weekend."

•

A married couple went to the hospital to have their baby delivered.

Upon their arrival, the doctor said he had invented a new machine that would transfer a portion of the mother's labor pain to the father. He asked if they were willing to try it out. They were both very much in favor of it.

The doctor set the pain transfer to 10 percent for a starter, explaining that even 10 percent was probably more pain than the father had ever experienced. But as the labor progressed, the husband felt fine and asked the doctor to go ahead and bump it up a notch. The doctor then adjusted the machine to 20 percent pain transfer. The husband was still feeling fine. The doctor checked the husband's blood pressure and was amazed at how well he was doing. At this point, they decided to try for 50 percent. The husband continued to feel quite well. Since the pain transfer was obviously helping out the wife considerably, the husband encouraged the doctor to transfer *all* the pain to him.

The wife delivered a healthy baby with virtually no pain. She and her husband were ecstatic. When they got home, the mailman was dead on the porch.

•

The missionary realizes that one thing he never taught the natives was how to speak English, so he takes the chief for a walk in the forest.

He points to a tree and says to the chief, "Tree."

The chief looks at the tree and grunts, "Tree."

The missionary is pleased with the response. They walk a little farther, and he points to a rock and says, "Rock."

Hearing this, the chief looks and grunts, "Rock."

The missionary is really getting enthusiastic about the results when he hears a rustling in the bushes. As he peeks over the top, he sees a couple of natives having heated sex.

The missionary is really flustered and quickly responds, "Riding bicycle."

The chief looks at the couple briefly, pulls out his blowgun, and kills them.

The missionary goes ballistic and yells that he has spent years teaching the tribe how to be civilized and kind to each other, so how could the chief kill these people in cold blood that way?

The chief replies, "Riding *my* bicycle."

•

A guy walks into a pub and sees a sign hanging over the bar that reads:

Cheese Sandwich: $1.50
Chicken Sandwich: $2.50
Hand Job: $5.00

Checking his wallet for the necessary payment, he walks up to the bar and beckons to one of the three exceptionally attractive blondes serving drinks to an eager-looking group of men.

"Yes?" she inquires with a knowing smile. "Can I help you?"

"I was wondering," whispers the man, "are you the one who gives the hand jobs?"

"Yes," she purrs, "I am."

"Well, wash your f***ing hands, I want a cheese sandwich!"

•

An eighteen-year-old girl tells her mother that she has missed her period for two months. Worried, the mother goes to the drugstore and buys a pregnancy kit. The result shows that the girl is pregnant.

Shouting, cursing, and crying, the mother says, "Who was the pig that did this to you?"

The girl picks up the phone and makes a call. Half an hour later a Ferrari stops in front of the house. A mature, distinguished man with gray hair, impeccably dressed in an expensive suit, gets out and enters the house. He sits in the living room with the father, the mother, and the girl and tells them:

"Good morning. Your daughter has informed me of the problem. However, I cannot marry her because of my personal family situation, but I will take charge. If a girl is born, I will bequeath her two retail stores, a town house, a beach villa, and a million-dollar bank account. If a boy is born, my legacy will be a couple of factories and a two-million-dollar bank account. If it is twins, a factory and one million dollars each. But, if there is a miscarriage, what do you suggest I do?"

The father, who has remained silent, places a hand firmly on the man's shoulder and tells him, "You'll screw her again!"

•

Two women went out one weekend without their husbands. As they came back right before dawn, both of them drunk, they felt the urge to pee. They noticed the only place to stop was a cemetery. Scared but drunk, they decided to go there anyway.

The first one did not have anything to clean herself with, so she took off her panties, cleaned herself, and discarded them.

The second, not finding anything either, thought, *I'm not getting rid of my panties*, so she used the ribbon of a flower wreath to clean herself.

The morning after, the two husbands were talking to each other on the phone, and one said to the other, "We have to be on the lookout. It seems that these two were up to no good last night. My wife came home without her panties."

The other one said, "You're lucky. Mine came home with a card stuck to her ass that read, 'We will never forget you.' "

•

A beautiful woman loved growing tomatoes, but couldn't seem to get her tomatoes to turn red. One day while taking a stroll she came upon a gentleman neighbor who had the most beautiful garden full of huge red tomatoes.

The woman asked the gentleman, "What do you do to get your tomatoes red?"

The gentleman responded, "Well, twice a day I stand in front of my tomato garden and expose myself, and my tomatoes turn red from blushing so much."

The woman was so impressed, she decided to try the same thing with her tomato garden. So twice a day for two weeks she exposed herself to her garden, hoping for the best.

One day the gentleman was passing by and asked the woman, "By the way, how did you make out? Did your tomatoes turn red?"

"No," she replied, "but my cucumbers are enormous."

•

A lady calls the local newspaper to insert a notice in the obituary column. She tells the writer all about Jake, her late husband—about his early days, his struggles, his successes, his philanthropies, the family, the children, and on and on.

The newspaperman interrupts, "Madam, we charge 5 dollars per word."

"So just put in 'Jake died.'"

"Madam, we have a five-word minimum."

"All right, so put in 'Jake died, Mercedes for sale.'"

•

A young guy goes out on the town with his friends and spies the girl of his dreams across the dance floor. Having admired her from afar, he finally gets up the courage to talk to her. Everything goes better than expected, and she agrees to accompany him on a date the following Saturday evening. Saturday night the man arrives at her house with flowers and candy.

To his surprise, she answers the door in nothing but a towel. "I'm sorry," she exclaims, "I am running a bit late. Please come in and I will introduce you to my parents, who will entertain you while I finish getting dressed. I should warn you, though, they are both deaf-mutes."

With this she ushers him into the living room, introduces him to her parents, and promptly disappears. As you can imagine, this is a little uncomfortable as both the parents are completely silent. Dad is sitting in his armchair watching golf on TV, and Mom is busy knitting.

After about ten minutes of complete silence, Mom jumps

from her chair, pulls up her skirt, pulls down her panties, and pours a glass of water over her fanny. Just as suddenly, Dad launches himself across the room, bends her over the couch, and takes her from behind. He then sits back down in his chair and balances a matchstick in front of his eye. The room is plunged back into eerie silence, and the young man is shocked beyond disbelief.

After about another ten minutes, the daughter returns fully dressed and ready for the evening. The date is an utter disaster as the young man is completely distracted by the earlier events.

At the end of the night, the girl asks, "What's the matter? Have I done something wrong?"

"No, it's not you," he replies. "It's just that the strangest thing happened while I was waiting for you, and I am still a bit shocked. First your mother jumps from her chair, lifts up her skirt, pulls down her panties, and throws a glass of water over her ass. Then, as if that weren't enough, your father races from his chair, leans her over the couch, and does her from behind. He then sits back down and places a matchstick by his eye."

"Oh, is that all?"

The man can't believe her casual response.

"That's how they communicate! Mom was simply saying, 'Are you going to get this asshole a drink?' and Dad was replying, 'No, f*** him—I'm watching the match.' "

•

A little town had a high birthrate that had attracted the attention of the sociologists at the state university. They wrote a grant proposal; got a huge chunk of money; hired a few additional sociologists, an anthropologist, and a family-planning and birth-control specialist; moved to town; rented offices; set up their computers; got squared away; and began designing their questionnaires and such.

While the staff was busy getting ready for their big research effort, the project director decided to go to the local drugstore for a cup of coffee. He sat down at the counter, ordered his coffee, and, while he was drinking it, told the druggist what his purpose was in town and asked him if he had any idea why the birthrate was so high.

"Sure," said the druggist. "Every morning the six-o'clock train comes through here and blows for the crossing. It wakes everybody up, and . . . well . . . it's too late to go back to sleep, and it's too early to get up!"

•

Joe went to a small town last week. He had only fifteen bucks and desperately wanted to get laid. At the first whorehouse, he was turned down, yet warned not to visit Sandy Sandpaper. At the second, third, and fourth whorehouses, he was as unsuccessful as at the first and duly warned. Still desperate for a quick lay, Joe ultimately decided to pay a visit to Sandy Sandpaper.

Joe knocked, and Sandy, a vivacious woman, opened the door. She assured him that $15 would suffice for the night. A few minutes into the festivities, Sandy asked, "How does it feel?"

"A little rough, like sandpaper."

"Just a minute." Sandy made her way to the bathroom.

After a few minutes, Sandy emerged, and she and Joe started right where they had left off.

"Now how does it feel?" asked Sandy.

"Terrific. What did you do?" asked Joe, at the height of his pleasures.

"Oh, I just picked the scabs and let them drain a little."

•

A guy goes into this restaurant every morning and looks at the menu, but always orders the same thing. Ham and eggs. So one morning the waitress decides to scratch it off the menu.

The guy comes in as usual and starts to look at the menu.

The waitress sees him just looking and looking and goes over to him and says, "I'm sorry, but I scratched what you like."

The man then says, "Well, that's okay, but wash your f***in' hands before you bring me my ham and eggs!"

•

Having lunch one day, a sex therapist said to her friend, "According to a survey we just completed, ninety percent of all people masturbate in the shower. Only ten percent of them sing."

"Really?" asked the friend.

The therapist nodded. "And do you know what song they sing?"

The friend shook her head. "No."

The therapist replied, "I didn't think so."

•

Several years ago the U.S. army funded a study to determine why the head of a man's penis is larger than the shaft. The study took two years and cost $180,000. The study concluded that the head is larger than the shaft so as to provide the woman with more pleasure during sex.

After the results were published, NOW decided to conduct their own study on the same subject. They were convinced that the results of the federal study were incorrect. After three years of research and costs in excess of $250,000, they concluded that the head of a man's penis is larger than the shaft to provide men with more pleasure during sex.

Not long after, the national marketing director of Hooters,

faced with a threatened OSHA inquiry, decided to conduct his own study. Over one weekend, with a net profit of $2,200 in tips, the study found that the head on a man's penis is larger than the shaft so as to prevent his hand from flying up and hitting him in the forehead.

•

A man enters a barbershop for a shave. While the barber is foaming him up, he mentions the problems he has getting a close shave around the cheeks.

"I have just the thing," says the barber, taking a small wooden ball from a nearby drawer. "Just place this between your cheek and gum."

The client places the ball in his mouth, and the barber starts giving the man the closest shave he has ever experienced. After a few strokes, the client asks in garbled speech, "And what if I swallow it?"

"No problem," says the barber. "Just bring it back tomorrow like everyone else does."

•

The jumbo jet is just coming into an airport on its final approach. The pilot comes on over the intercom.

"This is Captain Johnson. We're on our final descent, and I want to thank you for flying with us today. I hope you enjoy your stay in New York."

He forgets to switch off the intercom. The whole plane can now hear the conversation in the cockpit.

The copilot says to the pilot, "Well, Skipper, whatcha gonna do in New York?"

"Well," says the skipper, "first I'm gonna check into the hotel and take a crap. Then, I'm gonna take that new stewardess out for supper, you know, the one with the huge tits. I'm gonna wine and dine her, take her back to my room, and screw her all night."

Everyone in the plane is trying to get a look at the new stewardess. She's so embarrassed that she runs from the back of the plane toward the cockpit to turn the intercom off. Halfway down the aisle, she trips over an old lady's bag and goes down.

The old lady leans over and says, "No need to run, dear, he's gotta take a shit first!"

•

An attractive young lady was sitting in a fine restaurant one night waiting for her date. She wanted to make sure everything was perfect, so she bent down in her chair to get the mirror from her purse, but she accidentally farted quite loudly just as the waiter walked up.

Sitting up straight now, embarrassed and red-faced, knowing everyone in the place heard her, she turned to the waiter and demanded, "Stop that!"

The waiter looked at her drily and said, "Sure, lady, which way is it headed?"

•

A woman walks into the store and purchases one small box of detergent, one bar of soap, three individual servings of yogurt, and one stick of women's deodorant.

She then goes to the checkout line.

Cashier: "Oh, you must be single."

Woman: "You can tell that by what I bought?"

Cashier: "No, you're f***ing ugly!"

•

Two leprechauns have a bet, and to settle it, they go to a convent.

Mother superior answers the door and says, "Oh my goodness! It's leprechauns!"

The first leprechaun replies, "Take it easy, Sister, I only

wanna ask you a question. Are there any nuns in your convent that are my size?"

"No, little man, no nuns in my convent are your size."

"All right then. Are there any nuns in all of Ireland that are my size?"

"No, little man, no nuns in all of Ireland are your size."

"All right then. One more question: Are there any nuns in the entire world that are my size?"

"No, little man, I am quite sure that no nuns in all of the world are your size!"

"Okay then."

The second leprechaun starts laughing his ass off. But through the laughter, he manages to say, "You see, I told you! You f***ed a penguin!"

•

A naive sailor is in a bar in London. He meets a wild girl, and she takes him upstairs. She takes off her pants and her panties.

He looks between her legs and says, "What's that?"

She says, "It's my lower mouth."

"What do you mean, your 'lower mouth'?"

"Just what I said, it's my lower mouth. It's got a mustache, and it's got lips."

"Has it got a tongue in it?"

"Not yet."

•

A man was on his first business trip to Japan, and he decided to check out the local whorehouse.

He walked in and was assigned a young girl with a body that got him "up" immediately.

As soon as they reached the room, he started ripping her clothes off and going to town.

Moaning and grunting, the girl was screaming in Japanese, *"Wasukima! Wasukima!"* He was sure that she was praising him for his good job, so he kept going harder than ever.

Later, he went golfing with his boss and a few clients.

As the clients were Japanese, he decided to impress them with his new knowledge of their language. When one of them got a hole in one, he raised his arms and shouted, *"Wasukima!"*

All of the men looked at him quizzically, and one of them asked, "Why are you shouting 'wrong hole'?"

•

One fall day, Bill was out raking leaves when he noticed a hearse slowly drive by.

Following the first hearse was a second hearse, which was followed by a man walking solemnly along, followed by a dog, and then about two hundred men walking in single file.

Intrigued, Bill went up to the man following the second hearse and asked him who was in the first hearse.

"My wife," the man replied.

"I'm sorry," said Bill. "What happened to her?"

"My dog bit her and she died."

Bill then asked who was in the second hearse.

The man replied, "My mother-in-law. My dog bit her and she died as well."

Bill thought about this for a while, then finally asked, "Can I borrow your dog?"

The man replied, "Get in line."

•

A man and a woman were waiting at the hospital donation center.

Man: "What are you doing here today?"

Woman: "Oh, I'm here to donate some blood. They're going to give me five dollars for it."

Man: "Hmm, that's interesting. I'm here to donate sperm, myself. But they pay me twenty-five dollars."

The woman looked thoughtful for a moment, then they chatted some more before going their separate ways. A couple of months later, the same man and woman met again in the donation center.

Man: "Oh, hi there! Here to donate blood again?"

Woman (shaking her head with mouth closed): "Unh-unh."

•

Back in the Old West, a chief came to town.

They were having a show that featured a ventriloquist. The ventriloquist saw the chief and decided to play a trick on him.

The chief came up to the stage and the ventriloquist said, "That's a nice horse you have there."

The chief said, "Good horse."

"Does he talk?"

Stoically the chief said, "Horse no talk."

The ventriloquist looked at the horse and said, "How's the chief treating you? Everything going all right?"

The horse (really the ventriloquist, obviously) said, "Well, the chief has been putting on a little weight lately, but all in all he treats me pretty well."

The chief, never having heard his horse talk, was surprised.

The ventriloquist said to the chief, "That your dog there? Good-looking dog."

The chief said, "Good dog."

"Can the dog talk, too?"

"Dog no talk."

The ventriloquist, looking at the dog, said, "How is the chief treating you?"

"Pretty good. I have to eat a lot of dust from the horse and the chief, but I get fed regularly and the chief doesn't beat me."

The startled chief eyed the dog suspiciously.

The ventriloquist looked at this sheep with the chief. "That your sheep?"

"Sheep *lies*!" exclaimed the chief.

•

Two good buddies, Bill and Bob, are way out in the boonies hunting and not having much luck.

Finally they decide to take a few minutes and rest a bit, and Bob decides that he has to pee.

Unfortunately for Bob, he doesn't look where he's pointing his pecker, and a rattlesnake bites him on the head of his dick!

Well, after several seconds of Bob's jumping, screaming, and begging, the snake finally lets go and slithers away into the grass.

Neither man knows how to treat a snakebite, so Bill decides that he should hike out and get to a doctor.

After several hours of hiking, Bill finally finds a doctor, who tells him that he must suck the venom out of the bite with his mouth. The doctor has a dirt bike on hand, which he loans to Bill to help rescue Bob.

So with the dirt bike, Bill gets to Bob in short order. When Bob sees Bill, he weakly asks, "What did the doctor tell you?"

"You're gonna die!"

•

A beautiful blonde walks into a bar and asks the bartender for a triple Jack Daniel's. She drinks it down in one gulp and orders another. After five more of the same, she falls on the floor blind drunk. All the men in the bar take advantage of this and screw her.

The next night she comes back and asks the bartender for a triple Jack Daniel's. She drinks it down and orders another. After five more of the same, she falls on the floor and passes out. All the men in the bar take advantage of this and screw her.

The third night she comes back again and the same thing happens.

On the fourth night, she comes back to the bar and asks the bartender for a martini.

The bartender says, "I thought you drink Jack Daniel's."

She replies, "Not anymore, it makes my pussy sore!"

●

The Lone Ranger and Tonto walked into a bar and sat down to drink a beer. After a few minutes, a big, tall cowboy walked in and said, "Who owns the big white horse outside?"

The Lone Ranger stood up, went face-to-face with the stranger, and said, "That horse is mine. Now, what's the problem?"

The cowboy looked at the Lone Ranger and said, "I just thought you'd like to know that your horse is nearly dead outside!"

The Lone Ranger and Tonto rushed outside, and sure enough Silver was ready to die from heat exhaustion. The Lone Ranger got the horse water. However, Silver still looked pretty sick.

Seeing this, the Lone Ranger began to run circles around the overheated animal in a desperate attempt to create a breeze to help him feel better. It seemed to make a difference, but the Lone Ranger began to tire. After fifteen minutes, he stopped and said, "Tonto, do you mind taking over for a few minutes?"

Tonto said, "Sure, *kemo sabe*," and took off running circles around Silver. Not able to do anything else but wait, the Lone

Ranger returned to the bar to finish his drink. A few minutes later, the cowboy came over and tapped the Lone Ranger on his shoulder.

Irritated, the Lone Ranger stood up and said, "Okay, what's wrong with my horse this time?"

The cowboy looked him in the eye and said, "Nothing, but it looks like you left your Injun runnin'."

●

An eighty-five-year-old couple, after being happily married for almost sixty years, died together in a car crash. They had been in good health the last ten years, mainly due to the old woman's interest in health food and proper diet.

When they reached the pearly gates, Saint Peter took them to their luxury mansion, which was decked out with a beautiful kitchen, master bedroom suite, and a fancy Jacuzzi.

The old man asked Saint Peter how much all this was going to cost. "It's free," Saint Peter replied, "this is heaven."

Next, they went out the backyard to survey the championship-style golf course that the home faced. They would have golfing privileges every day. In addition, the course changed to a new one daily, representing the greatest golf links on earth.

The old man asked, "So what are the greens fees?"

Saint Peter replied, "This is heaven, you play every day for free!"

Next they went to the clubhouse and saw the lavish buffet lunch with the best cuisine they had ever seen, and Saint Peter said, "You can eat whatever you like and never get fat and you never get sick in heaven."

With that, the old man had a fit, throwing down his halo, screaming wildly, and taking the Lord's name in vain. His wife and Saint Peter both tried to calm him down, asking what was wrong. The old man glared at his wife and said,

"This is all your fault! If it weren't for you stuffing me daily with those f***ing bran muffins, I could have been here years ago!"

•

An American man was being entertained by an African leader. They'd spent the day discussing what the country had received from the Russians before the new government kicked them out.

"The Russians built us a power plant, a highway, and an airport. Plus we learned to drink vodka and play Russian roulette."

The American frowned. "Russian roulette's not a friendly, nice game."

The African leader smiled. "That's why we developed African roulette. If you want to have good relations with our country, you'll have to play. I'll show you how."

He pushed a buzzer, and a moment later six magnificently built, nude women were ushered in. "You can choose any one of these women to give you oral sex," he told the American.

This gained the American's immediate attention, but before he made his choice, a thought occurred to him. "How on earth is this related to Russian roulette?"

The African leader said, "One of them is a cannibal."

•

A beautiful, sexy woman went up to the bar in a quiet pub. She gestured alluringly to the bartender, who approached her immediately. She seductively signaled that he should bring his face closer to hers. As he did, she gently caressed his full beard.

"Are you the manager?" she asked softly, stroking his face with both hands.

"Actually, no."

"Can you get him for me? I need to speak to him," she

said, running her hands beyond his beard and into his hair.

"I'm afraid I can't," breathed the bartender. "Is there anything I can do?"

"Yes. I need for you to give him a message." She ran her forefinger across the bartender's lips and slyly popped a couple of her fingers into his mouth and allowed him to suck them gently.

"What should I tell him?" the bartender said.

"Tell him," she whispered, "there's no toilet paper, hand soap, or paper towels in the ladies' room."

•

Two college coeds were having a beer. One said to the other, "Mary was so excited when she found out she was pregnant. She called me late one night after my boyfriend and I had already gone to bed."

"What on earth did she want?" her friend asked.

"Oh . . . she just said, 'I can't believe I have a person inside me!' I said, 'So do I. Could I call you back in an hour or so?'"

•

A guy is walking down the street and enters a watch shop. While looking around, he notices a drop-dead gorgeous female clerk behind the counter. He walks up to the counter where she is standing, unzips his pants, flops his dick out, and places it on the counter.

"What are you doing, sir?" she asks. "This is a clock shop!"

He replied, "I know it is and I would like two hands and a face put on this!"

•

A man was strolling on the beach one day when he came across a lamp lying in the sand. He picked it up and rubbed it. Sure enough, a genie popped out.

"I will grant you your one true desire," boomed the huge genie.

"Wow, that's fantastic!" exclaimed the man. "All my life I wanted a cock so big that it would touch the ground."

So, *poof!* The genie cut the man's legs off!

•

A guy is shipwrecked on a celebrity cruise and wakes up stranded on a desert island with Nicole Kidman. After a few weeks they are having passionate sex. This is all fine and dandy for a while, but the guy starts getting a bit depressed.

Nicole comes up to him on the beach one day and says, "What's the matter?"

He says, "Well, it's wonderful. I am on a tropical island with a beautiful woman whom I love, but . . . but . . . I miss my friends. I miss going down to the bar with them."

"Well, I'm an actress. Maybe if I get dressed in some of those male clothes that were left behind in the trunks, I can pretend to be one of your friends, and you can talk to me as if you were down at the bar."

It sounded a bit weird, but he thought he would try it. So she gets into the men's clothing and they sit down, and the guy goes, "Hey, Joe, you'll never guess who I've been f***ing!"

•

It was George the mailman's last day on the job after thirty-five years of carrying the mail through all kinds of weather to the same neighborhood.

When he arrived at the first house on his route, he was greeted by the whole family there, who roundly and soundly congratulated him and sent him on his way with a tidy gift envelope.

At the second house they gave him a box of cigars.

The folks at the third house handed him a selection of terrific fishing lures.

At the fourth house he was met at the door by a strikingly beautiful woman in a revealing negligee. She took him by the arm and led him up the stairs to the bedroom, where she blew his mind with the most passionate love he had ever experienced. When he'd had enough, they went downstairs, where she fixed him a giant breakfast: eggs, potatoes, ham, sausage, blueberry waffles, and fresh-squeezed orange juice.

When he was truly satisfied, she poured him a cup of steaming coffee. As she was pouring, he noticed a dollar bill sticking out from under the cup's bottom edge. "All this was just too wonderful for words," he said, "but what's the dollar for?"

"Well," she said, "last night I told my husband that today would be your last day, and that we should do something special for you. I asked him what to give you. He said, '*F**** him. Give him a dollar.' The breakfast was my idea."

•

A woman is picked up by Dennis Rodman in a bar. They like each other and she goes back with him to his hotel room.

He removes his shirt, revealing his tattoos, and she sees one on his arm that reads REEBOK. She thinks that's a bit odd and asks him about it.

Dennis says, "When I play basketball, the cameras pick up the tattoo and Reebok pays me for the advertisement."

A bit later, his pants are off and she sees PUMA tattooed on his leg. He gives the same explanation for the unusual tattoo.

Finally, the underwear comes off and she sees the word AIDS tattooed on his penis. She jumps back with shock.

"I'm not going to do it with a guy who has AIDS!"

"It's cool, baby, in a minute it's going to say ADIDAS."

•

One day, a guy with no arms and no legs was on a beach sunning himself when he saw three beautiful women approaching.

The first lady bent down and whispered in his ear, "Excuse me, have you ever been hugged before?"

He replied, "No," and she gave him a big hug.

The second lady bent down and asked, "Have you ever been kissed before?"

Again he replied, "No," and she gave him a big, juicy kiss on the lips.

The third lady bent down and asked, "Have you ever been f***ed before?"

For the third time he replied, "No," eyes alight.

"Well, you are now. The tide's coming in!"

•

A guy is on a blind date that seems to be going well. After a few drinks they return to her place. They sit on the sofa and start making out.

The guy, nibbling her ear, whispers, "I'd like a little pussy."

The girl pulls away, looks deeply into his eyes, and says, "Me, too, mine's as big as a house!"

•

The lord of the manor returned from his grouse hunt quite a bit earlier than expected. He entered the master bedroom to change and found her ladyship making passionate love to Sir Archibald.

The irate lord stood stiffly and loudly berated his wife for her infidelity. With thunder in his voice, he reminded her that he had taken her from a miserable existence on a local run-down farm, given her a fine home, provided her with servants, expensive clothes and jewels, and almost anything she desired.

By this time the woman was crying inconsolably, and his lordship turned his wrath on his supposed friend.

"And as for you, Reggie, you might at least stop while I'm talking!"

•

Three men were trying to guess the professions of their respective dates of the previous evening, judging by their bedroom performance and conversation.

The first insisted that his date had been a nurse, because she said, "Lie down and relax. This won't hurt a bit."

The second concluded that his must have been a schoolteacher, because she said, "Do it over and over until you get it right."

The third figured that his date must have been a stewardess, because all she had said was "Put this over your mouth and nose and continue to breathe normally."

•

An instructor was giving a course in human sexuality, during which he was discussing numerous items in the Kinsey report.

Audible gasps could be heard when he read out that a woman had several hundred orgasms in a single session.

Suddenly, a male voice from the back of the class shouted, "Wow, who was she?"

"Who the hell cares!" a female yelled. "Who was *he*?"

•

A sweet, beautiful, young would-be starlet comes to Hollywood to seek her fame and fortune. At her first power cocktail party she goes to the host and asks him, "Who's the most powerful man in the room?"

"That would be Jerry, over there by the caviar."

The young woman walks over to Jerry and says, "Excuse

me, Jerry, would you mind stepping back behind this column? I'd like to talk to you."

Jerry and the girl step behind the column and she says, "Jerry . . . I'm going to unzip your fly, take out your cock, and give you the best blow job you've ever had!"

Jerry smiles slightly and says, "Well, okay. But . . . what's in it for me?"

•

A woman and her boyfriend are in bed.

She says, "Stick a finger in my pussy."

He does.

She then says, "Stick your hand in it."

He sticks his whole hand in it.

Then the woman asks him to stick both hands into her vagina, and he complies.

"Now, lover boy," she says, "clap your hands."

"I can't, honey!"

"Tight, eh?"

•

A guy says, "I remember the first time I used alcohol as a substitute for women."

"Yeah, what happened?" asks the other guy.

"Well, I got my penis stuck in the neck of the bottle."

•

The blind daters had really hit it off, and at the end of the evening as they were beginning to undress each other in his apartment, the fellow said, "Before we go any further, Charlene, tell me—do you have any special fetishes that I should take into account in bed?"

"As a matter of fact," the girl said, smiling, "I do happen to have a foot fetish . . . but I suppose I'd settle for maybe seven or eight inches."

•

A man and a woman were sitting in a bar.

"First," said the confident young stud, "I'm going to buy you a few drinks and get you a bit loose."

"Oh, no, you're not," said the girl.

"Then I'll take you to dinner and ply you with a few more drinks," said the persistent bachelor.

"Oh, no, you're not!"

"Then I'll take you to my place and keep serving you drinks."

"Oh, no, you're not."

"Then I am going to make uncontrolled, passionate love to you."

"Oh, no, you're not," she said firmly.

"And I'm not going to wear a condom either!"

"Oh, yes, you are!"

•

A white man noticed the impressive length of the black man's penis at the adjacent urinal. "Sure wish I had one like yours."

The black man replied, "You can—just tie a string around it and hang a weight on the end of the string. Put the weight down your pant leg and you can have one like mine."

The white man thanked him for the suggestion and left. Some weeks later, they met again. The black man asked how the project was going.

"Great, I'm halfway there!"

"Really?" said the black man.

"Yes. It's turning black!"

•

Bill was standing in a lingerie store staring at a collection of Wonderbras.

The clerk noticed he had been there for some time and that

he appeared to be having trouble picking one out. She walked over and asked him if she could be of assistance.

Bill answered, "Well . . . if it's a Wonderbra, am I supposed to pick the size she is, or the size I want her to be?"

•

After my divorce, I found myself having to buy condoms, something I hadn't had to do for better than ten years.

The selection was overwhelming, and I asked the pharmacy clerk for some help.

He extolled the virtues of latex, ribbed, lubricated, colored, glow in the dark (assuming you can't find it any other way), magnum size, and more.

At last, as he was running out of breath, I asked which condom he recommended. He replied, "The condom made of lamb's intestine has a more natural feel."

I said, "Not to us city boys."

•

A traveling salesman runs out of gas in the country and walks to the nearest farmhouse. After explaining his dilemma, he is invited to stay the night as long as he does not mess with the host's daughter.

Well, of course, at one point during the night the girl comes to his room, and he takes her out to the farmer's car so the farmer won't hear them and makes love to her.

The next morning the salesman is glad to know the farmer has gassed up his car during the night. Since the farmer seems to know nothing of the encounter with the daughter, the salesman quickly leaves and heads for home.

Two months later the salesman returns home from work and finds a letter in the mail from the farmer:

Are you the dirty jerk who put the spots upon my dashboard and the footprints on my ceiling upside down?

Ever since you touched my Nellie,
She's had trouble with her belly.
Don't you think it's time you came around?

The salesman laughs and writes a letter to the farmer:

Yes, I'm the dirty jerk that put the spots upon your dashboard,
and the footprints on your ceiling upside down.
Ever since I touched your Venus,
I've had trouble with my penis.
Now, don't you think it's fifty-fifty all around?

•

The boyfriend said, "We're going to have a *great* time Saturday. I've got three tickets for the show."

"Why do we need three?" asked the girl.

"They're for your father, mother, and sister."

•

"Mr. Jones, I have reviewed this case carefully," the divorce-court judge said, "and I've decided to give your wife $775 a week."

"That's very generous and fair of you, Your Honor," the husband said. "And every now and then, I'll try to send her a few bucks myself."

•

Two cannibals—a father and a son—were elected by the tribe to go out and get something to eat. They walked deep into the jungle and waited by the path.

Soon, along came this little old man. The son said, "Oh, Dad, there's one."

"No," said the father. "There's not enough meat on that one to even feed the dogs. We'll just have to wait."

Well, a little later, along came this really fat man.

The son said, "Hey, Dad, he's plenty big enough."

"No," said the father, "we'd die of a heart attack from all the fat in that one. We'll just wait."

About an hour later, along came this absolutely gorgeous woman. The son said, "Now there's nothing wrong with that one, Dad. Let's eat her."

"No," said the father. "We'll not eat her either."

"Why not?"

"Because we're going to take her back alive and eat your mother."

•

A young man excitedly tells his mother he's fallen in love and is going to get married.

He says, "Just for fun, Ma, I'm going to bring over three women, and you guess which one I'm going to marry."

The mother agrees.

The next day, he brings three beautiful women into the house and sits them down on the couch and they chat for a while.

He then says, "Okay, Ma, guess which one I'm going to marry."

She immediately replies, "The redhead in the middle."

"That's amazing, Ma. You're right! How did you know?"

"I don't like her."

•

Henry was visiting a friend in the hospital. He was trying to stop smoking and was chewing on an unlit cigar when he got on the elevator.

A lady said to him with a snarl, "Sir, there is no smoking in here."

Henry said, "I'm not smoking, lady."

"But you have a cigar in your mouth."

"Lady, I've got on Jockey shorts, too, but I'm not riding a horse."

•

There are two old-maid sisters . . . both virgins. One Friday night Gladys looks at Betty and says, "I'm not going to die a virgin. I'm going out and I'm not coming home until I've been laid."

Betty says, "Well, make sure you're home by ten so I don't worry about you."

Ten o'clock rolls around and there's no sign of Gladys . . . eleven o'clock . . . twelve o'clock . . . Finally about twelve forty-five, the front door flies open and in runs Gladys . . . heading straight for the bathroom.

Betty, growing concerned, knocks on the door. "Are you okay, Gladys?"

No answer, so she opens the door, and there sits Gladys with her panties around her ankles, legs spread, and her head stuck between her legs looking at herself.

"What is it, Gladys? What's wrong?"

"Betty, it was ten inches long when it went in, and five inches when it came out. When I find the other half, you're gonna have the time of your life!"

•

I met a guy on the golf course who played to scratch using nothing more than a large weight on the end of a broom handle for everywhere except the green, and an old umbrella for putting.

At the nineteenth hole, I told him how impressed I was.

"I guess it's because I'm a genius," he replied casually. "I find things so easy that I have to make everything more difficult.

"Billiards, for example. I play with a rubber bung stuck on the end of a metal pole twisted like a corkscrew. I could still beat the local champ with one hand tied behind my back. I have to make it difficult or I get bored.

"Or rifle shooting," he went on. "I've taken the sights off the gun, I hold it one-handed—left-handed even though I'm right-handed—sight with my right eye, even though the gun's in my left hand, and stand on one leg while everyone else lies prone to hold the weapon stable. Even then, I could win easily whenever I want. Nothing's any fun unless I can make it into a challenge."

I was impressed. "Got any kids?"

"Yes, and before you ask . . . standing up in a hammock."

•

Dear Abby:

I have been engaged for almost a year. I am to be married next month. My fiancée's mother is not only very attractive but really great and understanding. She is putting the entire wedding together and invited me to her place to go over the invitation list because it had grown a bit beyond what we had expected it to be. When I got to her place, we reviewed the list and trimmed it down to just under a hundred . . . then she floored me. She said that in a month I would be a married man and that before that happened, she wanted to have sex with me. Then she just stood up and walked to her bedroom and on her way said that I knew where the front door was if I wanted to leave.

I stood there for about five minutes and finally decided that I knew exactly how to deal with this situation. I headed straight out the front door . . . there, leaning against my car, was her husband, my father-in-law to be. He was smiling. He explained that they just wanted to be sure I was a good kid and would be true to their little girl. I shook his hand and he congratulated me on passing their little test.

Abby, should I tell my fiancée what her parents did, and that I thought their "little test" was asinine and insulting to my character? Or should I keep the whole thing to myself, including that I was walking out to my car to get a condom?

•

Three women were roommates. One night they all had gone out on dates, and all came home at about the same time.

The blonde said, "You know you've been on a good date when you come home with your hair all messed up."

The brunette said, "No, you know you've been on a good date when you come home with your makeup all smeared."

The redhead reached under her skirt, removed her panties, and threw them up to the ceiling, where they stuck. She said, "Now *that's* a good date!"

•

An American soldier, serving in World War II, had just seen several weeks of intense action on the front lines against the Germans. He had finally been granted R&R and was on a train bound for London. The train was crowded, so the soldier walked the length of the train, looking for an empty seat. The only unoccupied seat was adjacent to a well-dressed, middle-aged lady and was being used by her little dog.

The weary soldier asked, "Please, ma'am, may I sit in that seat?"

The Englishwoman looked down her nose at the soldier, sniffed, and said, "You Americans. You are such a rude class of people. Can't you see my little Fifi is using that seat?"

The soldier walked away, determined to find a place to rest, but after another trip through the train found himself again facing the woman with the dog. Again he asked, "Please, lady, may I sit there? I'm very tired."

The Englishwoman wrinkled her nose and snorted, "You Americans! Not only are you rude, you are also arrogant. Imagine!"

The soldier didn't say anything else. He leaned over, picked up the little dog, tossed it out the window of the train, and sat down in the empty seat.

The woman shrieked and demanded that someone defend her and chastise the soldier.

An Englishman sitting across the aisle spoke up. "You know, sir, you Americans do seem to have a penchant for doing the wrong thing. You eat holding the fork in the wrong hand. You drive your autos on the wrong side of the road. And now, sir, you've thrown the wrong bitch out the window."

•

A man boards an airplane and takes his seat. As he settles in, he glances up and sees a very beautiful woman boarding the plane. He soon realizes she's heading straight toward him. Lo and behold, she takes the seat right beside his.

Eager to strike up a conversation, he blurts out, "Business trip or vacation?"

She turns, smiles, and says, "Business. I'm going to the annual Nymphomaniac Convention in Chicago."

He swallows hard. Here is the most gorgeous woman he has ever seen, sitting next to him, and she's going to a meeting of nymphomaniacs! Struggling to maintain his composure, he calmly asks, "What's your business role at this convention?"

"Lecturer. I use my experience to debunk some of the popular myths about sexuality."

"Really." He swallows hard. "What myths are those?"

"Well, one popular myth is that African-American men are the most well endowed, when, in fact, it's the Native American who is most likely to possess that trait. Another popular myth is that Frenchmen are the best lovers, when actually it is the man of Jewish descent. However, we have found that the best potential lover in all categories is the Southern redneck."

Suddenly, the woman becomes a little uncomfortable and

blushes. "I'm sorry, I shouldn't be discussing this with you. I don't even know your name!"

"Tonto!" the man says. "Tonto Goldstein! . . . But my friends call me Bubba!"

•

A farmer went to a livestock dealer and bought an anvil, a bucket, two chickens, and a goose. The farmer looked at his purchases and said, "Damn, I *walked* here. How am I gonna carry all this home?"

The livestock dealer said, "Why don't you put the anvil in the bucket, carry the bucket in one hand, and put the chickens under each arm and carry the goose in your other hand?"

"Hey, thanks!" the farmer said, and off he went. While walking home, he met a little old lady who told him she was lost.

She asked, "Can you tell me how to get to 1515 Mockingbird Lane?"

The farmer said, "Well, as a matter of fact, I live just down the road from there. Let's take my shortcut and go down this alley. We'll be there in no time."

"I am a lonely widow without a husband to defend me. How do I know that when we get in the alley, you won't hold me up against the wall, pull up my skirt, and ravish me?"

"Holy smokes, lady! I am carrying a bucket, an anvil, two chickens, and a goose. How in the world could I possibly hold you up against the wall and do that?"

She replied, "Set the goose down, cover him with the bucket, put the anvil on top of the bucket . . . and I'll hold the chickens."

•

A woman walked into a pharmacy and asked for a vibrator.

The pharmacist gestured with his index finger. "Come this way."

The woman replied, "If I could come that way, I wouldn't need a vibrator!"

•

A woman goes to her doctor and says she wants an operation because her vagina lips are much too large. She asks the doctor to keep the operation quiet because it's an embarrassing procedure and she doesn't want anyone to find out about it. The doctor agrees.

The next day, the woman awakens from her successful operation and finds three roses carefully placed beside her bed. Outraged, she immediately calls in the doctor and says, "I thought I asked you not to tell anyone about my operation!"

"Don't worry," he explains, "I didn't tell anybody. The first rose is from me because I felt bad that you had to go through all this by yourself. And the second rose is from the nurse who assisted me with the operation. She, too, had the same operation some time ago."

"Who is the third rose from?"

"That rose is from the guy upstairs in the burn unit. He wanted to thank you for his new ears!"

•

Little Johnny has just been toilet-trained and decides to use the big toilet like his daddy.

He pushes up the seat and balances his little penis on the rim.

Just then the toilet seat slams down, and little Johnny lets out a scream.

His mother comes running to find Johnny hopping round the room clutching his genitals and howling.

He looks up at her with his little tearstained face and sniffles, "K-k-k-k-kiss"—sniff—"it better."

Little Johnny's mother shouts, "Don't start your father's shit with me!"

•

A farmer's wife is at her lawyer's getting advice about a divorce.

"He makes excessive sexual demands on me, Mr. Jones."

"How do you mean?"

"Well, Mr. Jones," says the farmer's wife, "this morning I was looking at the chickens when he crept up behind me and had me from behind!"

"Chickens? Mrs. Smith, I didn't know you kept chickens."

"We don't, Mr. Jones. This was in the supermarket!"

•

Back in the olden days, a man was traveling through Switzerland. Nightfall was rapidly approaching, and the man had nowhere to sleep. He went up to a farmhouse and asked the farmer if he could spend the night.

The farmer told him that it would be all right, and that he could sleep in the barn. The man went into the barn to bed down, and the farmer went back into the house.

The farmer's daughter came down from upstairs and asked the farmer, "Who was that man going into the barn?"

"That's some fellow traveling through. He needed a place to stay for the night, so I said that he could sleep in the barn."

The daughter asked, "Did you offer the man anything to eat?"

"Gee, no, I didn't."

"Well, I'm going to take him some food."

The daughter went into the kitchen, prepared a plate of food, then took it out to the barn. The daughter was in the barn for an hour before returning to the house.

When she came back in, her clothes were all disheveled and buttoned up wrong, and she had several strands of straw tangled up in her long blond hair.

She immediately went up the stairs to her bedroom and went to sleep.

A little later, the farmer's wife came down and asked the farmer why their daughter went to bed so early.

"I don't know," said the farmer. "I told a man that he could sleep in the barn, and our daughter took him some food."

"Oh. Well, did you offer the man anything to drink?"

"Umm, no, I didn't."

The wife said, "I'm going to take something out there for him to drink."

The wife went to the cellar, got a bottle of wine, then went out to the barn. She did not return for over an hour, and when she came back into the house, her clothes were also messed up and she had straw twisted into her blond hair. She went straight up the stairs and into bed.

The next morning at sunrise, the man in the barn got up and continued on his journey, waving to the farmer as he left.

A few hours later, the daughter woke up and came rushing downstairs. She went right out to the barn, only to find it empty. She ran back into the house.

"Where's the man from the barn?" she eagerly asked the farmer.

Her father answered, "He left several hours ago."

"What?" she cried. "He left without saying good-bye? After all we had together? I mean, last night he made such passionate love to me!"

"What?" shouted the father. "He took advantage of you?" The farmer ran out into the front yard looking for the man, but by now the man was halfway up the side of the mountain.

The farmer screamed up at him, "I'm gonna get you! You had sex with my daughter!"

The man looked back down from the mountainside, cupped his hands next to his mouth, and yelled out, "I laid the old *ladee*, too!"

So that is how yodeling came about.

•

A huge, muscular man walks into a bar and orders a beer.

The bartender can't help but stare at the guy because in contrast to his large muscles, the man has a head the size of an orange.

The bartender hands the guy his beer and says, "You know, I'm not gay, but I want to compliment you on your physique, it really is phenomenal! But I have a question. Why is your head so small?"

The big guy nods slowly. He's obviously fielded this question many times.

"One day," he begins, "I was hunting and got lost in the woods. I heard someone crying for help. I followed the cries and they led me to a frog that was sitting next to a stream."

"No shit?" says the bartender, thoroughly intrigued.

"Yeah, so I picked up the frog and it said, 'Kiss me. Kiss me and I will turn into a genie and grant you three wishes.'"

"Keep going!" the bartender urged.

"I looked around to make sure I was alone and gave the frog a kiss. *Poof!* The frog turned into a beautiful, naked woman. She said, 'You now have three wishes.'

"I looked down at my scrawny, 115-pound body and said, 'I want a body like Arnold Schwarzenegger's.' She nodded, snapped her fingers, and *poof!* There I was, so huge that I ripped out of my clothes and was standing there naked! She then asked, 'What will be your second wish?'"

"What next?" begged the bartender.

"I looked hungrily at her beautiful body and replied, 'I want to make sensuous love with you here by this stream.'

She nodded, lay down, and beckoned to me. We made love right there by that stream for hours!

"Afterwards, as we lay there next to each other, sweating from our lovemaking, she whispered into my ear, 'You know, you do have one more wish. What will it be?'

"I looked at her and replied, 'How 'bout a little head?' . . . *Poof!*"

•

It's the spring of 1961 and Bobby goes to pick up his date. He's a pretty hip guy with his own car.

When he goes to the front door, the girl's father answers and invites him in. "Carrie's not ready yet, so why don't you have a seat?"

"That's cool," says Bobby.

Carrie's father asks Bobby what they're planning to do.

Bobby replies politely that they will probably just go to the soda shop or a movie.

Carrie's father responds, "Why don't you two go out and screw? I hear all the kids are doing it."

Naturally, this comes as quite a surprise to Bobby, so he asks Carrie's dad to repeat it.

"Yeah," says Carrie's father, "Carrie really likes to screw. She'll screw all night if we let her!"

Well, this just makes Bobby's eyes light up, and he immediately revises his plans for the evening.

A few minutes later, Carrie comes downstairs in her little poodle skirt and announces that she's ready to go.

Almost breathless with anticipation, Bobby escorts his date out the front door.

About twenty minutes later, a thoroughly disheveled Carrie rushes back into the house, slams the door behind her, and screams, *"Dammit, Daddy! The twist! It's called the twist!"*

•

A bunch of Indians capture a cowboy and bring him back to their camp to meet the chief.

The chief says to the cowboy, "You going to die. But we sorry for you, so give you one wish a day for three days. On sundown of third day, you die. What is first wish?"

The cowboy says, "I want to see my horse."

The Indians get his horse. The cowboy grabs the horse's ear and whispers something, then slaps the horse on the back. The horse takes off.

Two hours later, the horse comes back with a naked blonde. She jumps off the horse and goes into the tepee with the cowboy.

The Indians look at each other, figuring, "Typical white man—can only think of one thing."

The second day, the chief says, "What your wish today?"

The cowboy says, "I want to see my horse again."

The Indians bring him his horse. The cowboy leans over and whispers something in the horse's ear, then slaps it on the back. Two hours later, the horse comes back with a naked redhead. She gets off and goes into the tepee with the cowboy.

The Indians shake their heads, figuring, "Typical white man—going to die tomorrow and can only think of one thing."

The last day comes, and the chief says, "This your last wish, white man. What you want?"

The cowboy says, "I want to see my horse again."

The Indians bring him his horse.

The cowboy grabs the horse by both ears, twists them hard, and yells, "Read my lips! *Posse*, dammit! P-O-S-S-E!"

•

A guy is standing at a urinal when he notices that a midget is watching him.

Although the little fellow is staring at him intently, the

guy doesn't get uncomfortable until the midget drags a small stepladder up next to him, climbs it, and admires his privates at close range.

"Wow," comments the midget, "those are the nicest balls I have ever seen!"

Surprised—and flattered—the man thanks the midget and starts to move away.

"Listen, I know this is a rather strange request," says the little fellow, "but I wonder if you would mind if I touched them?"

Again the man is rather startled, but seeing no real harm in it, he obliges the request.

The midget reaches out, gets a tight grip on the man's balls, and says loudly, "Okay, hand over your wallet or I'll jump!"

•

Three guys are drinking in a pub when another man comes in and starts drinking at the bar.

After a while, he approaches the group of guys and, pointing at the one in the middle, shouts, "I've shagged your mum!" The other two guys look bewildered as the man resumes his drinking at the bar.

Ten minutes later he comes back and yells at the middle guy again, "Your mum sucked my cock!" Then he goes back to his drink.

Ten minutes later he's back again and announces, "*Oi!* I've had your mum up the ass!"

Finally the guy in the middle stands up and shouts, "Look, Dad, you're pissed, now bugger off home!"

•

A woman was having a passionate affair with an inspector from a pest-control company.

One afternoon they were carrying on in the bedroom together when her husband arrived home unexpectedly.

"Quick," said the woman to her lover, "into the closet!"

She bundled him in the closet stark naked. The husband, however, became suspicious and after a search of the bedroom discovered the man in the closet.

"Who are you?" the husband asked.

"I'm an inspector from Bugs-B-Gone."

"What are you doing in there?"

"I'm investigating a complaint about an infestation of moths."

"And where are your clothes?"

The man looked down at himself. "Those little bastards."

•

Police arrested Harry Jones, a forty-year-old white male resident of Atlanta, Georgia, in a pumpkin patch at 11:38 p.m. Friday.

Jones will be charged with lewd and lascivious behavior, public indecency, and public intoxication at the county courthouse on Monday.

The suspect allegedly stated that as he was passing a pumpkin patch, he decided to stop. "You know, a pumpkin is soft and squishy inside, and there was no one around here for miles. At least I thought there wasn't," he stated in a phone interview from the county courthouse jail.

Jones went on to state that he pulled over to the side of the road, picked out a pumpkin that he felt was appropriate to his purposes, cut a hole in it, and proceeded to satisfy his alleged "need."

"I guess I was just really into it, you know?" he commented with evident embarrassment.

Jones apparently failed to notice the Atlanta police car approaching and was unaware of his audience until officer Barbara Bobley approached him.

"It was an unusual situation, that's for sure," said Officer

Bobley. "I walked up to [Jones] and he's . . . just working away at this pumpkin."

Bobley went on to describe what happened when she approached Jones. She just went up and said, "Excuse me, sir, but do you realize that you are screwing a pumpkin?"

He got real surprised as you'd expect and then looked her straight in the face and said, "A pumpkin? Damn . . . is it midnight already?"

•

Morris wakes up in the morning.

He has a massive hangover and can't remember anything he did last night.

He picks up his bathrobe from the floor and puts it on. He notices something in one of the pockets—a bra.

He mutters, "Bloody hell, what happened last night?"

He walks toward the bathroom and finds a pantie in the other pocket of his robe.

Again he mutters, "What happened last night, what have I done? Must have been a wild party."

He opens the bathroom door, walks in, and looks in the mirror.

He notices a little string hanging out of his mouth, and his only thought is "Please, if there's a God, let this be a tea bag."

•

Two brothers have a lifelong dream to emigrate to America. They work hard and save their money.

After many years, they have saved enough money and finally emigrate to New York.

Before they begin building their new lives in America, they decide to see some of the famous places they dreamed of for so long: the Statue of Liberty, the Empire State Building, Rockefeller Center, and others.

Eventually, they make their way to Coney Island. As they

stroll down the beach, taking in all the newness of America, they see a large billboard that reads HOT DOGS, with a big arrow pointing down to a little hot dog stand.

Being hungry and seeing that having an American hot dog would be something new, they decide to try one. So they order two hot dogs and sit on a nearby bench to enjoy another piece of Americana.

The first brother sets his hot dog in his lap, unfolds the paper wrapper, looks at his hot dog for a moment, and suddenly wraps it back up. He then turns to his brother and says, "What part of the dog did you get?"

•

Paul was ambling through a crowded street fair when he decided to stop and sit at a palm reader's table. Said the mysterious old woman, "For fifteen dollars, I can read your love line and tell your romantic future."

Paul readily agreed, and the reader took one look at his open hand and said, "I can see that you have no girlfriend."

"That's true," said Paul.

"Oh my goodness, you are extremely lonely, aren't you?"

"Yes," Paul shamefully admitted. "That's amazing. Can you tell all of this from my love line?"

"Love line? No, from the calluses and blisters."

•

A woman walks into a drugstore and asks the pharmacist if he sells extra large condoms.

He replies, "Yes, we do. Would you like to buy some?"

She responds, "No, sir, but do you mind if I wait around here until someone does?"

•

Two strangers met on the golf course. They started playing and enjoyed the game. Partway around the course, one guy asked the other, "What do you do for a living?"

"I'm a hit man."

"You're joking!"

"No, I'm not." He reached into his golf bag and pulled out a beautiful Martini sniper's rifle with a large telescopic sight. "Here are my tools."

"That's a beautiful telescopic sight," said the other guy. "Can I take a look? I think I might be able to see my house from here." So he picked up the rifle and looked through the sight in the direction of his house. "Yeah, I can see my house all right. This sight is fantastic. I can see right in the window. Wow, I can see my wife in the bedroom. I can see she's naked! Wait a minute, that's my neighbor in there with her. He's naked as well! The bitch!" He turned to the hit man. "How much do you charge for a hit?"

"I do a flat rate. For you, one thousand dollars every time I pull the trigger."

"Can you do two for me now?"

"Sure, what do you want?"

"First, shoot my wife. She's always been mouthy, so shoot her in the mouth. Then the neighbor, he's a friend of mine, so just shoot his dick off to teach him a lesson."

The hit man took the rifle and took aim, standing perfectly still for a few minutes.

"Are you going to do it or not?" said the first guy impatiently.

"Just wait a moment, be patient," said the hit man calmly. "I think I can save you a thousand dollars here."

•

A white guy is walking along the beach when he comes across a lamp partially buried in the sand. He picks up the lamp and gives it a rub. Two genies appear, and they tell him he has been granted three wishes. The guy makes his three wishes and the genies disappear.

The next thing the guy knows, he's in a bedroom in a mansion surrounded by six beautiful women. He makes love to all of them and begins to explore the house. Suddenly he feels something soft under his feet. He looks down and the floor is covered in $100 bills. Then, there's a knock on the door. He answers it, and standing there are two people dressed in Ku Klux Klan outfits. They drag him outside to the nearest tree, throw a rope over a limb, and hang him by the neck until he's dead.

As the Klansmen are walking away, they remove their hoods, and it's the two genies. One genie says to the other one, "I can understand the first wish, having all these beautiful women in a big mansion to make love to. I can also understand his wanting to be a millionaire . . . but why he wanted to be hung like a black man is beyond me."

•

The matchmaker goes to see Mr. Avery, a confirmed bachelor for many years. "Mr. Avery, don't leave it too late. I have exactly the one you need. You only have to say the word and you'll meet and be married in no time!"

"Don't bother," replies Mr. Avery. "I've two sisters at home who look after all my needs."

"That's all well and good, but all the sisters in the world cannot fill the role of a wife."

"I said two sisters. I didn't say they were mine!"

•

Two voices—male and female—on a plane.

"I think everyone's asleep, let's go."

Sound of steps.

"This one is empty . . . no one's looking . . . you go in first."

"It's a bit cramped—let me sit down."

"Have you got the condom? Quick, put it on, sniff sniff."

"Ah, perfume—you think of everything."

"This is great." Long sigh.

Static on the loudspeaker, then a new voice: "This is the captain speaking, to those two people in the rear toilet. We know what you're doing and it is expressly forbidden by airline regulations. Now put those cigarettes out and take the condom off the smoke detector!"

•

The following is a father's advice to his son just moments before he gets on the bus that will carry him off to join the army.

"Son, you are getting ready to embark on a great adventure, as many of the men in our family have done since your great-great-grandfather did over a hundred years ago. There will be many dangers ahead that you will encounter—remember your training and obey your commanders. This will keep you alive during the arduous days of battle. Always stay with the plan; if you deviate from it, you will be in grave jeopardy. When the time of battle is over, be wary as you go into the towns and cities ahead because there are many hidden dangers lurking there. There will be many temptations to lure you away from your brothers-in-arms, and this could put you in danger even if it seems safe at the time. In every town there will be a street that will be most treacherous of all—there will be strong drink to dull your senses, loud and crude songs to suppress your hearing, and wild women of ill repute to enable your enemy to catch you off guard. My advice to you as a former soldier is simple. Whatever you do . . . *find that street!*"

•

14 Things to Do in Wal-Mart While Your Friends and Family Are Taking Their Sweet Time Shopping

1. Get twenty-four boxes of condoms and randomly put them in people's carts when they aren't looking.

2. Set all the alarm clocks in housewares to go off at five-minute intervals.

3. Make a trail of tomato juice on the floor to the rest-rooms.

4. Walk up to an employee and tell him/her in an official tone, "Code three, in housewares," and see what happens.

5. Go to the service desk and ask to put a bag of M&M's on layaway.

6. Move a CAUTION: WET FLOOR sign to a carpeted area.

7. Set up a tent in the camping department and tell other shoppers you'll invite them in only if they bring pillows from the bedding department.

8. When a clerk asks if she can help you, begin to cry and ask, "Why can't you people just leave me alone?"

9. While handling guns in the hunting department, ask the clerk if he knows where the antidepressants are.

10. Dart around the store suspiciously while loudly humming the theme from *Mission: Impossible.*

11. In the auto department, practice your Madonna look using different-sized funnels.

12. Hide in the clothing rack and, when people browse through, say, "Pick me! Pick me!"

13. When an announcement comes over the loudspeaker, assume the fetal position and scream, *"No! No!* It's those voices again."

And last but not least . . .

14. Go into a fitting room and yell loudly, "Hey! We're out of toilet paper in here!"

•

A couple attending an art exhibition at the National Gallery were staring at a portrait that had them completely confused. The painting depicted three black men totally naked sitting on a park bench. Two of the figures had black penises, but the one in the middle had a pink penis. The curator of the gallery realized that the couple were having trouble interpreting the painting and offered his assessment. He went on for nearly half an hour explaining how it depicted the sexual emasculation of African-Americans in a predominantly white, patriarchal society.

"In fact," he pointed out, "some serious critics believe that the pink penis also reflects the cultural and sociological oppression of gay men in contemporary society."

After the curator left, a Scottish man approached the couple and said, "Would you like to know what the painting is really about?"

"Now why would you claim to be more of an expert than the curator of the gallery?" asked the couple.

"Because I'm the guy who painted it. In fact, there's no African-American depicted at all. They're just three Scottish coal miners. The guy in the middle went home for lunch."

•

This guy sticks his head into a barbershop and asks, "How long before I can get a haircut?"

The barber looks around the shop and says, "About two hours."

The guy leaves.

A few days later the same guy sticks his head in the door. "How long before I can get a haircut?"

Again, the barber looks around at the shop full of customers. "About two hours."

The guy leaves.

A week later the same guy sticks his head in the shop. "How long before I can get a haircut?"

The barber looks around the shop. "About an hour and a half."

The guy leaves.

The barber looks over at a friend in the shop and says, "Hey, Bill, follow that guy and see where he goes."

In a little while Bill comes back into the shop laughing hysterically.

The barber asks, "Bill, where did he go when he left here?"

Bill looks up. "To your house."

•

A guy runs a stop sign and gets caught by a policeman.

Cop says, "License and registration please."

Guy says, "What for?"

"You didn't come to a complete stop at the stop sign."

"I slowed down and no one was coming."

"You still did not come to a complete stop. License and registration please."

"What's the difference?"

"The difference is you have to come to a complete stop. License and registration *please!*"

"If you can show me the difference between slow down and stop, I'll give you my license and registration."

Cop says, "Exit your vehicle, sir."

The cop takes out his nightstick and starts beating the shit out of the guy and says, "Do you want me to slow down or stop?"

•

A bar had a sign in the window advertising that they needed a piano player.

A scroungy-looking old guy, dressed like a bum, entered the bar and told the bartender he was interested in the job.

The bartender wasn't too impressed with his looks, but figured, what the heck, and pointed the old guy to the piano in the corner.

The old man sat down and started to play the most beautiful, melodious piece of music the people in the bar had ever heard. All talk stopped during the song, and when he finished, they all applauded.

"Hey, you're good," said the bartender. "What was that?"

"I call it 'Drop Them Pants Honey, I'm Gonna Take Ya Right Here.'"

"Interesting title," said the bartender. "Got another?"

The man broke into a foot-stompin' honky-tonk piece that brought the bar patrons to their feet clapping along until it was finished, at which time they again gave him a thunderous round of applause.

"You're really great! What do you call that one?" asked the bartender.

"That's a little ditty I call 'I Wanna Spank Your Bare Butt Baby, Till You Scream and Holler.'" The man then said, "If you'll excuse me, I'd like to use the restroom."

While he was gone, the bartender decided to offer him the job, starting immediately.

The man returned a moment or two later, and the bartender said, "If you want the job, it's yours." He looked down and noticed the man hadn't quite finished his trip to the restroom. "By the way, do you know your penis is hanging out for all the world to see?"

"Know it? I wrote it!"

•

A man walks into a bar one night and asks for a beer.

"Certainly, sir, that'll be one cent."

"*One cent*, that is way too cheap!" exclaims the guy.

The barman replies, "Yes."

So the guy glances over at the menu and asks, "Could I have a nice juicy T-bone steak, with french fries, and peas?"

"Certainly, sir, but all that comes to real money."

"How much money?"

"Four cents."

"*Four* cents!" exclaims the guy. "Where's the guy who owns this place?"

"Upstairs with my wife."

"What's he doing with your wife?"

"Same as what I'm doing to his business."

•

A man in a bar noticed an attractive set of blond Siamese twins. They started talking, he bought them a few drinks, and pretty soon they were laughing and joking, getting on really well. At closing time he asked them if they would like to go back to his place for a nightcap, and they both agreed.

Back at his apartment they enjoyed a few more drinks and started talking dirty. He suggested that they should go off to the bedroom, and the Siamese twins readily agreed. They all undressed, and soon he was having terrific sex with one of the twins. After he'd finished with the first one, the second one cried out, "My turn now," so he started to have sex with her.

The other Siamese twin suddenly noticed a saxophone in the corner of the bedroom and asked the guy if she could try it out, as she'd always wanted to play the saxophone. He said sure and carried on having sex with her twin while she tried to play "When the Saints Go Marching In" at full volume on the saxophone. The evening ended with the guy calling a cab for the Siamese twins. They all agreed that they should meet up again sometime.

Four days later the Siamese twins are walking down the street and one turns to the other and says, "Hey, isn't that the apartment that we went to with that guy the other night?"

"Yeah, I think it is," says the other one. "Shall we go up and see if he's in?"

"I'm not sure. Do you think he'll remember us?"

•

A widower lives with his daughter, a graduate student, in a small university town in the Midwest. The man comes home from work at the same time every day. One day, upon entering the house, he hears an awful racket coming from behind his daughter's bedroom door. He barges through the door only to see his daughter on her bed being "intimate" with a large, studded vibrator.

Before he can say a word, the daughter exclaims, "Look, Dad, I'm thirty-three years old, in graduate school, and all the good guys are married already. For all I know, this is the best I'll ever have, so just leave me alone!"

The father leaves the room, scratching his head, closing the door behind him.

A week or so later, the daughter comes home from school, enters the living room, and finds her dad sitting on the couch with a beer in one hand, watching football on TV, and with the vibrator on the couch next to him.

"Dad, what the hell are you doing?"

"Oh, just sitting here, watching the match and having a beer with my son-in-law!"

•

A boy and his date were parked on the back road some distance from town, doing what boys and girls do on back roads some distance from town, when the girl stopped the boy.

"I really should have mentioned this earlier, but I'm actually a hooker and I charge twenty dollars for sex."

The boy reluctantly paid her, and they did their thing.

After a cigarette, the boy just sat in the driver's seat looking out the window.

"Why aren't we going anywhere?" asked the girl.

"Well, I should have mentioned this before, but I'm actually a taxi driver, and the fare back to town is twenty-five dollars."

•

Over a beer, two guys are talking, discussing various sex positions. The first guy says his favorite position is "the rodeo."

The other guy asks, "What's the rodeo position, and how do you do it?"

The first guy says, "You tell your wife to get on the bed on all fours and do it doggie style. Once things start to get under way and she's really enjoying it, lean forward and whisper in her ear, 'Your sister likes this position, too,' and then you try to hang on for eight seconds."

•

A guy is hanging out in his favorite bar when he spots a fabulous babe walking in on the arm of some ugly dude. He asks the bartender about her and is delighted to discover that she's a prostitute. He watches her the rest of the night, amazed that someone so attractive could be available to him. The next night he goes back to the bar, and sure enough she shows up again, only this time alone. The guy gets up his nerve and approaches her.

"Is it true you're a prostitute?"

"Why, sure, big boy. What can I do for you?"

"Well, I dunno. What do you charge?"

"I get a hundred dollars for a hand job. We can negotiate from there."

"One hundred dollars! For a hand job? Are you nuts?"

"You see that Ferrari out there?" The guy looks out the

door, and sure enough, a shiny new Ferrari is parked outside. "I paid cash for that Ferrari with the money I made on hand jobs. Trust me, it's worth it."

The guy mulls it over for a while and decides what the hell. He leaves with her and gets the most unbelievable experience he has ever had. This hand job was better than any complete sexual experience he had ever had in his miserable life.

The next night he's back at the bar, waiting eagerly for her to show up. When she does, he immediately approaches her.

"Last night was incredible!"

"Of course it was. Just wait until you try one of my blow jobs."

"How much is that?"

"Five hundred dollars."

"Five hundred dollars! C'mon, that's ridiculous!"

"You see that apartment building across the street?" The guy looks out front at a twelve-story apartment building. "I paid cash for that building with the money I made on blow jobs. Trust me, it's worth it."

Based on the night before, the guy decides to go for it. He leaves with her and once again is not disappointed. He nearly faints—twice.

The next night he can hardly contain himself until she shows up. "I'm hooked, you're the best! Tell me, what'll it cost me for some pussy?"

She motions for him to follow her outside. She points down the street; between the buildings he can see Manhattan.

"You see that island?"

"Aw, c'mon! You can't mean that!"

She nods her head. "You bet. If I had a pussy, I'd own Manhattan!"

•

A team of archaeologists were working in Jerusalem when they found a slab of rock with five figures carved on it. In order, the figures were:

1. A woman
2. A donkey
3. A shovel
4. A fish
5. A Star of David

After months of studying the rock and the figures on it, the lead archaeologist took the rock and went on a lecture tour. He said the carvings were thousands of years old, but even so, they revealed a lot about the people of that time.

1. The woman being placed first in the line of figures indicates that women were held in high esteem. It was most likely a family-oriented culture.
2. The donkey indicates that they had domesticated animals.
3. The shovel shows that they were highly intelligent, as they knew how to make tools.
4. The fish shows that they knew how to augment the crops they raised by reaping from the sea.
5. The Star of David of course indicates that they were a religious group of people.

A little old man in the front row finally got the attention of the speaker. When acknowledged, he said, "I'm sorry to blow your conclusions, but you were reading it left to right. In Hebrew we read from right to left. The way it really reads is, 'Holy mackerel, dig the ass on that woman!' "

•

A police officer pulls a guy over for speeding and has the following exchange:

Officer: "May I see your driver's license?"

Driver: "I don't have one. I had it suspended when I got my fifth DUI."

Officer: "May I see the owner's card for this vehicle?"

Driver: "It's not mine, I stole it."

Officer: "The car is stolen?"

Driver: "That's right. But come to think of it, I think I saw the owner's card in the glove box when I was putting my gun there."

Officer: "There's a gun in the glove box?"

Driver: "Yes, sir. That's where I put it after I shot and killed the woman who owns this car and stuffed her in the trunk."

Officer: "There's a *body* in the *trunk*?"

Driver: "Yes, sir."

Hearing this, the officer immediately calls his captain. The car is quickly surrounded by police, and the captain approaches the driver to handle the tense situation.

Captain: "Sir, can I see your license?"

Driver: "Sure, here it is."

It's valid.

Captain: "Whose car is this?"

Driver: "It's mine, Officer. Here's the owner's card."

The driver owns the car.

Captain: "Could you slowly open the glove box so I can see if there's a gun in it?"

Driver: "Yes, sir, but there is no gun in it."

Captain: "Would you mind opening your trunk? I was told you said there's a body in it."

Driver: "No problem."

The trunk is opened and there is no body.

Captain: "I don't understand it. The officer who stopped you said that you told him you did not have a license, stole the car, had a gun in the glove box, and that there was a dead body in the trunk."

Driver: "Yeah, I'll bet the lying SOB told you I was speeding, too."

•

A man with no arms walked into a bar and asked for a beer. The bartender shoved the foaming glass in front of him.

"Look," said the customer, "I have no arms—would you please hold the glass up to my mouth?"

"Sure." The bartender did.

"Now, I wonder if you'd be so kind as to get my handkerchief out of my pocket and wipe the foam off my mouth."

"Certainly." And it was done.

"If you'd reach in my right-hand pants pocket, you'll find the money for the beer." The bartender got it.

"You've been very kind," said the customer. "Just one thing more. Where is the men's room?"

"Out the door, turn left, walk two blocks, and there's one in a filling station on the corner."

•

During the Great Depression, a man walked into a bar one day. He went up to the bartender and said, "Bartender, I'd like to buy the house a round of drinks."

The bartender said, "That's fine, but we're in the middle of a depression, so I'll need the money first."

The guy pulled out a huge wad of bills and set them on the bar. The bartender couldn't believe what he was seeing. "Where did you get all that money?"

"I'm a professional gambler."

"There's no such thing! I mean, your odds are fifty-fifty at best, right?"

"Well, I only bet on sure things."

"Like what?"

"Well, for example, I'll bet you fifty dollars that I can bite my right eye."

The bartender thought about it. "Okay."

So the guy pulled out his false right eye and bit it.

"Aw, you screwed me," said the bartender, and paid the guy his $50.

"I'll give you another chance. I'll bet you another fifty dollars that I can bite my left eye."

The bartender thought again. "Well, I know you're not blind, I mean, I watched you walk in here. I'll take that bet."

So the guy pulled out his false teeth and bit his left eye.

"Aw, you screwed me again!" protested the bartender.

"That's how I win so much money, bartender. I'll just take a bottle of your best scotch in lieu of the fifty dollars."

With that, the guy went to the back room and spent the better part of the night playing cards with some of the locals. After many hours of drinking and card playing, he stumbled up to the bar. Drunk as a skunk, he said, "Bartender, I'll give you one last chance. I'll bet you five hundred dollars that I can stand on this bar on one foot and piss into that whiskey bottle on that shelf behind you without spilling a drop!"

The bartender once again pondered the bet. The guy couldn't even stand up straight on two feet, much less one.

"Okay, you're on," he said.

The guy climbed up on the bar, stood on one leg, and began pissing all over the place. He hit the bar, the bartender, himself, but not a drop made it into the whiskey bottle.

The bartender was ecstatic. Laughing, he said, "Hey, pal, you owe me five hundred dollars!"

The guy climbed down off the bar. "That's okay. I just bet the guys in the card room a thousand bucks each that I could piss all over you and the bar and you'd be laughing the whole time!"

•

A guy is driving through the countryside and suddenly develops car trouble. The highway is rather deserted, and having no other choice, he pulls his car over. Fortunately, he spies a farmhouse a little ways up and walks there in the hope of using a phone to call for help.

At the house, a farmer answers the door and, hearing the man's plight, welcomes him to use the phone. While the man is on the phone calling a towing service, he notices something odd in the farmer's backyard: a pig with a wooden leg.

Waiting for the tow truck, the two men strike up a conversation. The man can't help his curiosity and asks, "Was that a pig with a wooden leg I saw in your yard?"

"Sure was."

"I have to know, why does the pig have a wooden leg?"

"Well, that's a very special pig. One day, I tripped and sprained my ankle near the highway. That pig pulled me from harm's way and went to the house, got my wife, and let her know I was in trouble."

"Wow," the man says, "I don't know of many dogs that could do that. That is a special pig. But, please tell me, why does the pig have a wooden leg?"

"Well, as I was saying, that's a very special pig. One day the missus and me were asleep in bed when the house caught on fire. That pig ran upstairs, jumped on the bed, woke both of us up, and, sure as I'm talking to you today, saved our lives."

"I understand that pig is very special," the man says, getting a little frustrated, "but please tell me—why does the pig have a wooden leg?"

"Well, a pig as special as that, you wouldn't want to eat him all at once now, would you?"

•

A young guy walks into a store, walks up to the manager's office, knocks on the door, and when the manager comes out, says, "Hi, I'm looking for a job. Ya got any jobs?"

The manager says, "Actually, we do have something now. Come with me and I'll get you started right away."

The manager takes the kid into the hardware and variety section and stands him behind the counter and explains to him that when someone comes in looking for something, he is to go and get the item for the customer, but he must also sell the customer something else that is relevant to the item he/she is purchasing. The kid doesn't understand, so the manager decides to show him how.

Just then, a customer walks into the store and asks the manager for some grass seed, but before the customer walks out with the seed, the manager asks, "Sir, we have lawn mowers on special at the moment, would you be interested?"

The customer protests that he has just purchased grass seed, but when the manager points out that he is going to need a mower, and he realizes that it's a good deal on the mower, he changes his mind, buys one, and walks out of the store a happy customer.

The manager turns to the kid and says, "Okay, do you understand now?" The kid nods his head emphatically, so the manager walks off and leaves him to it.

A short time later that day, a guy comes into the store looking a bit embarrassed and tells the kid that he wants a box of tampons for his girlfriend, so the kid runs off and gets them, but before the guy can walk away, the kid says, "Excuse me, sir, would you like to buy a lawn mower, they're on special at the moment."

The guy is perplexed. "I just bought a box of tampons, what the hell would I want a lawn mower for?"

"Well, sir, your weekend's f***ed, you might as well mow the lawn."

•

A young man joined the army and signed up to be a paratrooper. After weeks of training he got his first jump out of a plane. He watched people ahead of him go, and when it was his turn to jump, he got scared and sat back down.

The squad leader barked to the young man, "If you don't jump out of this plane, I'll stick my dick up your ass!"

A few weeks later the young man returned home and told his father what happened. His father asked, "Did you jump?"

The boy said, "A little at first."

•

A missionary is sent into the deepest depths of Africa to live with a tribe. He spends years with the people, teaching them to read, write, and have good Christian values. One thing he particularly stresses is the evil of sexual sin.

"Thou must not commit adultery or fornication!"

One day the wife of one of the tribe's noblemen gives birth to a white baby. The village is shocked and the chief is sent by his people to talk with the missionary.

"You have taught us of the evils of sexual sin, yet here a black woman gives birth to a white child. You are the only white man who has ever set foot in our village. Anyone can see what's going on here!"

The missionary replies, "No, no, my good man. You are mistaken. What you have here is a natural occurrence, what is called an albino. Look to thy yonder field. See a field of white sheep, and yet amongst them is one black one. Nature does this on occasion."

The chief pauses for a moment, then says, "Tell you what. You don't say anything about the sheep, I won't say anything about the white baby."

•

A sixty-year-old man walks into a big drugstore and up to the girl at checkout #3. He asks, "Do you guys have condoms here?"

She says, "Sure. What size are you?"

"I don't know."

"Well, just let me check." The cashier unzips his pants, takes a feel, then says over the intercom, *"Extra large condoms to checkout number three, please. Extra large condoms to checkout number three."*

A stock boy brings the condoms. The man pays for them and leaves.

Later, a thirty-year-old man walks into the store and up to checkout #3. He asks the girl, "Do you sell condoms here?"

The cashier replies, "Sure, but what size do you need?"

"Well, I don't know."

"Just let me check here." She unzips his pants, takes a couple of tugs, and then says over the intercom, *"Large condoms to checkout number three, please. Large condoms to checkout number three."*

A stock boy brings the condoms. The man pays for them and leaves.

Seeing this, a fifteen-year-old boy who hopes to get lucky goes up to the girl at checkout #3 and asks sheepishly, "Um, uh, do you guys sell any condoms here?"

"Yep. What size do you need?"

"I don't know."

She unzips his zipper for a feel, pauses, and says over the

intercom, *"Cleanup at checkout number three, please. Cleanup at checkout number three!"*

•

God saw Adam was alone in the Garden of Eden and asked if he and Eve had been having sex. Adam admitted that, yes, they had just been "intimate."

God asked where Eve was and Adam answered that she was down by the river, washing herself.

"Drat," sayeth the Lord. "Now I'll never get the smell out of the fish!"

•

A deaf-mute walks into a pharmacy to buy condoms. He has difficulty communicating with the pharmacist and cannot see condoms on a shelf.

Frustrated, the deaf-mute finally unzips his pants, places his dick on the counter, and puts down a $5 bill next to it.

The pharmacist unzips his pants, does the same as the deaf-mute, then picks up both bills and stuffs them in his pocket. Exasperated, the deaf-mute begins to curse the pharmacist wildly in sign language.

"Look," the pharmacist says, "if you can't afford to lose, you shouldn't bet."

•

This man gets his prescription for Viagra and goes home to get ready for when his wife arrives. He calls her on the phone, and she says, "I'll be home in an hour."

"Perfect," he replies. Because the doctor told him to take his Viagra an hour before sex, he takes the pill and waits. Well, the hour goes by, the man is ready to go, but no wife!

She calls him and says, "Traffic is terrible. I won't be there for about an hour and a half."

The man, frustrated, calls his doctor for advice. "What should I do?"

The doctor replies, "It would be a shame to waste it. Do you have a housekeeper around?"

"Yes."

"Well, maybe you can occupy yourself with her instead."

The man replies with dismay, "But I don't need Viagra with the housekeeper."

•

A young man is showing off his new sports car to his girl-friend. She is thrilled at the speed.

"If I do two hundred miles per hour, will you take off your clothes?" he asks.

"Yes!" exclaims his adventurous girlfriend.

As he gets up to two hundred, she peels off all her clothes. As he is unable to keep his eyes on the road, the car skids on some gravel and flips over. The naked girl is thrown clear, but he is jammed beneath the steering wheel.

"Go ahead and get help!" he cries.

"I can't. I'm naked and my clothes are gone!"

"Take my shoe and cover yourself."

Holding the shoe over her pubes, the girl runs down the road and finds a service station. Still holding the shoe between her legs, she pleads to the service station proprietor, "Please help me! My boyfriend's stuck!"

The proprietor looks at the shoe and says, "There's nothing I can do . . . he's in too far!"

•

Mrs. Cohen, Mrs. Levy, and Mrs. Goldberg are discussing their sons.

Mrs. Cohen says, "Now, my Sheldon, what a man! A world-famous lawyer, he has big-shot clients, a mansion in Beverly Hills, a summer home in Hawaii. He has a beautiful wife, and everything a man could want in the world."

Mrs. Levy says, "That's nice. Let me tell you about my

son Jonathan. He is a doctor, a world-famous researcher. He travels across the world on conferences, talks, and lectures. He was nominated for a Nobel Prize in medicine. What a man!"

Mrs. Goldberg says, "My Hershel, he's an engineer. Now, he makes $35,000 a year, and he's not famous. But his pee-pee is so long, you can line up ten pigeons in a row on it."

The ladies sip their tea for a while.

Then, Mrs. Cohen says, "Actually, I got a confession to make. Sheldon's an up-and-coming lawyer in Los Angeles, but he doesn't have a mansion or a summer home. He's a bright young man with a good future."

Mrs. Levy says, "Well, I've got a confession, too. Jonathan is a good doctor, and he got his share of scholarships, but a Nobel Prize winner he isn't."

They both look expectantly at Mrs. Goldberg.

"Well, all right, I'll tell the truth, too. The last bird gotta stand on one leg."

•

Four farmers were seated at the bar in a tavern. At the table next to them sat a young girl.

The first man said, "I think it's *woomb*."

The second replied, "No, it must be *wooombh*."

The third said, "You both have it wrong—it's *woom*."

The fourth stated, "No, it has to be *woommmmbbb*."

At this, the young lady could stand it no longer. She got up, walked over to the farmers, and said, "Look, you hayseeds, it's *womb*. That's it, that's all there is to it." Then she left.

Eventually, one of the farmers broke the silence by saying, "Well, I don't know. A slip of a girl like that, I don't see how she could know. I'll bet she's never even heard an elephant fart."

•

A boy goes in to buy condoms for the first time. The man behind the counter says, "That'll be $2.98 plus tax."

The boy says, "Tax? Don't these things stay on by themselves?"

•

Three sisters wanted to get married, but their parents could not afford three weddings, so all of them wed on the same day. They also couldn't afford to go on honeymoons, so they all stayed home with their new hubbies.

That night the mother got up because she couldn't sleep. When she walked past her oldest daughter's room, she heard screaming. Then as she passed her second daughter's room, she heard laughing. Finally, as she passed her youngest daughter's room, she couldn't hear anything.

The next morning when the men left, the mother asked her oldest daughter, "Why were you screaming last night?"

The daughter replied, "Mom, you always told me if something hurt, I should scream."

"That's true."

The mother looked at her second daughter. "Why were you laughing so much last night?"

The daughter replied, "Mom, you always said if something tickled you, you should laugh."

"That's also true."

Then the mother looked at her youngest daughter and asked, "Why was it so quiet in your room last night?"

The youngest daughter replied, "Mom, you always told me I should never talk with my mouth full!"

•

Back in the good old days in Texas, when stagecoaches and the like were popular, three people were in a stagecoach one day: a true red-blooded, born-and-raised Texas gentleman, a tenderfoot city slicker from back East, and a beautiful and well-endowed Texas lady. The city slicker kept eyeing the lady, and finally he leaned forward and said, "Lady, I'll give you ten dollars for a blow job."

The Texas gentleman looked appalled and pulled out his pistol and killed the city slicker on the spot.

The lady gasped and said, "Thank you, suh, for defendin' mah honor!"

Whereupon the Texan holstered his gun and said, "Your honor, hell! No tenderfoot from back East is gonna raise the price of a woman in Texas!"

•

A couple gets caught making out in a car by a cop.

The cop says, "What do you think you're doing?"

The guy says, "Officer, we were just necking."

The cop says, "Yeah? Then you better put your neck back in your pants and get the hell out of here."

•

Three morticians were having a few drinks and started discussing their hardest cases. The first said, "I believe I had the hardest. I had a young man who ran his car into a tree. It took a week before I could show him."

The second smiled. "That's nothing. I had this couple who got hit by a train. It took two weeks before I could show them."

The third grinned. "You two didn't have anything! I had a woman who jumped off a ten-story building. She landed on a fire hydrant. It took me three weeks to get the smile off her face."

•

A dusty cowboy rides up to the saloon, gets off his horse and ties it to the hitching post, then slaps the dust off his jacket and chaps. He walks around to the back of the horse, puckers up his lips, and kisses the horse directly on the asshole. He then walks into the saloon, walks up to the bar, and says to the bartender, "Whiskey!"

The bartender pours him a glass of whiskey and says to the cowpoke, "Say there, pardner, I noticed when you got off your horse, you went behind it and kissed it right on the asshole. Why'd you do that?"

"Chapped lips."

"Chapped lips? Is that a cure for chapped lips?"

"No," says the cowpoke, "but it sure as hell stops you from lickin' 'em."

•

Two cannibals are wandering around in the desert for days without food. They're hungry and desperate. To their delight, they stumble upon a dead human carcass, pristine from any scavengers, so they sink their teeth into the dead flesh, tearing it apart, one starting from the head and one from the toes.

After a few minutes, the guy at the head yells to the cannibal at the bottom, "Hey, how's it going down there?"

The cannibal at the bottom says, "This is great, I'm having a ball."

The guy at the top says, "Slow down and enjoy it; you're eating too damn fast."

•

A blind man went to the lumberyard for a job. The boss didn't want to just tell him no, so he told him that if he could pass a test, he'd hire him.

He had one of his employees take the man out back to identify some lumber. He brought the man to a pile of pine paneling; the man walked around the pile and sniffed, correctly identifying it as pine paneling. The employee thought, *How did he do that?*

Next he took him to a pile of two-by-fours. These he also

correctly identified after sniffing around a bit. Now they were all amazed. They decided it was time to trick him. They brought out the receptionist and laid her buck naked on her back. The blind man walked around and sniffed. Obviously puzzled, he walked around and sniffed and walked around and sniffed some more. Scratching his head, he told them to flip it over. They did so and the sniffing continued. Suddenly he started laughing and said, "You think you've got me, don't you? Well, I know what that is. That's the shithouse door off a tuna boat!"

•

A big Texan ambles into a men's room and does a double take at the little guy standing at the next urinal. He's holding his "snake" with two hands and smiling.

The Texan asks, "How long is that snake, fella?"

"Fourteen inches."

"Is that fourteen inches soft?"

"Yes."

"Well, how long is it when it's hard?"

The little guy answers proudly, "I don't know—it takes so much blood, I faint!"

•

A medical student specializing in pathology truly wanted to excel in his studies. Without fail, he would visit the school's path lab daily following his classes to do extra work.

One evening he uncovered a cadaver only to notice a cork plugging its rectum. Curious, he removed the cork only to hear, *"On the road again, I just can't wait to get on the road again . . ."*

Startled, he replaced the cork. Curiosity soon got the best of him, and he once again removed the cork. Again he heard the same tune: *"On the road again, I just can't wait to get on the road again . . ."*

He could stand it no more. He replaced the cork, covered the cadaver, and raced upstairs to his professor's office. He persuaded the man to accompany him back to the lab. Once there, the student again uncovered the cadaver and displayed the corked rectum. The professor looked unfazed. When the student removed the cork, the same tune emanated: *"On the road again, I just . . ."*

The professor looked bored and started to walk away.

The student was aghast at this casual response and said, "Don't you find this amazing?"

The professor replied, "Not really, almost any asshole can sing country and western."

•

A sailor pulled into a little town, and every hotel room was taken. He pleaded to the hotel manager, "I've got to have a room somewhere, or just a bed, I don't care where."

"Well, I do have a double room with one occupant—an air force guy," admitted the manager, "and he might be glad to split the cost. But to tell you the truth, he snores so loudly that people in adjoining rooms have complained in the past. I'm not sure if it's worth it to you."

"No problem," the tired navy man assured him, "I'll take it."

The next morning the sailor came down to breakfast bright-eyed and bushy tailed. "How'd you sleep?" asked the manager.

"Never better."

The manager was impressed. "No problem with the other guy snoring then?"

"Nope, I shut him up in no time."

"How'd you manage that?"

"He was already in bed, snoring away, when I came into the room. I went over, gave him a kiss on the cheek, said, 'Good night, beautiful,' and he sat up all night watching me."

•

A man is walking around New York with his wife. They find a perfume shop, the wife goes in, and he waits outside.

A hooker comes along and says to him, "Like to come home with me, buddy?"

"For how much?"

"One hundred dollars."

"I'll give you five bucks."

The hooker swears at him and walks away.

A little later, the man's wife comes out of the shop and they continue their walk.

As they round the corner, there stands the same hooker. She takes one look at the man and his wife and says, "*Ha!* See what you get for five bucks!"

•

At a dance at a local college, a guy from America asks a girl from Sweden to dance. While they're dancing, he gives her a little squeeze and says, "In America we call this a hug."

She says, "Yaah, in Sveden we call it a hug, too."

A little later, he gives her a peck on the cheek. "In America we call this a kiss."

"Yaah, in Sveden we call it a kiss, too."

Later that evening after quite a few drinks, he takes her out on the campus lawn and has sex with her. "In America we call this a grass sandwich."

"Yaaah, in Sveden we call it a grass sandwich, too, but we usually put more meat in it."

•

An attractive woman from New York was driving through a remote part of Texas when her car broke down. An Indian on horseback came along and offered her a ride to a nearby town.

She climbed on the horse and they rode off. The ride was

uneventful . . . except, every few minutes the Indian would let out a whoop so loud that it would echo from the surrounding hills.

When they arrived in town, he let her off at the local service station, yelled one final "Yahoo!" and rode off.

"What did you do to get that Indian so excited?" asked the service station attendant.

"Nothing, I merely sat behind him on the horse, put my arms around his waist, and held on to his saddle horn so I wouldn't fall off."

"Lady, Indians ride bareback."

•

Tired of the boring "squares" she'd been laying, a gal decided to find out if bikers were really the heavy "cocksmen" that she heard they were.

So she picked up a gigantic biker and went with him up to his pad. Stripped and ready, anxiously awaiting some real action, she was astonished to see that his fully erect dick was only two inches long.

"Who," she demanded scornfully, "do you think you're gonna satisfy with that?"

Grinning confidently, the biker replied, "Me!"

•

One day a man walked into a dentist's office for some dental work. The dentist said, "Sir, you have a tooth I must pull. What type of painkiller would you like?"

The man looked at the dentist. "None, thanks, I have experienced the second-greatest pain in my life."

"Sir, pulling this tooth will be painful. I suggest a painkiller."

The man looked back at the dentist. "I have experienced the second-greatest pain in my life. Nothing else will ever compare."

"Sir, I'm telling you, use a painkiller."

The man again said, "I have experienced the second-greatest pain in my life. I do not need painkillers. Now pull the tooth."

"Okay, you asked for it. But first, tell me, what was the second-greatest pain in your life?"

"Yes, I remember it well. I was hunting, and while walking through the woods, the urge came upon me and I headed over to a tree. Well, I started to do my thing, and when the first part dropped, it set off a large bear trap that was hidden in the snow, which closed on my balls. That was the second-greatest pain in my life."

"Ouch! But what was the first-greatest pain in your life?"

"When I reached the end of the chain."

●

A guy arrives at the pearly gates, waiting to be admitted. Saint Peter is leafing through the Big Book to see if the guy is worthy of entering. After several minutes, Saint Peter closes the book, furrows his brow, and says, "I don't see that you ever really did anything great in your life, but I don't see anything really bad either. Tell you what. If you can tell me of one *really* good deed that you did in your life, I'll let you in."

The guy thinks for a minute. "Okay, well, there was this one time when I was driving down the highway and I saw a gang assaulting this poor girl. I slowed down, and sure enough, there they were, about ten of 'em torturing this woman. Infuriated, I got out of my car, grabbed a tire iron out of my trunk. The gang members formed a circle around me. I walked straight up to the leader of the gang. He was a huge guy with a studded leather jacket and a chain running from his nose to his ear. I hit him over the head with the tire iron, then I turned around and yelled to the rest of them, 'Leave this poor innocent girl alone! You're all a bunch of sick, deranged animals! Go home before I really teach you all a lesson in pain!'"

Saint Peter, duly impressed, says, "Wow! When did this happen?"

"About ten minutes ago."

•

Morris complained to his friend Irving that lovemaking with his wife was becoming routine and boring.

"Get creative, Morris. Break up the monotony. Why don't you try playing doctor for an hour? That's what I do," said Irving.

"Sounds great, but how do you make it last for an hour?"

"Hell, just keep her in the waiting room for fifty-five minutes."

•

Once, in a small town, lived a man named Jack. Everyone in town knew Jack was an optimist. Whenever placed in a terrible situation, he would say, "It could have been worse."

Everyone in town was tired of hearing Jack say that, so one day they decided to lie to Jack.

They went up to him and said, "Jack, the baker found his wife in bed with another man last night! He shot the man and then himself! Isn't that terrible?"

Jack said, "Well, yes, it's terrible, but it could have been worse!"

The townspeople said, "How could *anything* possibly be worse?"

"Well, if it had been Monday night, I would be dead!"

•

A man complained to his friend, "My elbow hurts. I'd better go to the doctor."

"Don't do that," volunteered his friend. "There's a new

computer at the drugstore that can diagnose any problem quicker and cheaper than a doctor. All you have to do is put in a urine sample, deposit ten dollars, and the computer will give you your diagnosis and plan of treatment."

The man figured he had nothing to lose, so he took a sample of urine down to the drugstore. Finding the machine, he poured in the urine and deposited $10. The machine began to buzz and various lights flashed on and off. After a pause, a slip of paper popped out, stating, *You have tennis elbow. Soak your arm in warm water twice a day. Avoid heavy labor. Your elbow will be better in two weeks.*

That evening as the man contemplated this breakthrough in medical science, he began to suspect fraud. To test his theory he mixed together some tap water, a stool sample from his dog, and urine samples from his wife and teenage daughter. To top it all off, he masturbated into the jar. He took this concoction down to the drugstore, poured it in the machine, and deposited $10.

The machine went through the same buzzing and flashing routine as before, then printed out: *Your tap water has lead. Get a filter. Your dog has worms. Give him vitamins. Your daughter is on drugs. Get her in rehab. Your wife is pregnant. It's not your baby. Get a lawyer. And if you don't stop jerking off, your tennis elbow will never get better.*

•

An eccentric billionaire wanted a mural painted on his library wall, so he called in an artist. Describing what he wanted, the billionaire said, "I am a history buff, and I would like your interpretation of the last thing that went through General Custer's mind before he died. I am going out of town on business for a week, and when I return, I expect to see it completed."

Upon his return, the billionaire went to the library to examine the finished work. To his surprise he found a painting of a cow with a halo. Surrounding this were hundreds of Indians in various stages and positions of lovemaking.

Furious, he called the artist in.

"What the hell is this?" screamed the billionaire.

"Why, that's exactly what you asked for," said the artist smugly.

"No! I didn't ask for a mural of pornographic filth. I asked for a mural interpreting Custer's last thought!"

"And there you have it. I call it *Holy Cow, Look at All Those F***ing Indians.*"

•

Two Dutch girls are riding their old, rickety bikes down the streets of Amsterdam one late afternoon. As it turns closer to dusk, the increasing darkness of the streets starts making the two girls a little nervous. One girl leans over to the other and says, "You know, I've never come this way before."

The other girl says, "It's the cobblestones!"

•

Two nude statues, of a man and a woman, stand across from each other in a secluded park. A few hundred years after they've been put in place, an angel flutters down to them.

With a wave of his hand, suddenly the statues have been given life, and they step down from their pedestals.

The angel says, "I have been sent to grant the mutual request you both have made after hundreds of years standing across from each other, unable to move. But be quick—you only have fifteen minutes before you must become statues again."

The man looks at the woman, and they both blush and giggle, then run off into some underbrush. An intense rustling comes from the bushes, and seven minutes later, they both come back to the angel, obviously satisfied.

The angel smiles at the couple. "That was only seven minutes—why not go back and do it again?".

The former statues look at each other for a minute, then the woman says, "Why not? But let's reverse it this time. You hold down the pigeon, and I'll shit on it."

•

An old man gets on a crowded bus and no one gives him a seat. As the bus shakes and rattles, the old man's cane slips on the floor and he falls.

As he gets up, a seven-year-old kid, sitting nearby, turns to him and says, "If you put a little rubber thingy on the end of your stick, it wouldn't slip."

The old man snaps back, "Well, if your daddy had done the same thing seven years ago, I would have a seat today."

•

"Good evening, ladies," Sherlock Holmes said as he passed three women eating bananas on a park bench.

"Do you know them?" Dr. Watson asked.

"No, I've never met the nun, the prostitute, or the bride we just passed."

"Good Lord, Holmes, how in the world did you know all that?"

"Elementary, my dear Watson. The nun ate the banana by holding it in one hand and using the fingers of the other hand to properly break the fruit into small pieces.

"The prostitute grabbed it with both hands and crammed the whole thing in her mouth."

"Amazing!" Watson exclaimed. "But how did you know the third was a newlywed?"

"Because she held it with one hand and pushed her head toward it with the other."

•

Young Dave was courting Mabel, who lived on an adjoining farm out West in cattle country. One evening as they were sitting on Dave's porch watching the sun go down over the hills, Dave spied his prize bull doing his business on one of the cows. Dave sighed in contentment at this idyllic rural scene and figured the omens were right for him to put the hard word on Mabel.

He leaned in close and whispered in her ear, "Mabel, I'd sure like to be doing what that bull is doing."

"Well then, why don't you?" Mabel whispered back. "It is *your* cow."

•

Bob was driving home after a day at the construction site over the Golden Gate Bridge at about 90 mph.

Wouldn't you know, a cop jumped out and clocked him with radar. Bob pulled over like a good citizen.

The cop walked up to the window and said, "You know how fast you were going, *boy*?" Ignoring Bob, the officer continued, in his normal charming fashion, "That's speeding and you're getting a ticket and a fine!"

The cop took a good look at the young Bob and said, "You don't even look like you have a job! Why, I've never seen anyone so scruffy in my entire life!"

Bob said, "I've got a job! I have a good, well-paying job."

The cop leaned in the window, and with the smell of day-old doughnuts on his breath, said, "What kind of a job would a bum like you have?"

"I'm a cunt stretcher."

"What you say, *boy*?"

"A cunt stretcher."

"What's a cunt stretcher do?"

Bob explained, "Girls call me up and say they want to be

stretched, so I go over there and start with a couple of fingers, then a couple more, and then one whole hand. Then two. Then I pull them farther and farther apart until it's six feet across."

The cop, absorbed with the images in his mind, let down his guard. "What the hell do you do with a six-foot cunt?"

Bob nonchalantly commented, "You give it a radar gun and stick it at the end of a bridge!"

•

A young man is staying on a farm with his aunt and uncle for the summer. One morning the aunt and uncle walk into the kitchen and see the young man drinking an extremely large glass of milk.

The young man says, "I took the liberty of milking your cow this morning! It took me a while to get her started up. She must be old and stubbly."

The uncle says with a confused look, "Um, son, we don't have a cow. . . . We have a bull!"

•

Three women are in a gym locker room dressing up to play racquetball when suddenly a guy runs through the room wearing nothing but a bag over his head.

He passes the first woman, who looks down at his penis. "He's not *my* husband," she says.

He passes by the second woman, who also looks down at his penis. "He's not *my* husband either."

He passes the third woman, who also looks down as he runs by her.

"Wait a minute," she says, "he's not even a member of this club."

•

An Australian, an American, and an Irishman were prisoners in a German POW camp. The commandant was a mean bastard and was going to shoot his three captives unless their combined dick length was at least twenty inches.

The three POWs had their cocks measured, and their combined dick length was twenty inches exactly, so they were spared.

Later on, the three were talking, and the Australian said, "Well, if it wasn't for my ten-inch dick, we'd all be dead."

The American said, "Nah, if it wasn't for my eight-inch dick, then we'd all be dead."

Then the Irishman said, "If I didn't have a hard-on, we'd all be dead."

●

Three conventioneers, having finally managed to convince their wives to go back to the hotel, located a house of ill repute.

The madam was crestfallen. "Sorry, fellows, all the girls are busy. No one left but me."

"Gee, we spent most of the evening getting rid of our wives and we're leaving tomorrow. Isn't there anything you can do?"

"Well, there's always *me*, I give specials."

The first guy decided he'd go for it, and when he came back downstairs, he had a grin ear to ear.

"How was it? How much was it?"

"It was great! I got the twenty-five-dollar special. She had this can of Reddi-wip, and she sprayed it all around and then licked it off."

The second fellow didn't hesitate, bolted up the stairs, and was back after a while, grinning like the first.

"How was it? How much was it?"

"It was super! I got the fifty-dollar special. Same as Jack, the Reddi-wip, but she had some chopped walnuts that she sprinkled on it. Nibbled off the walnuts and licked off the Reddi-wip, faantaaastic!"

The third could not be constrained; he raced up the stairs and came back shortly thereafter, chin between his knees.

"Gosh! What happened? What went wrong?"

"Well, I got the seventy-five-dollar special, kinda like what you guys got, but she starts with a pineapple ring. Then there's the Reddi-wip, the chopped walnuts, but she's got some chocolate sprinkles and a cherry she puts on top. Damn, it looked so good I ate it myself."

•

A businessman was getting ready to go on a long business trip. He knew his wife was flirtatious with an extremely healthy sex drive, so he thought he'd buy her a little something to keep her occupied while he was gone.

He went to a store that sold sex toys and looked around. He thought about a life-size sex doll, but that was too close to another man for him. He was browsing through the dildos, looking for something special to please his wife, and started talking to the old man behind the counter.

He explained his situation.

"Well, I don't really know of anything that will do the trick. We have vibrating dildos, special attachments, and so on, but I don't know of a thing that will keep her occupied for weeks, except . . ."

"Except what?" the man asked.

"Nothing, nothing."

"C'mon, tell me! I need something!"

"Well, sir, I don't usually mention this, but there is the Voodoo Penis."

"So what's up with this Voodoo Penis?"

The old man reached under the counter and pulled out an old wooden box, carved with strange symbols and erotic images. He opened it, and there lay an ordinary-looking dildo.

The businessman laughed and said, "Big damn deal. It looks like every other dildo in this shop!"

"But you haven't seen what it'll do yet." He pointed to a door. "Voodoo Penis, the door."

The Voodoo Penis miraculously rose out of its box, darted over to the door, and started pounding the keyhole. The whole door shook wildly with the vibrations, so much so that a crack began to form down the middle. Before the door split, the old man said, "Voodoo Penis, return to box!"

The Voodoo Penis stopped, levitated back to the box, and lay there quiescent once more.

"I'll take it!" said the businessman. The shopkeeper resisted, saying it wasn't for sale, but finally surrendered to $738 in cash. The guy took it home to his wife, told her it was a special dildo. To use it, she only had to say, "Voodoo Penis, my crotch."

He left for his trip satisfied that things would be fine while he was gone. After he'd been gone a few days, his wife was unbearably horny. She thought of several people who would willingly satisfy her, but then she remembered the Voodoo Penis. She undressed, opened the box, and said, "Voodoo Penis, my crotch!"

The Voodoo Penis shot to her crotch and started pumping. It was absolutely incredible, like nothing she'd ever experienced before. After three mind-shattering orgasms, she was exhausted and decided she'd had enough.

She tried to pull it out, but it was stuck in her, still thrusting. She tried and tried to get it out, but nothing worked. Her husband had forgotten to tell her how to shut it off. Worried, she decided to go to the hospital to see if they could help. She put her clothes on, got in the car, and started to drive, quivering with every thrust of the dildo. On the way, another incredibly intense orgasm made her swerve all over the road.

A police officer saw this and immediately pulled her over. He asked for her license, then asked how much she'd had to drink. Gasping and twitching, she explained, "I haven't had anything to drink, Officer. You see, I've got this Voodoo Penis thing stuck in my crotch and it won't stop screwing me!"

The officer looked at her for a second, shook his head, and in an arrogant voice replied, "Yeah, right . . . Voodoo Penis, my ass!"

•

Three men stand before Saint Peter awaiting admission into heaven. However, Saint Peter has been informed that heaven will only admit 33 percent of applicants today.

The admissions standard: Who died the worst death?

So Saint Peter takes each of the three men aside in turn and asks him how he died.

First man: "I'd been suspecting for a long time that my wife was cheating on me. I decided to come home early from work one afternoon and check to see if I could catch her in the act. When I got back to my apartment, I heard the water running. My wife was in the shower. I looked everywhere for the guy, but couldn't find anyone or any trace that he had been there. But the last place I looked was out on the balcony. I found the guy hanging from the edge, trying to get back in! So I started jumping up and down on his hands, and he yelled, but he didn't fall. So I ran inside and got a hammer and crushed his fingers with it until he fell twenty-five floors screaming in agony. But the fall didn't kill the guy—he landed in the bushes! So I dragged the refrigerator from the kitchen—it weighed about a ton—pulled it to the balcony, and hurled it over the edge. It landed right on the guy and killed him. But then I felt so horrible about what I had done, I went back into the bedroom and shot myself."

Saint Peter nodded slowly as the man recounted the story. Then, telling the first man to wait, he took the second aside.

Second man: "I lived on the twenty-seventh floor of this apartment building. I had just purchased this book on exercises and was practicing them on my balcony, enjoying the sunshine, when I lost my balance and fell off the edge. Luckily, I only fell about two floors before grabbing another balcony and holding on for dear life. I was trying to pull myself up when this guy came running onto what must have been his balcony and started jumping up and down on my hands. I screamed in pain, but he seemed really irate. When he finally stopped, I tried to pull myself up again, but he comes out with this hammer and smashes my fingers to a pulp! I fell, and I thought I was dead, but I landed in these bushes. I couldn't believe my second stroke of luck, but it didn't last—the last thing I saw was this enormous refrigerator falling from the building, and it landed on top of me and crushed me."

Saint Peter comforted the man, who seemed to have several broken bones. Then he told him to wait and turned to the third man.

Third man: "Picture this. You're hiding, naked, in a refrigerator . . ."

•

One day, a recently married man goes to the attic of his new home to put a few things in storage. While he is there, he notices a large steamer trunk sitting in the corner. When he tries to open it, he finds it is locked.

Puzzled and curious, he calls his new bride up to the attic and asks her about the trunk. She tells him that it is hers and that it only contains some personal things. He accepts her answer and eventually forgets all about it.

Three years later when he is cleaning out the attic, he runs across the trunk and again asks his wife what's in it. She again tells him that it contains only personal things, but this time he is more persistent.

So she sits him down and reminds him that she makes him happy when he's feeling down, that she keeps the house meticulously clean, that she cooks him fantastic meals seven days a week, and that she gives him all the sex he wants, anytime he wants it. Then she tells him if he is happy with all of those things, he should forget about the trunk because she will not talk about it.

"Fair enough," says the husband, and he finishes cleaning out the attic.

On their twenty-fifth wedding anniversary, he pulls the trunk down the stairs, into the middle of the living room floor, and calls to his wife.

"Honey, we've been married for twenty-five years, and I think it's time we had a heart-to-heart talk. What the hell is in that trunk?"

The wife immediately protests, reminding him once again about the clean house, the good food, and the great sex.

"I don't care," he tells her. "After twenty-five years we ought to be able to talk about anything. Now open this god-damn trunk!"

So, she takes a key from a chain hanging around her neck and opens the trunk. Inside are three ears of corn and $25,000 in cash.

"Jesus Christ!" shouts the surprised husband. "What's going on here? Where did all of this come from?"

"Well, sweetie," replies the wife, "you said we could talk, so I'll tell you what you want to know. Over the years, I tried to stay faithful to you, but I wasn't always successful. Every time that I cheated on you, I put an ear of corn into the trunk."

The husband cannot believe the shocking confession that he has just heard, but after mulling it over in his mind for a few moments, he says to his wife, "All right, I admit I'm not too thrilled about this, but I did say we should be honest with each other, and I guess I can live with three infidelities in twenty-five years. But where did all the money come from?"

"Well, whenever the trunk got full, I sold the corn."

•

Fred had not been feeling well, so he went to his longtime doctor. The doctor did some tests and walked back into the room.

"Fred, I have some bad news for you, and I really don't know how to tell you. I've rerun all the tests and double-checked the results. You are going to die of cancer. There is no cure. You have about six to eight weeks to live."

"Well, Doc, I am glad you told me straight out. Now I can get all of my personal affairs in order."

The doctor felt bad about Fred and, the next day at the gym, heard two guys talking.

"Did you hear about Fred?"

"Yeah, I heard that he is dying of AIDS."

This really upset the doctor and he rushed over to a telephone to call Fred.

"Hello, Fred? Did you understand what I told you yesterday?"

"Of course, Doc. I am dying of cancer and have six to eight weeks to live."

"But I just heard two of your friends say you were dying of AIDS."

"Yeah, Doc, I know. You see, after I am gone, I don't want anyone screwing my wife!"

•

A man was having problems with premature ejaculation so he went to his doctor to ask about a cure.

The doctor said, "When you feel like you are getting ready to ejaculate, try startling yourself."

That same day the man went to the store and bought himself a starter pistol. All excited to try the doctor's suggestion, he ran home to his wife. He found her in bed, naked and waiting. As the two began, they found themselves in the 69 position. The man, moments later, felt the sudden urge to ejaculate and fired the starter pistol.

The next day, the man went back to the doctor, who asked, "How did it go?"

"Not that well. When I fired the pistol, my wife shit on my face, bit my penis, and my neighbor came out of the closet with his hands in the air!"

•

As a painless way to save money, a young couple agreed that every time they had sex, the husband would put his pocket change into a china piggy bank on the bedside table. One night while being unusually athletic, he accidentally knocked the piggy bank onto the floor and it smashed.

To his surprise, among the masses of coins there were handfuls of $5 and $10 bills. He asked his wife, "What's up with all the bills?"

She replied, "Well, not everyone is as cheap as you are."

•

Mary and Betty were friends that worked in the same office. At lunch, Betty confided to her coworker that she had had an awful row with her husband the night before.

"What was it about?" asked Mary.

"He was going through a closet, looking for something, and found my birth control pills."

"Well, what's the problem with that?"

"He had a vasectomy two years ago!"

•

One night a man heard howls coming from his basement and went down to discover a female cat being raped by a mouse. Fascinated by what he saw, the man gained the mouse's confidence with some cheese, then took him next door. The mouse repeated his amazing performance by raping a German shepherd.

The man, excited by this, was dying to show someone his discovery. He rushed home and woke up his wife, but before he could explain, she saw the mouse, screamed, and covered her head with the blanket.

"Don't be afraid, darling," said the man. "Wait until I tell you about this."

"Get out of here," cried his wife. "And take that sex maniac with you!"

•

A man and woman were traveling in their car. The man was driving when a police officer pulled them over. The officer walked up to the window and said, "Did you know you were speeding back there?"

The lady, who was almost deaf, said to her husband, "What did he say? What did he say?"

The man turned to his wife. "He said I was speeding."

The officer then said, "Where are you from?"

The wife then said, "What did he say? What did he say?"

The man turned to his wife. "He wanted to know where we came from." He turned to the officer. "We're from Chicago."

The officer then said, "Shit, you know, I had my worst f*** ever in Chicago."

The lady said, "What did he say? What did he say?"

The man turned back and said, "He says he thinks he knows you."

•

On their honeymoon, Harriet says to her new husband, "Eddie, how many women have you slept with?"

"If I tell you, you'll freak out."

"No, I won't."

"Okay. One, two, three, four, five, six, seven . . . you . . . nine, ten, eleven, twelve, thirteen . . ."

•

A knockout young lady decided she wanted to get rich quick, so she found herself a rich seventy-three-year-old man, planning to love him to death on their wedding night.

The courtship and wedding went off without any problem, in spite of the half-century age difference. The first night of their honeymoon, she got undressed and waited for him to come out of the bathroom to come to bed.

When he emerged, however, he had nothing on except a rubber to cover a twelve-inch erection and was carrying a pair of earplugs and a pair of nose plugs. Fearing her plan had gone desperately amiss, she asked, "What are those for?"

"There are two things I can't stand: the sound of a woman screaming, and the smell of burning rubber!"

•

This guy decides he's going to play a little joke on his wife. As she steps out of the shower, he grabs one of her breasts and says, "If you firmed these up a bit, you wouldn't have to keep using your bra." He laughs and laughs.

The next morning, he again catches her as she finishes her shower and grabs her ass and says, "If you firmed this up a bit, you wouldn't have to keep using your girdle." Again he laughs and laughs and laughs.

The next morning as he steps out of the shower, his wife

grabs his penis and says, "If you firmed *this* up a bit, I wouldn't need to keep sleeping with your brother."

•

A man comes home from work to find his wife packing her suitcase.

"What the hell are you doing?" he asks.

"I'm leavin' you for a better life."

"Where do you think you're going?"

"I'm going to Las Vegas. I hear they pay $400 for a blow job there."

The man thinks for a minute, then gets his suitcase out and starts packing his clothes.

"What the hell are you doing?" his wife asks.

"I'm going to Las Vegas, too. I want to see how you live on $800 a year!"

•

A groom passes down the aisle of a church to take his place by the altar, and the best man notices that the groom has the biggest, brightest smile.

The best man says, "Hey, man, I know you're happy to be getting married, but what's up—you look so excited."

"I just had the best blow job I have ever had in my entire life, and I am marrying the wonderful woman who gave it to me."

The bride comes walking down the aisle, and she, too, has the biggest, brightest smile.

The maid of honor notices this and says, "Hey, girlfriend, I know you're happy to be getting married, but what's up—you look so excited."

"I have just given the last blow job of my entire life."

•

I worked for a while at Wal-Mart selling sporting goods. As an employee of Wal-Mart, you are sometimes required to make storewide pages, e.g., "I have a customer in hardware who needs assistance at the paint counter." One night a tentative female voice said over the intercom, "I have a customer by the balls in the toy department who needs assistance."

•

Three old ladies named Gertrude, Maude, and Tillie were sitting on a bench having a quiet conversation when a flasher approached from across the park.

The flasher came up to the ladies, stood right in front of them, and opened his trench coat.

Gertrude immediately had a stroke. Then Maude also had a stroke.

But Tillie, being older and feebler, couldn't reach that far.

•

What do you get when you stand a blonde on her head?

A brunette with bad breath!

•

I was in Alabama in 1987, and I got lost.

I pulled into a town I couldn't believe still existed in the eighties. A dusty dirt road, a little old wooden store that actually said GENERAL STORE, and that was it. A little old man was sitting in front of the store in a rocking chair.

I said to him, "What do you folks do around here?"

"We don't do nothin' but hunt 'n' f***."

"What do you hunt?"

"Somethin' to f***."

•

A guy gets on an elevator with a big, fat woman.

He says, "Can I smell your snatch?"

"No."

"Then it must be your feet."